DESERT ACCOMMODATIONS

The History of Lodging in Phoenix

1872 - 1972

Laurence Bell

Poverty Island Publishing House

U.S.A.

Copyright © 2014 by Laurence Bell. All rights reserved.

No part of this book may be reproduced in any form whether written, electronic, by recording, or by photocopying, without the written permission of the publisher or author. The exception would be in the case of brief quotations embodied in critical articles or reviews, and pages where permission is specifically granted by the publisher or author.

Although every precaution has been taken to verify the accuracy of the information contained herein, the author and publisher assume no responsibility for any errors or omissions. No liability is assumed for damages that may result from the use of information contained within.

ISBN 978-0-9906842-0-6

Published by:

Poverty Island Publishing House
Chicago, Illinois

Printed in the United States of America

Library of Congress Control Number: 2014915698

For all general information, please contact Poverty Island Publishing House:
info@povertyislandpublishing.com

Initial Proofreading: Callie LaMarche

Copy Edit: Book Helpline

Cover Design: Littera Designs

Inspiration: Kay Emig

Dedication

To my parents,

    who have always encouraged me to

        learn, explore, and appreciate.

Contents

Section 1: A History of Lodging   1

Section 2: Listing of Lodging Facilities   23

Section 3: Listing by Address   423

Bibliography   459

Introduction

This book describes the first one hundred years of the lodging industry in Phoenix, Arizona. The first section is a brief synopsis of the general business climate and growth opportunities through the years. It also contains a listing of lodging franchises that existed in the area. Section 2 is a listing of all lodging facilities that were located within the modern-day city limits of Phoenix. The section includes facilities that offered overnight lodging at some point in their history. Many apartment businesses are included because they did rent to the transient market at one time. Larger lodging houses and boarding houses have been included as they were an important part of the area's lodging industry. Interesting historical happenings are included when possible. Section 3 is a listing of lodging facilities arranged by address. This section is included to make locations easy to find.

Every effort has been made to keep the research accurate. Information has been obtained from as many historical sources as possible and cross-referenced when appropriate. Sources are listed in the bibliography. Most dates were obtained from city directories and newspaper advertisements.

Section 3 makes it easy to find locations by address. However, many of the facilities that exist now are private property. Many are now in less desirable parts of town. It is best to exercise caution and to respect property ownership when visiting the locations. Property owners and tenants are not always interested in the history of the property and many times do not like being photographed. Of course many people are friendly and welcoming as well.

Section One

A History of Lodging in Phoenix, Arizona

Prehistoric Phoenix

The first people in the Phoenix area to require lodging were the Hohokam, the area's first settlers. The Hohokam people appear to have arrived in the Salt River Valley about 1 AD. They survived through farming, and as their culture grew, their expertise in irrigation increased. The Hohokam skillfully built irrigation canals throughout the Salt and Gila River Valleys. They built mounds at regular intervals along the canals, likely for monitoring the canal system. Adobe structures including "big houses", large multi-story buildings, were constructed as part of their infrastructure. Within the current boundaries of the city of Phoenix, many canals, mounds, and buildings were built by the Hohokam. By 1450 AD the Hohokam abandoned the area. Many theories exist as to why they left, but most agree that years of drought played a part.

Considering the construction projects and the large area the Hohokam covered, it seems obvious that they must have had transient visitors. Unfortunately, the Hohokam had no known written language, so we don't know how they handled visitors. Did they stay in the "big houses"? Did they camp in the desert or stay with people in their homes? Any of these are possibilities. Surely the Hohokam lodged guests in some fashion hundreds of years before the city of Phoenix existed.

Early Native Americans in Phoenix

After the Hohokam abandoned the area, Native Americans, specifically the Pima and the Maricopa, occupied the space. It is widely believed that the Pimas are the descendants of the Hohokam people. This makes sense since the Pima occupied the area immediately after the Hohokam and were present when Europeans made first contact. The specific Pima people that lived in the Phoenix area were the On'k Akimel O'odham, which means the "Salt River People". These people lived in very small, semi-permanent villages along the Salt River. At the time, the Salt River ran with water all year long as the dams and diversions were not yet built.

The Maricopa people originally lived along the banks of the Colorado River in southwestern Arizona, but were forced to leave due to warring tribes. They relocated within the same region as the Pima, who accepted the Maricopas and welcomed them to live alongside them. The two groups were so close that they joined forces to defeat their enemies, the Yuma and Mohave, in the last exclusively Native American battle in the United States, the Battle of Pima Butte. The battle took place in 1857 just south of Phoenix near Pima Butte, north of the modern town of Maricopa.

A preserved Hohokam "Big House" near Coolidge, Arizona
Buildings similar to this existed in the Phoenix area as well. (Photo by Author 2012)

By the time European settlers became abundant in the area, the two peoples had become inseparable. In 1879 President Rutherford Hayes created the Salt River Pima-Maricopa Indian Community by executive order. The Salt River Pima and Maricopa people were relocated to the community located just east of Scottsdale.

The early On'k Akimel O'odham and accompanying Salt River Maricopas would have had a need to house transient guests. No known lodging facility existed in the time period to service them. It's likely that travelers were welcomed into family homes or camped nearby.

Early Phoenix

In 1867 Jack Swilling of Wickenburg noticed the series of ancient canals and mounds still visible in the desert, and the quality of the soil in the Salt River Valley. Swilling soon organized a canal construction company and began working in the valley. By 1868 crops were being grown, and a small settlement was in place east of the current downtown area. After some discussion, the name 'Phoenix' was selected to identify the new settlement. This name seemed fitting as the new town was being built on the ruins of a Hohokam village much like the mythological bird, the Phoenix, who renews itself from its own ashes.

In 1868 Yavapai County created an election precinct in the area so the settlers could vote. By 1870 it was decided that Phoenix would be located a couple miles west at the present downtown location. The area was surveyed and streets and blocks were laid out. On the 24th and 25th of December of 1870, the townsite lots were auctioned and sold to the highest bidder. Most lots were quickly subdivided, and land was further sold or traded. What would become the modern city of Phoenix was born.

The first commercial buildings built in the new town appeared in 1871. Soon general stores, saloons, banks, and churches were built. The first hotel in the city of Phoenix arrived by 1872. Built by John Gardiner and named the "Phoenix Hotel", the facility was built using single-story adobe construction and included a pool. The Phoenix Hotel was located at the northwest corner of Washington Street and Third Street, where the Phoenix Symphony Hall is now located.

Phoenix grew in a stable and well-planned manner. The town was originally based on agriculture rather than mining, making growth slow and controlled, rather than boom and bust. Expansion of the area was boosted in 1887 with the completion of rail service to Phoenix. Further boosting the economy, the territorial capital was moved to Phoenix in 1889. By 1892 there were eight hotels in Phoenix as well as several rooming houses. Rooming houses were important lodging facilities before auto courts and motels came along. They provided more affordable transient housing than hotels, although they didn't provide the services or amenities. Rooming houses, or lodging houses, could be purpose-built facilities, or converted family homes in which individual rooms were rented. Some provided food or other services such as laundry.

The economy of the city of Phoenix grew in many ways during the late 1800s and early 1900s. Rail service to Phoenix provided a way for businesses to import and export goods easily. This allowed industrialization to begin in town. The mainstay business, agriculture, continued to grow with more and bigger crops. Tourism also started to influence the economy as people began to realize they could escape the winter in Phoenix. A few Health Resorts, or Sanitariums, opened to house winter guests whose doctors had sent them to Phoenix due to a number of ailments. Of course growth in the business economy and population resulted in an increased need for lodging. By 1920 Phoenix touted at least 39 facilities that advertised themselves as hotels. There were at least an additional 80 facilities which were either small hotels or rooming houses in the city. Only a few of these properties were more than a few blocks from the city center.

A view down Center Street, now Central Avenue, circa 1909 (Author's Collection)

The rapid growth of the downtown area lodging facilities peaked in the late 1920s. The culmination occurred with the building of two additional large, multi-story facilities, the San Carlos and Westward Ho hotels. These hotels joined other large, existing hotels downtown such as the Jefferson, Adams, and Luhrs hotels. Soon the downtown area and its lodging facilities growth would level off. The Great Depression, combined with the new mobility of automobiles, would allow travelers to utilize cheaper facilities farther from downtown.

The Automobile Era

In 1908 the Ford Motor Company introduced the Model T. This new vehicle set the stage for a future boom in automobile transportation by making the car affordable and available. It took some time for automobile tourism to become popular as there was no infrastructure. Some fearless drivers set out without roads, and some built very Spartan roads, in more of an adventure than just transportation. This adventurous spirit of exploration became more prevalent with the advent of the auto trail.

Auto trails were the country's first set of overland roads built specifically for automobiles. Most of the trails were advertised and maintained by associations created for that purpose. The associations existed mainly to promote travel and tourism along the route. The gain was, of course, capturing the traveling dollar. The auto trails utilized names instead of numbers, and were marked along the way with either the name or initials of that trail. Phoenix benefited from the auto trails more than most cities because the ruggedness of the Arizona terrain forced the trails to converge. If a traveler was to take the southern route across the United States, it was very likely the traveler would end up in Phoenix. Auto trails that were routed to Phoenix included the Bankhead National Highway, the Old Spanish Trail, the Atlantic-Pacific Highway, the Dixie-Overland Route, the Borderland Route, and the Lee Highway. All of these trails were routed down Van Buren Street to downtown Phoenix.

As the auto trails became popular, the auto travelers started arriving in Phoenix. At first the travelers only had the choice of hotels or rooming houses for overnight stays. However, these facilities were not built to accommodate the new travelers. Safe parking was not available since hotels were built for train or stage travelers. The condition of auto travelers after a day on the dusty and hot highway was not what hotels expected of its patrons. Further, hotels were considered expensive to most of the auto travelers. The immediate solution for the travelers was to bring along camping equipment. Travelers would camp along the roads at any point at which they wanted to stop. This phenomenon was quickly noticed by enterprising individuals, and the auto camp was created.

Auto camps were simple facilities meant to serve the new automobile traveler. These facilities included basic needs such as water, parking, camping areas, and restrooms. Often a grocery store, gas station, or restaurant was located at or near the camp. Auto camps were an easy business to start as once the property was procured, the capital investment was very small. Enforcement of private property laws and restrictions on camping along the roadways soon drove the travelers to the camps. Many municipalities created auto camps to help contain the traffic and gain any economic impact the travelers would produce. Many auto camps appeared in Phoenix in the early 1920s. The earliest known camp was Camp Montezuma, on East Van Buren, as the facility was already in place as a former health resort. Phoenix also boasted a municipal auto camp located at Christy Park in the Six Points area near the fair grounds.

In 1925 state and federal officials realized the difficulties being created by auto trails and their promoters. A confusing array of named trails had been created that crisscrossed the country haphazardly. Many of the roads were redundant and followed the same routing as other trails. This was because the promoters of each trail needed to advertise a route that went some distance, many times coast to coast. A limited number of roadways created the routing redundancies. A Joint Board on Interstate Highways was created, and they decided to adopt a numbering system instead of a named system. Redundant roadways would be eliminated as much as possible. By 1926 the new system was in place. In Phoenix the roads still converged, but were reduced to US Highways 60, 80 and Arizona 89. In 1934 US Highway 70 was also extended through Phoenix. These roads all entered Phoenix from Tempe along Van Buren. Highways 60, 70, and 89 exited to the west along Grand Avenue to Wickenburg. Highway 80 was routed south on Seventeenth Avenue from Van Buren to Buckeye Road where a right turn would lead to Gila Bend. This routing lasted for decades.

As the automobile traffic continued to increase, and travelers became more sophisticated, auto courts were created. Initially auto courts were simple groups of cabins rented as units with parking. Auto courts quickly became popular in the Phoenix area. Most were built along the major highway routes through the city. Once again, Camp Montezuma was the first known court as it had buildings for transient rental already built when the auto courts became popular. Auto courts changed through the years from simple cabins to larger cottage buildings, some with multiple rooms. One of the larger early auto courts in Phoenix was the Autopia Motor Park located on East Van Buren. The facility offered garages and multiple room units. Soon the major roads into town were lined with auto courts.

Central Avenue and the Adams Hotel circa 1930 (Author's Collection)

About 1930, as the Great Depression loomed, the downtown hotels entered a period of slow growth. A combination of the poor economy and cheap available rooms near town were the major causes of the slowdown. The construction of the Westward Ho and San Carlos hotels had also added many new rooms to the downtown. New hotels did continue to open, but at a slower rate. Most existing downtown properties continued to survive as long as they were modernized when needed. However, the downtown rooming houses virtually disappeared as they had already been in decline due to the new auto courts. Slow growth of downtown lodging facilities lasted until just recently with the revitalization of the area.

Lodging growth through the 1930s and early 1940s was limited mainly to new, smaller courts. Facilities built in this timeframe were mostly of the cabin-style construction. This type of construction was popular, but limited the maximization of land use. Even cabin-style courts evolved through the years so that by the 1940s, most included covered parking between the buildings. Early cabin courts were updated by adding a single roof over the existing cabins to create a parking area in between. During this era there was enough available land to build new courts without eliminating earlier buildings. Growth generally took place from the city center outwards and near tourist draws.

Lodging facility construction almost always follows demand. Phoenix was special in that it had more going for it than just the pass-through traffic. As the area became industrialized, people also came to Phoenix for commercial business as well as for business related to the state government. Beyond those sources of traffic, the area was a natural tourist location due to its climate. Enterprising individuals created businesses that were draws in themselves. The Reptile Gardens and Joyland Park are just a couple of examples of such tourist traps. The western terrain itself was a popular draw to Americans as well. Today's Papago Park and city zoo was the Papago Saguaro National Monument until 1930. It seemed tourists were drawn to anything western at the time as it was still exotic.

Post War Growth

As World War II came to an end, the economy was in high gear, and Phoenix entered a spectacular motel growth period. Courts continued to be built along major roads, and even in more distant areas, at a very fast rate. Eventually lodging facilities were abundant several miles away from town. In many areas "motel rows" appeared. Virtually all of Van Buren Street from about Twentieth Avenue to Fiftieth Street was covered with courts. Grand Avenue and Seventeenth Street also had their motel rows.

As the major thoroughfares became full, the competition among motels increased. New motels were built using strip-style construction that maximized capacity by eliminating the space between cabins. Later, two- and three-story motels appeared using "motor inn" construction. This was multi-story strip construction utilizing exterior entrances. Older cabin courts were modernized by filling the spaces between the cabins with either false walls or additions to make them appear as strip-style motels. By the early 1960s, large resorts built in motor inn style became prevalent in the city. Many early courts gave up their real estate for the new, larger facilities.

1892 Map of Phoenix showing lodging facilities available at the time

Competition among motels was prevalent in other ways as well. Signage was updated from plain front lit signs to neon signs. Those neon signs were replaced by bigger and brighter neon signs. At one time East Van Buren Street looked much like the Las Vegas strip due to the vast amount of neon signs. Motels also competed by using themes. Early courts generally used Spanish/Mexican or Western styling in their architecture as well as climate influenced names like the Sun Villa. The Log Cabin Motel was an early user of a theme with its early American décor. Later, however, much more extreme themes were used. The Western theme was pushed to its fullest with facilities such as the Western Village. Colonial themes were utilized by the Hiway House and Ramada Inn chains. Arabian themed motels included the Egyptian and the Caravan properties. The most flamboyant of the themed hotels were those that utilized Polynesian themes such as the Samoan Village and the Kon Tiki.

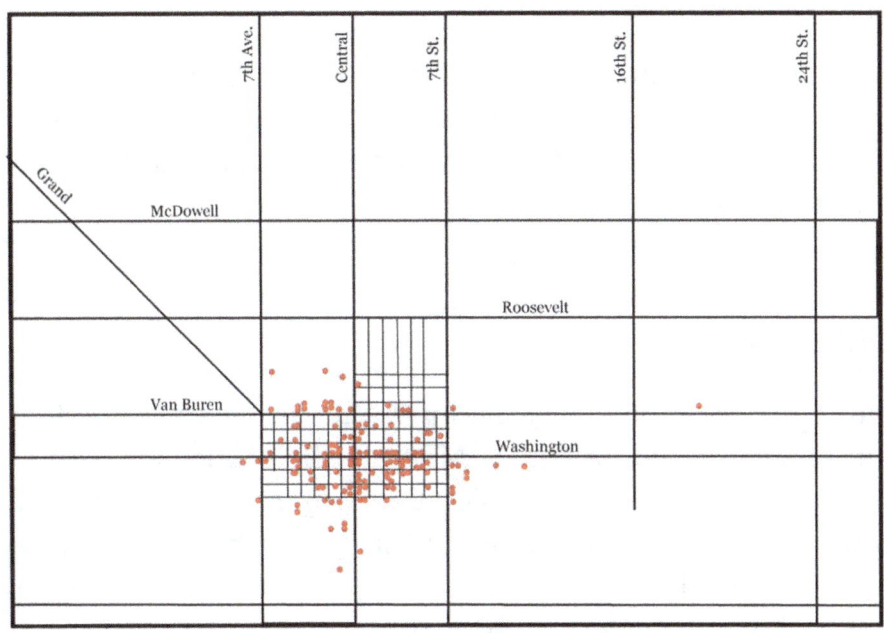

1920 Map of Phoenix showing growth of lodging facilities

Neon motel signs along Van Buren Street circa 1942 (Courtesy Library of Congress)

Flamboyance of theme due to competition reached its peak in the late 1960s. This was the point when most properties were doing well no matter their age. The motel rows were destination locations for travelers, and it seemed as though it would never end. However, things were about to change.

Decline of Older Motels

In the early 1970s motels built along the long-established entryways to Phoenix began to decline economically. Many of the properties along these routes were very old, but even the newer facilities began to have difficulties due to routing changes and the building of freeways. Limited access freeway construction began in the 1950s with the Black Canyon Highway. The first section of this highway opened in 1960. It would soon be designated I-17, and serviced the stretch from McDowell to Dunlap Streets. By 1963 the freeway was extended south to Durango Street and then east to Fortieth Street. This east-west stretch was originally in the freeway master plan as part of Interstate 10. I-10 was intended to meet I-17 at the Durango Curve. Bridges were actually built during the initial construction at the Durango Curve to facilitate the future I-10 interchange and later removed. This initial freeway construction did not affect traffic into the city core as I-10 was incomplete both south of town and west of town.

I-10 construction approached Phoenix in phases. From the west, the freeway arrived in Tonapah by 1973. It previously terminated just thirty miles from the California border where Highway 60 now meets I-10. By 1974 the freeway extended to the Goodyear area. South of town, construction was completed between Casa Grande and Phoenix by 1972. The opening of this stretch of freeway was the trigger for existing motel decline. Prior to the opening of this portion, traffic still followed the decades-long routing through Tempe, down Van Buren Street and west, following either Grand Avenue or Seventeenth Street and Buckeye Street. After the Casa Grande to Phoenix stretch opened, traffic completely bypassed the existing routes by exiting at Nineteenth Avenue and following the access road to Buckeye Road. Traffic was sent west on Buckeye to meet back up with I-10 at Goodyear.

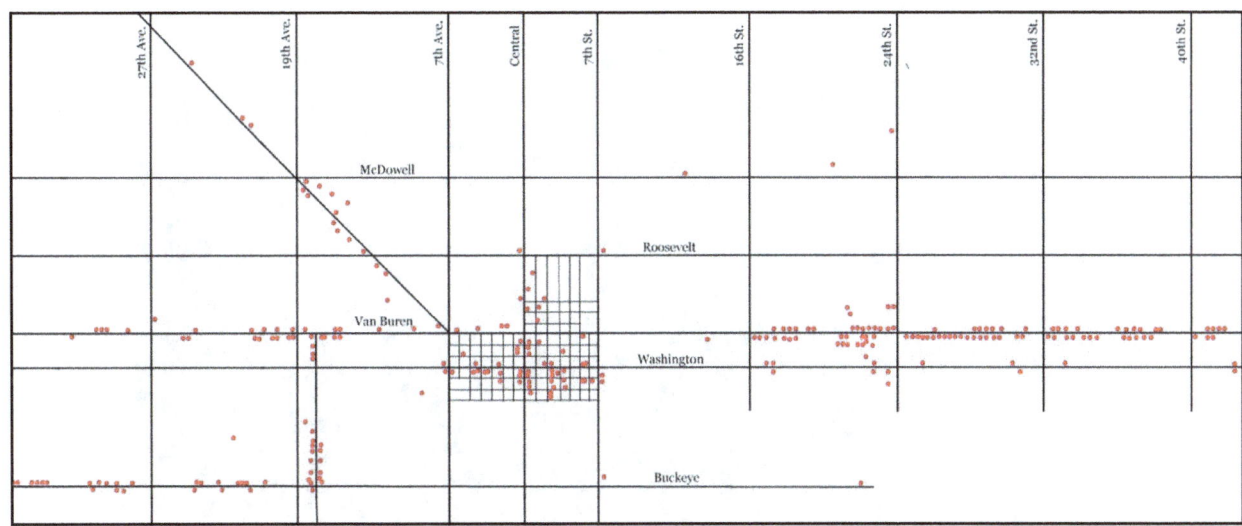

1960 map of Phoenix showing lodging locations. Major highways are obvious as they are lined with motels.

Many people in Phoenix realized the damage that was about to happen to local existing businesses. These people waged a war on the completion of Interstate 10. Due to their efforts, funding was delayed and I-10 was not completed until 1990, although I-10 was open to the I-17 interchange (the stack) by 1988. These efforts were too late to save the existing businesses as the traffic had already been rerouted in 1972.

After the traffic had been rerouted, the effects were quickly seen. New motel construction began along the new corridor, mainly at freeway exits, which drew traffic away from harder to reach properties. Older properties, feeling the economic impact, entered a survival mode. Many went to weekly rate structures or switched to an apartment-style business structure. Many of the smaller, older properties were closed completely. Eventually the larger, resort-type properties would succumb as well. Some of these larger properties found other uses as homeless shelters or, in the case of the Hiway House, a women's prison. Ultimately most of the remaining motels became run down and utilized their facilities to accommodate the prostitution trade. This was most prevalent along Van Buren Street, and prostitution is what most residents still think of when Van Buren Street is mentioned. The downtown hotels were affected by the interstate highways in the same manner. Downtown hotels began to close, including the Westward Ho which was closed by 1979.

The Desert Inn Motel on West Van Buren Street being demolished in 2012 (Photo by Author)

Starting in the 1990s and continuing today, a process of demolishment and reuse began. While a drive down Van Buren Street or Grand Avenue today still affords views of older motels, the vast majority of lodging properties have been demolished. Reuse of the real estate is beginning to revitalize many of the older areas. Some of the older but still viable properties have been renovated, and even a few new properties have been built. Downtown the addition of sports complexes and University campus extensions has revitalized the downtown lodging facilities as well.

Chains in Phoenix

Many motel chains appeared in Phoenix as the consistency they provided became more popular. Referred to as "flags" in the business, these chains take three basic forms: owned, referral, and franchised. Owned chains are those where the properties are owned by one individual or corporation. Many owners have more than one property, but a chain would only be present if the facilities are similarly branded and advertised. A referral chain exists if a group of hotels join under a flag to refer business to each other. The flag itself is not for profit, and fees are paid only for expenses. The third major type of chain is the franchised facilities. In this business model, the franchisor is a for profit organization that allows individual owners to utilize its flag for a fee. A franchise co-ownership business model was popular in the 1960s. This allowed for joint ownership between the franchise and the motel operator. Listed here are the chains that existed in Phoenix prior to 1972.

<u>Alsonett Hotels</u> – Charles H. Alberding was a hotel owner and operator from the 1940s until his death in 1989. He owned between 20 and 50 properties during those years at any one time. Hotels owned by Alberding were operated under the name Alsonett Hotels. The name was used in advertising and press releases. Alsonett was not the legal entity, but rather a marketing name derived in the early years while Alberding had partners. The Alberding, Gibson, and Connett names were the inspiration for the marketing name. In reality, each hotel was owned by its own corporation and was expected to operate on its own merits. Alsonett Hotel headquarters were located in Tulsa, Oklahoma, while Alberding lived in Chicago, Illinois. Alberding owned hotels throughout the United States. Arizona properties were the Jokake Inn, Paradise Inn, and the Royal Palms Inn. For most of Alberding's career his hotels were kept in very good condition. Towards the end of his life the properties were known for a lack of capital investment, and hotels became less than first class.

<u>AutoLodge</u> – The AutoLodge Corporation was a California company organized in 1955 that built motels in the southwest of the United States. After or during construction, the company would locate co-owners for each property. An agreement would normally include a fifty percent co-ownership with the managing owner. The AutoLodge in Phoenix was located at 804 East Van Buren.

<u>Best Western Motels</u> – Founded in 1946 by M.K. Guertin, Best Western Motels began as a loose organization in which innkeepers would refer guests to the next Best Western on their route. The first Best Western locations were in the western United States, which explains the name. By 1964 Best Western had become the largest chain in the country. In 1966 Best Western located its headquarters in Phoenix, where it still exists today. Properties in Phoenix that were members of Best Western include the Kon Tiki, the Desert Inn, the Desert Hills, and the Sea Breeze. Best Western properties are able to keep their individual names and identity.

Caravan Inns – Caravan Inn was a division of Western Hotels, which operated hotels in Hawaii, Colorado, Guatemala, and many other locations. Western Hotels began in 1930 as a hotel management firm in Washington State. The company changed its name to Westin Hotels in 1981 and still functions under that name. Caravan Inns were Arabian themed hotels of which several were built in western states. The Caravan Inn locations in Phoenix were located at 3333 East Van Buren Street and 1501 Grand Avenue.

Flamingo Hotels – Michael Robinson started the Flamingo Hotel chain when he opened the first Flamingo in Texas in 1951. Soon Robinson was building properties throughout the southwest. Eventually Robinson would make Phoenix his home and place the Flamingo headquarters there as well. The Flamingo chain became affiliated with both the Hiway House and Ramada Inn chains since Robinson was involved in both endeavors. It appears that Flamingo Hotels began selling off its properties in the 1960s. The Flamingo Hotel in Phoenix was located on East Van Buren Street and retained its Flamingo name for decades.

Friendship Inns – Friendship Inns was a referral chain headquartered in Salt Lake City. The chain began in 1961 and targeted lower end properties that had difficulty meeting other franchisors requirements. Motels accepted were still nice as Friendship Inns required an AAA rating for membership. The chain was sold to Econo Lodge in 1989, and became part of Choice Hotels when Econo Lodge was purchased in 1990. The Friendship Inns were converted to other Choice brands, and the flag was eliminated. The Friendship Inn in Phoenix was the former Imperial 400 at five points on Seventh Avenue near Van Buren Street. Today the location operates as a Friendship Inn, but it is not part of any chain.

Hiway House – The Phoenix-based Hiway House motel chain was created in 1956 by Del Webb. Webb owned a large Arizona construction company and was one of the original investors in the Ramada Inn chain. Locations were built in California, Arizona, New Mexico, and Texas. The chain was affiliated with the Flamingo chain for a short while until 1958 when the two chains were separated. In 1961 Webb sold off the chain to a group of investors under the new name, Hiway House Hotels. By 1964 Webb had repossessed the chain due to non-payment. However, the chain still had financial problems and went into receivership in 1966. By the early 1970s the chain was dissolved, and the properties sold off. Two Hiway House hotels were built in Phoenix: The Hiway House located on East Van Buren Street and the Hiway Inn on Grand Avenue.

Holiday Inns - Holiday Inn of America was created when Kemmons Wilson built the first location in the Memphis area in 1952. Wilson soon partnered with Wallace Johnson, and together they built three more Holiday Inns in Memphis. In 1957 Wilson organized the Holiday Inn Franchise system. By 1968 there were over 1,000 Holiday inns in the United States. Holiday Inns in Phoenix were located at 2247 East Van Buren Street, and 2201 South Twenty-Fourth Street. The Holiday Inn located on South Seventh Avenue predated the franchise system and was not part of Holiday Inn of America.

Hyatt Hotels – The Hyatt Hotels brand began when Jay Pritzker purchased the Hyatt House Hotel in 1957. The previous owners were Hyatt von Dehn and Jack Crouch. The facility was a small airport motor inn property located in Los Angeles, California. Soon the Hyatt Corporation went public and began its first expansion phase. The company had three divisions which were Hyatt House, Hyatt Chalet, and Hyatt Lodges. Hyatt expanded all over the United States and internationally over the next few decades. By 1982 all public interest in the company had been purchased by the Pritzker family. Today the company operates as Hyatt Hotels Corporation. In Phoenix there was a Hyatt Chalet located on East Van Buren near the downtown area.

Imperial 400 Hotels – The Imperial 400 motel chain was organized in 1959 and built its first motel in 1961 in the Los Angeles, California, area. The chain would utilize a theme of "Royal Accommodations at Thrifty Rates" and kept rates lower than competitive properties. Each property was built using a similar design with a distinctive roof placed over the lobby. The chain utilized a co-ownership franchise business model in which managing owners could buy into the individual property. Most co-owners would hold twenty-five to fifty percent interest. One percent of gross sales went into a national advertising fund. In the early 1960s, Imperial 400 Hotels embarked on a very ambitious expansion plan hoping for at least 160 properties by the end of 1965. In 1965 Imperial 400 Hotels entered into a bankruptcy under Chapter 11 reorganization. After emerging from bankruptcy, the company continued to operate motels under many names. The company was purchased by RPD Hotels in 1998. Phoenix Imperial 400 Motels included one at 201 North Seventh Street and one at 3830 East Van Buren Street.

Kelly Inns – Howard T. Kelly organized Kelly Inns about 1967, with headquarters in Phoenix. Kelly was the former Vice President of Rodeway Inns of the

Southwest. In that capacity he had helped to open the first Rodeway Inn at 424 West Van Buren Street in Phoenix. That property was to become a Kelly Inn by 1967. Kelly Inns sold franchises throughout the western states, as well as co-ownerships in both new motels and conversions. The company also managed motels, apartments, and office buildings. The management arm of the company was involved with the Coliseum Inn on Grand Avenue.

Manger Hotels – Julius Manger entered the hotel business in the very early 20th century. He owned properties mainly in the northeast United States, including the Hay-Adams in Washington, DC, and the Windsor in New York City. When Manger died in 1937, he was the biggest private owner of hotels in the United States. Early Manger hotels were not part of a chain as they did not standardize an advertised name or signage. In later years Manger-owned hotels would carry their individual names and a sign identifying them as a Manger Hotel. It appears Manger Hotels was dissolved in the 1970s. In Phoenix the Desert Sun Motel on Grand Avenue was a Manger Hotel and signed as such for a time.

Master Host Inns – In 1953 the new referral chain Master Host Motor Hotels was organized. The Fort Worth, Texas, based chain grew quickly, becoming a national flag. The chain was known for having the strictest quality standards. A property had to meet those standards and have a convention center, banquet facilities, and suites to be accepted. The company changed its name to Master Host Inns in the late 1960s. Most Master Host properties utilized a unique individual name along with the Master Host flag. Some properties were flagged as simply "Master Host Inn", but it was not normal practice. The flag continues to operate today in the same upper-mid tier. Motels that were part of the Master Host Inns chain in Phoenix included the Western Village and the Samoan Village.

Milner Hotels - The Milner Hotel chain began in 1936 and started with the Detroit, Michigan, property. The company initiated an aggressive growth model through lease agreements of existing hotels. By 1939 there were 110 hotels in the chain. Earle Reed Milner, the founder, worked his way up from a soap company office boy to hotel magnate. By the mid-1940s his chain was the largest in the world. All Milner Hotel properties at the time were named either Earle, Reed, or Milner Hotel.

In 1947 Earle Reed Milner died. At the time the chain had 178 hotel properties. Milner left a $4.5 million estate which took 14 years to settle. Contests from the Salvation Army and Milner's second and third wives delayed the disbursements. The Salvation Army claimed the will was changed just prior to Milner's passing to give them most of the estate. Eventually it was decided that seventy percent of the estate would go to Milner's son Earle Ronald. The rest would be divided among the heirs of Milner's third wife, who drowned in 1954, and six other children.

In 1959 the chain began entering the motel market through new construction. Hotel stays had declined due to the increased motel market across the country. The number of properties in the chain was also declining. In 1963 the chain had 70 properties, down from nearly 200 just a few years earlier. By 1973 that number had dropped to 40.

Today the Milner Hotel chain still operates with three locations. It advertises itself as the "World's First Hotel Chain".

Porter House Motels – In 1961 Phoenix contractor and real estate agent J.R. Porter announced the creation of the new Porter House Hotel chain through a public offering of stock in the new company. The new chain opened its first location in Show Low, Arizona, in May 1962. Other properties followed in Flagstaff, Arizona; Blythe, California; and Phoenix, Arizona. In Phoenix, the chain purchased the Desert Sun Hotel at 1325 Grand Avenue from Manger Hotels and converted it to a Porter House Hotel. The Phoenix location became the company's world headquarters. The company offered franchise agreements utilizing a percent of ownership concept. However, the four company-owned locations appear to be the only Porter House hotels to ever fly the flag. In 1966 the headquarters location was no longer a Porter House hotel, and the chain faded away.

Ramada Inns – Ramada Inns was organized in 1953 by a group of investors that included Marion Isbell, Michael Robinson, and Del Webb. The Phoenix headquartered chain opened its first hotel in Flagstaff in 1954. Isbell ran restaurants in Illinois, Robinson owned the Flamingo Hotel chain, and Webb owned a large construction company in Phoenix. The Ramada Inn headquarters and reservation center was located on East Van Buren Street for many years. Ramada went through a series of ownership changes and today is part of

Wyndham Worldwide. Ramada Inn locations in Phoenix included the flagship property on East Van Buren and the Sahara Hotel downtown.

Ranger Motels – Ranger Motels was organized in the early 1960s. The chain catered to larger independent motels who wished to gain the benefits of chain membership. Ranger boasted 25 members in 1963 when it placed its headquarters in Phoenix. Phoenix members included the Egyptian, Kon Tiki, and the chain's headquarters at the Bali-Hi. In 1967 the Ranger Motels Corporation was dissolved.

Rodeway Inns – Rodeway Inns was a Phoenix headquartered chain that originated in 1962 with the first property located on West Van Buren. The chain was initially an owned chain where all properties were owned and managed by the company. The chain was initiated by Michael Robinson and Joe Simmons. Robinson was previously involved in the founding of the Flamingo Hotel and Ramada Inn chains. In 1971 the Vantage Company purchased the chain, and the business model soon changed to franchising rather than ownership. The Rodeway chain changed hands a few times and eventually became a Choice Hotels brand in 1990. Rodeway locations in Phoenix included one at 424 West Van Buren Street and one at 3400 Grand Avenue.

Romney Hotels – In 1961 Wayne Romney organized Romney International Hotels in Phoenix. Romney's properties quickly grew to five locations. In 1968 Romney joined forces with Jack R. Young and Associates out of San Diego. The next few years brought rapid expansion with 42 properties owned by 1971. Western Financial Corporation purchased Romney International that year. Initially Western purchased more properties, but by 1975 the company had started selling off locations. The last 22 properties were sold to a group of Romney International executives. The company's name was changed to Paragon Hotel Corporation in 1984 and still functions as such today. Phoenix hotels operated by Romney International included the Egyptian Motor Hotel, the Romney Motor Hotel, and the Romney Sun Dancer. Most of the properties owned by Romney International don't fit the "chain" definition with an obvious affiliation with other hotels. However, those with the Romney name attached to them do.

Sheraton – In 1937 Ernest Henderson and Robert Moore purchased their first hotel marking the birth of Sheraton Hotels. The partners quickly added properties to their portfolio. By 1965 the company had become international and touted over 100 hotels under its flag. Sheraton built its reputation on upscale, full service properties. The Sky Riders Hotel in Phoenix gained a Sheraton flag in 1965, marking the company's first appearance in the valley. The Sheraton Sky Riders Hotel was a franchised location owned by a Chicago-based group.

TraveLodge – TraveLodge was an early motel chain which was organized in 1939. By 1940 its first motel opened in San Diego with headquarters located in El Cajon, California. The chain was started by Scott King and was positioned as a budget chain. The facilities offered excellent prices at the cost of limited amenities. Today TraveLodge is part of Wyndham Hotels and offers more than just budget accommodations. TraveLodge locations in Phoenix included one at 965 East Van Buren Street and one at 402 West Van Buren Street.

Vagabond – Vagabond Motor Hotels opened their first motel in 1958. The chain built hotels throughout the western United States. Vagabond used a cartoon drawing of a hobo laying down resting as their logo. The flag went through a series of owners, including Imperial Hotels, but is still in business today as a franchise system. It does business regionally in western states. The Vagabond Motor Hotel in Phoenix was located at 3644 East Van Buren Street.

The Modern Era

Chain motels and franchised properties became much more prevalent by the late 1970s. Most travelers had experienced a poorly maintained motel, and chains offered safety in quality. All successful chains have property standards that individual motels must conform to. It was natural that travelers would be drawn to them. In turn, property owners felt they needed a flag to compete.

Unfortunately, this shift towards chains also eliminated the majority of creativity experienced with independent motels. Each property in a chain needs to be as similar to others as possible, which requires a conservative approach. Themed motels lost their appeal as the market changed. Unlike the early motels, today's facilities are usually cookie cutter designs that will likely never instill a feeling of nostalgia.

Section Two

Listing of Lodging Facilities

The following is an alphabetical list of lodging facilities built in the current Phoenix city limits between 1872 and 1972. Pictures and details about each property are listed if possible.

A Motel – See Cottonwood Court

ABC Court circa 1950 (Author's Collection)

ABC Court – 3541 East Van Buren Street

The ABC Court was built in 1941 using cabin court construction and Spanish design. The stucco walled cabins included covered parking for automobiles between the buildings. With two units per cabin, the facility contained a total of 12 units.

The ABC Court was closed and demolished in 1960 to make room for the new Desert Sky Motor Inn.

Adalade Hotel – See Bonner Hotel

Adams Court – 1609 East Adams Street

The Adams Court was accepting guests by 1947. The facility consisted of eight brick duplex cottages built along the east and west property lines. This resulted in 16 kitchenette rental units. By 1959 the court had moved to a long-term rental business plan.

The court was demolished in the 1990s. Today it is a parking area for a body shop.

Adams Hotel circa 1900 (Courtesy Library of Congress)

Adams Hotel circa 1925, rebuilt after the 1910 fire (Author's Collection)

Adams Hotel lobby circa 1925 (Author's Collection)

Adams Hotel – 50 East Adams Street

The Adams Hotel was opened in 1896 by John Adams. Adams arrived in Phoenix in 1894 and purchased the property for the future hotel at that time. He had been a lawyer of some note in Chicago. The first Adams Hotel was a four-story wood frame and brick structure which contained 150 rooms. The complex also included a restaurant and roof garden. It was the largest building in Phoenix at the time and received many accolades. John Adams received immediate notoriety due to his investment in the city and even served as mayor of Phoenix. The hotel became very popular with Phoenix visitors and the territorial governmental officials. It was well known that much legislation took place at the hotel.

In May 1910 the Adams Hotel was destroyed by fire. The building and its contents were a total loss. However, all of the hotel guests and employees escaped death. This included the Territorial Governor, his wife, and daughter. Within days a committee was formed to arrange financing to rebuild the Adams. Barry Goldwater, father of the future presidential hopeful and founder of Goldwater's Department Store, was on the committee. An ad was placed in the newspaper stating that the property was not for sale. Soon construction was started on the new hotel. However, in early 1911, the investors decided to stop construction until a vote on alcohol prohibition took place. They stated that if city prohibition was to take place, the facility would be converted to another use. Prohibition was not passed, and the hotel's construction continued. The new Adams Hotel was bigger and better than its predecessor. The new facility was advertised as "absolutely fireproof" and utilized concrete construction. It included 250 sleeping rooms and two dining rooms. A pool was located on the roof.

The Adams was sold in 1973 to Mr. and Mrs. Albert Spensor and imploded in August of that year. A complicated array of companies was created under the Spensor's ownership using the name Vita-Adams Investment Company. A joint venture between Vita-Adams and the Prudential Insurance Company (PIC) was created, and monies borrowed for construction. Even before the new hotel was complete, problems arose. Vita-Adams refused to provide additional funding to complete the hotel per the original agreement. PIC dissolved the joint venture and finished the hotel, which was opened in early 1975. The parties entered an agreement in July of 1975 to settle their disputes. PIC received title to the Adams Hotel, a Vita-Adams company was given a lease to operate the hotel, and the Vita Company would finish and furnish what was left to complete at the hotel. However, in October 1975, some of the Vita-Adams companies declared Chapter XI bankruptcy. The parent company, Vita-Adams Investment Company, also filed for bankruptcy protection in February 1976. This resulted in lengthy court battles in the bankruptcy, district, and United States Court of Appeals.

Adams Hotel final building constructed in 1975. Now the Renaissance Phoenix (Photo by Author 2012)

The new hotel consisted of 532 rooms, a restaurant, convention center, pool, and shops. It utilized contemporary design in its construction. Distinctive "brows" adorn each exterior window creating a look similar to a cheese grater. By 1982 the Adams became the Phoenix Hilton. Later it became the Wyndham Phoenix. Today the hotel operates as the Renaissance Phoenix.

The former Admiral Motel, now apartments (Photo by Author 2014)

Admiral Motel – 5403 South Central Avenue

One of the buildings that became part of the Admiral Motel was already built by 1955. It was rented as apartments at the time. By 1959 three duplex buildings had been built, creating the six-unit motel.

The facility stopped operating as a hotel by 1969 and embraced an apartment business model. The Admiral Motel's original buildings still exist today as apartments.

Ahoy Tourist Motel – See Orange Auto Court

Air Line Modern Cottage Court – 2220 East Buckeye Road

By 1942 the Air Line Modern Cottage Court was in business. As the name would suggest, the court was located close to Sky Harbor Airport. The facility utilized one-bedroom wood frame cabins as rental units. They were given a stucco coating to provide a modern look. One of the cabins was lost to fire in 1943. The facility also catered to the trailer business by providing spaces and rental trailers. By 1950 the Court had become the Fifty-Nine Trees Court.

By 1960 the court was no longer in business. In 1962 the cabins were sold and moved off the property. Today the area is a parking lot.

Airport Haven Court – 2198 East Buckeye Road

By 1940 cabins were being rented at 2198 Henshaw (Buckeye) Road. They quickly took on the name Airport Haven Court because of their proximity to Sky Harbor Airport. The facility was built in cottage court style with three room buildings.

By 1963 the court became the Airport Haven Apartments as they moved to a long-term rental business model. By 1979 the facility was demolished, and the real estate became part of the airport access road easement.

Desert Pool Motel, formerly the Airways Motor Hotel circa 1960 (Author's Collection)

Airways Motor Hotel - 2922 East Van Buren Street

The Airways Motor Hotel was opened in 1948 with auto court style facilities. The individual cabins were created in a Mediterranean style with stucco walls and tile roofs. The court was built at the same time and in similar style to the adjacent Villa Motor Hotel. They were likely under the same ownership.

The Relax Inn, formerly the Airways Motor Hotel, today (Photo by Author 2012)

The Airways Motor Hotel operated from 1948 to 1955. At that time the facility was renamed the Desert Pool Motel. The motel used its pool facilities to compete within what was known as "motel row" on East Van Buren. The new sign was even shaped like the pool as an added draw. The motel operated under the Desert Pool name until 1980 when it was renamed the Fantasyland Motel. The name changed again in 1999 to the Relax Inn.

The Airways still exists today as the Relax Inn. The facility's original office and pool have been demolished, and the office relocated to the first cabin.

Alameda Court – 330 North Twenty-Third Street

The Alameda Court was in business by 1938. The facility consisted of a small cabin court with one- and two-room apartments. The cabins were arranged in a row behind the larger owner's home. By 1948 the court became known as Miller

Auto Court, although the Alameda name may have stuck around as well. The cabins were owned by the Miller family from inception.

By 1952 the cabins were being rented to long-term tenants only. The cabins were demolished in the late 1950s, and the home followed shortly afterwards. Today a modern apartment complex occupies the space.

Alamo Auto Court – 3751 East Van Buren Street

Built in cabin court style, the Alamo Auto Court was open by 1932. The facility also included a service station and trailer court. Demolition of the Alamo took place in the mid-1950s, and the Bill Johnson's Big Apple Restaurant was built in its place. Today the Big Apple still utilizes the Alamo's former space.

Alamo House – See Steinegger Lodging House

Alamo Motel – See Hutch Motel

Alamo Plaza Motor Court circa 1940 (Author's Collection)

Alamo Plaza Motor Court – 2835 East Van Buren Street

The Alamo Plaza Motor Court was housing transient guests by 1939. The facility was built using individual cottages with covered parking between them. The buildings were arranged in a U-shape with a central courtyard.

Alamo Plaza Hotel Courts was the first hotel chain in the United States. The chain had locations all over the southeast and Texas. It appears that the Alamo Plaza in Phoenix was not part of the chain. Rather, the motel likely "borrowed" the name as Alamo Plazas were popular when the Phoenix motel was built.

The Alamo Plaza remained in business until 1992, and the buildings were demolished by 1995. A tire store now occupies the space where the Alamo Plaza Motor Court once stood.

Alanoma Lodge – 3308 West Buckeye Road

By 1948 what would become the Alanoma Lodge was in business as the Route 80 Motel. By 1950 it took on the Alanoma name. The motel was small with only six units.

By 1962 the Alanoma was closed, and it was razed in short order. Today the area is a tire store.

Aldridge Court – 10023 North Twelfth Street

By 1949 the Aldridge Court was in operation. The facility consisted of four rental buildings and owner's quarters. Six rentals were available. By 1952 the court became known as Fredley's Motel.

By 1961 the court moved to an apartment business plan. It was demolished by 1992. Today the property is undeveloped.

Alexander Hotel – See Jefferson Rooming House

Alhambra Court – See Grand Avenue Court

Alhambra Rooming House – 246 West Adams Street

The Alhambra Rooming House was in operation by 1891 and likely earlier. By 1899 it had become the Kelso House. The facility located on the corner of Adams and Third Streets also had a restaurant.

In 1906 Mrs. Kelso closed the Kelso House. All business was sent to the Sixth Avenue Hotel. Mrs. Kelso went to handle the restaurant in the Sixth Avenue location.

A large modern building is located on the real estate today. The rooming house no longer stands.

Alice Guest Lodge – 1001 North Third Street

The Alice Guest Lodge was the former Arizona Apartments. It was converted to transient lodging by 1949. It was a two-story building built in apartment-hotel-style. The facility was owned by former State Senator and Gubernatorial Candidate, Marvin Smith.

The Lodge was closed by 1963 and demolished soon after. Today most of the property is involved in the easement of the road. The junction of Roosevelt Street and Third and Fourth Avenues was changed for better traffic flow. This took up much of the Alice Guest Lodge real estate.

All States Auto Court – 906 North Fifteenth Avenue

By 1928 the All States Auto Court was operating. It was built in the cabin court style popular at the time. About 10 cabins existed on the site. A larger central building contained owner's quarters and a store. That building was destroyed by fire in November 1936. Injuries were minimal. A new building was built to replace the damaged one.

The former All States Auto Court offices (Photo by Author 2014)

The facility closed in the 1950s, and the cabins were removed. The main building still exists today as offices for an auto body shop.

Allen's Court – 1439 South Seventh Street

Allen's Court was a small cabin court consisting of seven or eight cabins. The facility was in operation by 1949. The court operated intermittently as apartments and as a motel.

The court was demolished in the early 1980s. The area is industrial today.

Al's Apartment Motel – See Market Motel

Alturas Hotel – 233 East Washington Street

The Alturas Hotel opened in the fall of 1911. It was built as a replacement for the Gregory House, which had burned down in early 1911. The new construction was included in the new business area called the Kersting Block. The Alturas was included in the construction, but may have been built in a slightly different location. The new hotel was a two-story brick building. By 1923 the facility became the Salt River Hotel.

In 1941 there was some excitement at the Salt River Hotel in the form of a shootout. After two guests were assaulted in the hotel by other guests, the police were summoned. Upon arrival, one of the suspects fled to the roof. When police followed, a short gun battle ensued. The suspect eventually surrendered, and no one was injured. The suspect had just been released from prison in Utah. He later stated he could not remember the incident because he was intoxicated.

In 1967 a guest suffered second degree burns in his room. The man set his clothing on fire with a cigarette. He attempted to extinguish the fire with the wine he was drinking. The wine also caught fire, and he had to put the fire out with his hands.

By 1982 the hotel was no longer accepting guests. Today the area is part of the Collier Center complex.

Alwilda Lodge – 385 North Sixth Avenue

The Alwilda Lodge was in operation by 1959. It was a large home utilized for room rentals. Renters had kitchen access as well as sleeping quarters. The facility was utilized as far back as the 1920s as a boarding house. A garage apartment was located in the rear.

The lodge no longer accepted guests after 1972. It was razed in the 1980s. Today it remains a vacant lot.

Ambassador Hotel – 534 West Washington Street

By 1940 there was a boarding house and rooms for rent at 534 West Washington. The facility soon became known as the Ambassador Hotel. The hotel was a two-story building of unknown size. By 1948 the hotel was no longer in business.

In 1963 the Elgin Hotel opened on the property. It may have utilized the existing building or it may have been new construction. The Elgin Hotel name was a long-standing name that had previously been used in two locations in the city. In 1971 the Elgin closed, and its contents were sold.

Today the Fox Television building uses the real estate formerly utilized by the Ambassador Hotel.

American Camp – 1601 East Van Buren Street

The American Camp was one of the early auto camps that popped up in Phoenix. The facility catered to the new automobile traveler by providing a camping location and basic needs. Most of the early camps either disappeared quickly, or had to add cabins or trailer facilities to survive. The American Camp catered to both. The camp opened in 1925 and was demolished by 1949.

A fast-food restaurant now stands on the property once utilized by the American Camp.

American Hotel – See Wharton Hotel

Amuzu Hotel – 210 East Washington Street

The Amuzu Theatre was operating in Phoenix by 1915. The Amuzu Hotel utilized the theatre's second floor. By 1932 the Amuzu Theatre closed and the Hidalgo (later the Rex) Theatre opened next door at 212 East Washington. (It is possible the Amuzu became the Hidalgo with a new address.) The hotel ceased operations by 1933, but it operated as a rooming house for some time. It was listed for sale in 1936 as a rooming house.

The Phoenix Symphony Hall is on the property today.

Angela Hotel – See Best-Yet Motel

Angelo's Court – See MaryBill Court

Angeles Hotel – See Virginia Rooming House

Anglin Motel – 9315 Cave Creek

The Anglin Motel began as a home and three apartments in the early 1950s. By the mid-1950s it was advertised as the Western Motel Apartments, and it had five units by 1960. The facility operated as apartments-only by 1962. It was demolished in the 1980s.

Today a used car lot is located at the address.

Majestic Hotel, formerly the Anheuser Hotel circa 1925 (Courtesy Arizona State Library, Archives and Public Records, History and Archives Division, Phoenix, #97-0956)

Anheuser Hotel – 22-24 East Washington Street

The Anheuser Hotel was open by 1914. The building was a two-story brick structure which included a restaurant. By 1918 the name of the hotel changed to the Majestic Hotel. The Majestic was out of business by 1937.

Today the modern One North Central Building is on the property.

Annex Hotel – See Central Avenue Hotel

Annex Hotel – See Jefferson Rooms

Annex Hotel – 311½ West Washington Street

The Annex Hotel was a two-story brick building adjacent to the Arizona Hotel. The lower portion of the building held the Arizona Buffet restaurant for many years. The second floor featured sleeping rooms known as the Annex Hotel. The hotel was advertised from 1931 to 1940.

In 1968 the building was sold at auction and demolished. Today the area is used by a parking facility.

Antry's Auto Court – 2004 East Van Buren Street

Antry's Auto Court was in operation by 1941. The facility was built in cabin court style with individual cottages used as rental units. A decade earlier the property had been used for a short time as an auto camp with a now unknown name. That camp had closed by 1931.

In 1947 the Antry's name was changed to the Twin Palms Court. The name lasted only until 1949 when the court's name became the L-Bar-K Motel.

The L-Bar-K operated until 1966 when it was closed. Today the property is a used car lot.

Apache Hotel circa 1940 (Author's Collection)

Apache Hotel – 515 North Central Avenue

The Apache Hotel was opened in 1920 on the site of the former Annex Hotel. The hotel was a four-story, modern hotel built at a cost of 1.2 million dollars. The Apache was modernized and expanded in 1939. The new construction included a twenty-foot addition to the entire front of the building. This gave the building a brand new look. It also included a new lobby area and 25 additional rooms. The existing rooms were also remodeled at the time.

The Apache Hotel closed in 1986. It was demolished soon thereafter to make a parking lot. The area is currently part of the Walter Cronkite School of Journalism.

Apartment Hotel – See Royal Crest Lodge

Arbor Court – 8511 North Central Avenue

The Arbor Court was a small cottage court with an unknown opening date. By 1939 it was certainly in business. The facility was located in the picturesque "Orange District", and was bounded at the rear by the Arizona Canal. Cottages consisted of three rooms.

By 1953 the court was no longer operating, but the Arbor Buffet continued to function. The courts buildings were demolished by the late 1950s.

Today a restaurant still exists on the Arbor Buffet site. The parking lot to the south is where the court once existed.

Arcade Hotel – See Lemon Hotel

Arcadia Lodge – East Camelback Road

Jarvis Hunt, a Chicago Businessman, built a residence for himself near the foothills of Camelback Mountain in the early 1930s. By 1938 Hunt had built and opened the Arcadia Lodge on the property. The lodge was listed among the best lodges in Arizona and was a popular restaurant as well. After 1943 there is no more mention of the Lodge in the historical record.

The Arcadia Lodge was located on Camelback Road seven miles east of Central Avenue. It was likely located near Arcadia Road.

Aricopa Motel – 4311 East Van Buren Street

By 1949 the Aricopa Motel was in operation. The facility utilized multiple single-story buildings with various room styles. Twenty-seven rooms included single units, multiple room apartments, and eight kitchenettes. By 1952 the Aricopa changed its name to the Stagecoach Inn Motel.

Stagecoach Inn, formerly the Aricopa Motel, circa 1955 (Author's Collection)

The Stagecoach operated until 1985 when it stopped accepting transient guests. The facility was demolished shortly afterward. Today the property is a parking lot.

Arizona Ambassador Hotel circa 1955 (Author's Collection)

Arizona Ambassador Hotel – 335 West Maryland Avenue

The Arizona Ambassador was a rural resort operating by 1948. The facility utilized six large, apartment-style buildings for rental units. It featured a large entertainment area with a pool, playground, shuffleboard, and badminton court. Hotel amenities included a restaurant and lounge.

The Arizona Ambassador was closed and demolished in the early 1980s. Today the hotel has been replaced by residential housing.

Arizona Auto Court – 2308 (2500) Grand Avenue

By 1937 the Arizona Auto Court was renting cabins. The facility grew through the years, and by 1952 the complex included 18 units, a gas station, grocery store, and living quarters. By 1956 the auto court had become more of a trailer court, and its name changed to Vans Trailer Court. The cabins were demolished at the time.

Today a modern gas station resides on the property.

Arizona Biltmore Hotel circa 1930 (Author's Collection)

Arizona Biltmore Hotel – 2400 East Missouri Avenue

Charles and Warren McArthur were the original owners and constructors of the Arizona Biltmore Hotel. It was opened as a luxury resort on February 23, 1929. The hotel featured modern concrete construction and amenities such as stables, tennis courts, and a golf course.

The building was designed by the owners' brother, Albert Chase McArthur. Albert worked under Frank Lloyd Wright at one time, and Wright was brought in to collaborate. The scope of Wright's influence on the construction is hotly debated today. Certainly he was utilized to help design the precast concrete blocks the building is made of, now called "Biltmore Block". Wright claimed ownership of the process and was paid for its use. It was discovered later that Wright did not hold the patents on this type of construction, and litigation ensued. In any event, the hotel shows striking Wright influence.

The Arizona Biltmore Hotel (Photo by Author 2014)

The McArthurs had difficulty initially, and control of the hotel fell to one of the principal investors, William Wrigley. Wrigley was the owner of the William Wrigley Jr. Company, which manufactured Wrigley's Gum. He was also owner of the Chicago Cubs. Full ownership of the Biltmore was finalized in July 1931 with a court order of foreclosure that cleared the property's title. Wrigley built a mansion next to the hotel as his primary residence. On January 26, 1932,

Wrigley died of heart failure in Phoenix. He had suffered an earlier heart attack on Catalina Island about a year before. Wrigley also owned Catalina Island and was buried there.

The Wrigley family continued to own and operate the Arizona Biltmore until 1973 when it was sold to Talley Industries. Talley began renovations on the hotel, but a fire ravaged the building as they began. A decision was made to rebuild, and the hotel reopened for its regular season in September without losing any business.

The Arizona Biltmore played innkeeper to many famous guests, including Marylyn Monroe, Clark Gable, and Frank Sinatra. Every United States President from Herbert Hoover to George W. Bush has been to the Biltmore. Ronald and Nancy Reagan held their honeymoon at the hotel. The hotel has kept its upscale, luxury appeal by modernizing its timeless design through the years. It remains today one of Phoenix's premier hotel properties.

Arizona Hotel circa 1925 (Courtesy McClintock Collection, Arizona Room, Phoenix Public Library)

Arizona Hotel – 10 South Third Avenue

The Arizona Hotel was in business by 1923. The facility utilized brick construction and consisted of 105 rooms on five stories. It contained a lounge and cafe as well. In 1935 the hotel underwent a major renovation. A Carrier-Brunswick air conditioning system was installed at a cost of $25,000. The total cost of the 1935 remodel was $50,000. New furnishings were installed and the lobby enlarged to make a new entrance. The lobby could now be accessed from either Third Avenue or Washington Street.

In 1943 the hotel was purchased by a Mr. and Mrs. Porter and two other relatives known as the Porter sisters. The deed, however, only included the couple. By 1959 the Porters sere separated, and several legal proceedings took place including a divorce and division of property. Due to the complicated nature of the proceedings, a receiver was placed at the hotel to maintain its operation. The court cases lasted until 1965 before the issues were resolved.

By 1968 the hotel was closed. It was demolished in short order to create a parking lot. Today the property still holds a parking facility.

Arizona Lodging House – 420 West Harrison Street

The Arizona Lodging House was operating by 1903. The address listed until 1915 was 417 West Harrison Street. It's possible the facility was moved to a location across the street. The other possibility is that the house was just addressed incorrectly. The house operated until it was razed to make room for the Phoenix Union Station. The station opened in 1923. Today the Union Station building still stands on the property.

Arizona Manor Hotel – 2390 East Camelback Road

The Arizona Manor Hotel was in operation by 1951. The facility was an upscale, full service resort. It included a health salon with massages and steam baths. An upscale restaurant was located on the property as well. Celebrities were known to vacation at the Arizona Manor.

Arizona Manor Hotel circa 1955 (Author's Collection)

The Arizona Manor was closed by 1983 and demolished. The Biltmore Financial Center was built on the site and remains there today.

Arizona Motel circa 1940 (Author's Collection)

Arizona Motel circa 2012 (Photo by Author)

Arizona Motel – 2625 East Van Buren Street

The Arizona Motel was built as a cabin-style court and opened in 1938. The facility utilized a Spanish-influenced facade with stucco walled buildings. The Arizona Motel has withstood the changing economies and the decline of Van Buren Street. It still stands as the Arizona Motel today.

The Santa Fe Apartments, formerly the Arizona Motor Inn, today (Photo by Author 2012)

Arizona Motor Inn – 908 South Seventeenth Avenue

The Arizona Motor Inn was opened in 1937. The facility consisted of nine cottages and a large owner's home and office. Spaces between the cabins were covered to make carports.

By 1983 the facility became the Santa Fe Villas apartments and still exists as such today.

Arizona Palms Motel circa 1960 (Author's Collection)

Arizona Palms – 3725 East Van Buren Street

The Arizona Palms Motor Hotel opened in 1952. The facility was constructed in the standard single-story, strip motel style. The original construction was an L-shape with a central courtyard. Subsequent expansions resulted in a U-shaped building with pool facilities in the courtyard area.

The Western Lodge, formerly the Arizona Palms, today (Photo by Author 2012)

The Arizona Palms conducted business until 1990 when its name was changed to the Thrifty Inn. The motel's name was changed again in 2005 to the Western Lodge and still functions as such, although it appears to be open intermittently.

Arizona Ranch House circa 1960 (Author's Collection)

Arizona Ranch House – 5614 North Central Avenue

The Arizona Ranch house was originally built as a private residence. In 1948 it was converted to a resort with 11 rooms, a dining room, and pool. In 1958 four more rooms were added, and the dining room was expanded.

The rural ranch feel and upscale rooms became popular, and by 1961 another major expansion occurred. This time a new pool was built in the rear of the facility, and a new dining room was built over the existing pool. The old pool was converted to a pond where guests could catch their own fish to be cooked in the restaurant. It's likely the Arizona Ranch House was the first to utilize infrared heaters to make the outdoor dining area more comfortable. The owner predicted that other restaurants would also want heated patios for guest comfort. Of course his prediction came true and outdoor heaters are very prevalent in Phoenix today.

The motel stopped accepting guests by 1988. It was demolished in the mid-1990s. Today the area is residential with modern homes built on the site.

Arizona Twilighter circa 1955 (Author's Collection)

Arizona Twilighter – 4310 North Fifth Avenue

The Arizona Twilighter was opened as an upscale apartment hotel in January 1953. The facility contained multiple buildings arranged to create a "park-like" atmosphere. A large pool and kitchen facilities were included. The hotel immediately accepted both transients and long-term leases.

Upon the opening, the Arizona Twilighter offered one dollar per night rates to those suffering economically. This was on a limited basis, of course. The property operated as both a hotel and apartments at first, but by the mid-1960s it accepted only long-term renters.

The facility was demolished in the 1980s. Today modern apartments are located on the property.

Arrow Motel – See Polly Court

Astor Hotel – See Stacy Hotel

Atherton Court – 909 South Thirty-Fifth Avenue

The Atherton Court was in operation by 1948. The facility utilized single-story, strip-motel design, which was new at the time. It was built in a U-shape with parking in the center. By 1952 the court was renamed the Nine-O-Nine Court. In the mid-1950s the court shifted more towards an apartment business model and stopped advertising to the tourist market.

The original Atherton Court building still exists today and operates as apartments.

Attaway House – See Gordon Rooming House

Aut-O-Tel Camp – 2841 East Van Buren Street

The Aut-O-Tel Camp was in operation by 1931. The facility was built in cabin court style, which was popular at the time. With 14 cottages and 16 trailer pads, the Aut-O-Tel catered to both types of transient guests. By 1938 the facility was renamed the Suhuaro Court (later the Saguaro Court).

The Suhuaro Court operated until 1957 when its property became part of the Red Barn Motel. The area is now a vacant lot.

Auto Rest Court – See Motel Inn

AutoLodge Motel circa 1965 (Author's Collection)

AutoLodge Motel – 804 East Van Buren Street

The AutoLodge Motel was opened in January 1962. The facility was built in two-story motor hotel style. It included 32 units and a manager's quarters. The AutoLodge was part of a chain being built by the National AutoLodge Corporation. The company built motels utilizing a co-ownership type of concept. Motels were built by National AutoLodge, and co-owners were found to invest at fifty percent as managing partners.

The AutoLodge operated until 1991 when its name changed to the Economy Inn. The facility held the Economy Inn name until its demolition in 2000. The real estate is now part of the Marriot Spring Hill Suites property.

Autopia Motor Hotel circa 1930 (Author's Collection)

Autopia Motor Hotel circa 1930 (Author's Collection)

Autopia Motor Park - 3901 East Van Buren Street

Autopia Motor Park was built in 1928 at a cost of over $110,000. That is the equivalent of about 1.5 million dollars in 2014. The Autopia was a multiple building complex built in cabin court style with 58 units. The facility was the city's first large tourist court, with property that extended from Van Buren Street to Washington Street. Entry was available from both streets, but frontage was on Van Buren.

The Autopia was an early example of the trend away from auto camps towards the more civilized accommodations of an auto court. With most of the comforts of home, the facility's early advertising capitalized on the ability to stay without setting up camp. The motor park provided electricity, hot and cold water, daily housekeeping, multiple room apartments, and private garages.

The Autopia operated until 1950 when the court's name was changed to the Continental Guest Lodge. The name was again changed in 1952 to the Tropicana Motel. Around 1960 the Tropicana closed permanently. The facility was demolished and the land used for many future businesses. One use was the Samoan Village Motel, which was built on a portion of the property.

Today the property where the Autopia was located is part of the Gateway College campus.

Avalon Rooms – See Wharton Hotel

Avon (The) – See Polk House

Aztec Motor Court – 3613 (3603) East Van Buren Street

The Aztec Motor Court was in business by 1939. The facility contained 16 units presented in a Spanish style which utilized an adobe exterior and tile roofs. Construction was of the cabin court style. The Aztec Motor Court was a long-lived facility lasting until 1987. The cabins were demolished in short order.

Today the real estate is used for an adult business.

Bachelor Court – See Jody's Court

Bagdad Inn circa 1965 (Author's Collection)

Bagdad Inn, now the New Day Center (Photo by Author 2012)

Bagdad Inn - 3335 East Van Buren Street

The Bagdad Inn was open by 1960 and utilized real estate previously used by the Sharon Court. This was another property with the popular Arabian theme prevalent throughout the United States at the time. The facility was built using two-story, motor inn style construction and included 100 rooms. All of the rooms in the Bagdad featured a king size bed.

The Bagdad operated independently for some time, but by 1967 it had become part of the Caravan Inn East. The motel was separated from the Caravan property again in 1996 and gained a Super 8 flag. In 2007 the facility was purchased along with the old Caravan East by the United Methodist Outreach Ministries (UMOM) to be used as homeless housing.

The original Bagdad Inn building still exists as part of the UMOM's New Day Center.

Bali-Hi Motor Hotel circa 1960 (Author's Collection)

Bali-Hi Motor Hotel – 1515 Grand Avenue

The Bali-Hi Motor Hotel was opened in 1955 on the property of the former Palm Garden Auto Court. The facility was built using two-story, motor inn style construction. It contained 65 rental units, a coffee shop, restaurant, and lounge. The Bali-Hi was considered one of the premier motor hotels in Phoenix at the time of its construction.

The Teen Challenge, formerly the Bali-Hi Hotel, today (Photo by Author 2012)

The Bali-Hi became the headquarters for the Ranger Hotels chain in 1963. The chain joined larger independent motels to gain the economic benefits a large buying group could provide. Other Phoenix members included the Egyptian and the Kon Tiki.

For several years the Bali-Hi operated the adjacent Caravan Inn as part of the Bali-Hi. It was eventually sold off and became a separate entity.

In 1960 the FBI arrested a fugitive doctor at the Bali-Hi. The medical doctor was staying at the motel under an assumed name. He was a former president of the Naturopathic Physicians Association, but had gone into hiding while continuing to perform abortion procedures. At the time abortions were illegal in the United States.

The Bali-Hi was closed as a motel by 1991. Today the original Bali-Hi building still exists. It operates as a Teen Challenge induction center. Teen Challenge is a faith-based substance abuse recovery organization.

Bank Exchange Hotel – 136 East Washington Street

The Bank Exchange Hotel was opened in 1879 by Emil Ganz. The hotel was Ganz' first endeavor in Phoenix, and he went on to be Mayor of the city and President of the National Bank of Arizona. The early hotel was a two-story structure built using wood frame and brick. In April 1885 a large fire took place in downtown Phoenix. Several businesses were destroyed along Washington Street including the Bank Exchange Hotel. The hotel was not rebuilt as Ganz moved on to his other interests. Interestingly, Ganz' granddaughter, Joan, was a co-creator of the famous Sesame Street television series.

An address for the Bank Exchange is somewhat elusive. Inaccurate information is included in many sources. However, it is clear that the hotel was located opposite the City Hall, and the real estate was later used for the Popular Dry Goods Company Building. This puts the address at 136 East Washington.

Today the address is a wine and martini bar.

Barbara Court – 2148 West Buckeye Road

By 1948 the Barbara Court was accepting guests. The court was built in an unknown style, but it was small and named after the owner. It did include kitchenettes and went through a remodel in 1959.

By 1981 the Barbara Court was closed as a motel. It was demolished by 1995, and the real estate is a vacant lot today.

Barstow Rooms – 401 West Jefferson Street

The Barstow Rooms was a rooming house located at Jefferson Street and Fourth Avenue. The facility was a house and likely built originally as a residence. By 1905 rooms were being rented in the home. Eventually, it became the Barstow with 10 rental rooms and 10 cots. Renting cots only was popular at times for people who just wanted to get some sleep but not rent a room. By 1950 the area became a service station location and then a parking lot.

Today the area is a parking structure.

Bassler Hotel – See Sixth Avenue Hotel

Bayliss Hotel – 381 North Second Avenue

The Bayliss Hotel was in operation by 1949. It consisted of six units. Apartments were rented at the address as early as the 1920s. This may have been the same building, or the Bayliss may have been a new construction.

By 1983 the property became the Downtowner Hotel but was closed by 1986. It was demolished in the 1990s. Today a storage facility is located on the property.

BB Motel – 2608 West Van Buren Street

In 1949 the Irma Apartments became the BB Motel. The motel was a single building with apartments inside. By 1972 the facility had become known as the Avalon Motel. Its name changed again by 1978 to the Englund Motel. By 1980 the facility had moved to an apartment business model under the name Avalon Apartments. The facility was demolished in 2006.

Today the area is an undeveloped lot.

Sun Valley Motel, formerly the Beach Court, circa 1950 (Author's Collection)

Beach Court – 3641 (3701) East Van Buren Street

The 19-unit Beach Court was opened by 1932. The facility utilized cabin court style with individual cottages for each unit. Office and manager's quarters were located at the front center of the property. In 1946 the court changed its name to the Sun Valley Motel, most likely in an attempt to modernize its advertising.

The Sun Valley closed permanently and was demolished by 1996. Today the property is a parking lot.

Beasley Hotel – See Dorris Hotel

Bel Aire Motel – 1814 West Van Buren Street

The Bel Aire Motel was in operation by 1948. It consisted of multiple large buildings containing rental units. By 1967 the buildings were being moved off the property, and the facility was closed.

Today a bank is located at the address.

Bell Hotel – See French Rooming House

Bell Motel – See Star Auto Court

Bellevue Court – See Calico Cat Court

Belmont Court – 4 South Eighteenth Avenue

The Belmont Court was accepting guests by 1931. It was situated directly behind the State Capitol building. The facility consisted of six buildings and an owner's home. The buildings were arranged in two rows of three with the residence placed in the rear.

By the late 1950s the court began operating as apartments only. The buildings were demolished in the 1970s to create a parking lot. It remains so today.

Benson Lodge – 620 North Second Street

The Benson Lodge opened in 1939. It contained 30 rental rooms and offered food as well. By 1949 the facility became the Palms Hotel. By 1968 it became the Sagebrush Inn and by 1969 the Sullivan Hotel. The facility began operating as a boarding house by 1972.

Palms Hotel, formerly the Benson Lodge, circa 1950 (Author's Collection)

The facility was demolished in the early 1980s. Modern condominiums are located on the property today.

Best Rest Court – 2812 (2750) Grand Avenue

By 1943 cottages were being rented at what would become the Best Rest Court. Details about the court are not known other than it doubled as a used car lot. By 1951 the court was gone, and the area had become an equipment sales company.

Today the real estate is part of the Grand Avenue and Twenty-Seventh Avenue interchange easement.

Best-Yet Motel – 2114 West Buckeye Road

By 1948 the Best-Yet Motel was in business. It was a cabin court of good size and included at least some kitchenettes. By 1963 the facility had become the Warren Motel. Its name changed again by 1968 to the Angela Hotel.

The motel was closed and demolished by 1990 and is undeveloped today.

Bide-A-Wee Court – 530 North Eighteenth Street

By 1930 a tourist camp was established at 530 North Eighteenth Street. Three cabins were quickly added, and the name became the Bide-A-Wee Court. By 1940 the facility took on the name of the owner, Wilson's Court. Eight house trailer spaces were added to the complex along with the cabins and the owner's residence.

In 1943 Willard Blackwood, a guest at the tourist court, was arrested for the murder of Lawrence Smith. Smith operated a service station on Washington Street. Blackwood shot Smith in the head after an argument, rendering the man dead. The argument took place over the alleged theft of gasoline on the part of Blackwood. Blackwood pumped gas into his car while no attendants were on duty.

By 1948 the court was no longer advertised to short-term renters. The area is a parking lot today.

Bide-A-Wee Place - 1110 North Sixteenth Street (Park Road)

The Bide-A-Wee Place was two miles north of town on what is now Sixteenth Street. The area was rural at the time, and the facility was mainly a furniture manufacturer. Along with the furniture they had cottages on the property for rent. There were several cottages in different configurations. About 1923 the cottages began being marketed as "duplex apartments". The facility was demolished in the 1950s to make room for the Sacred Heart Home for the Aged.

Today the assisted living building still exists on the property but it is vacant. Restoration work is being performed on the building as of 2014.

Bill's Cottage Court – 1811 East Washington Street

Bill's Court was in business by 1932. As the name would imply, it consisted of 14 individual cottages. They were aligned in two rows with parking in the center. By 1948 the facility became Bucks Court.

The facility was out of business by 1956. Industrial buildings are located on the property today.

The former Biltmore Motel, now offices (Photo by Author 2014)

Biltmore Motel – 2512 East Thomas Road

The Biltmore Motel was operating by 1949 as the Stratford Arms Apartments. By 1952 the facility operated as both a motel and apartments under the name Biltmore Motel. The motel was constructed in the familiar U-shape utilizing three buildings with Spanish influenced architecture. It was unusual, however, that the parking was situated on the outside of the U. A central green space for pedestrian traffic only was placed between the buildings. Units had doors located on both sides for access to the courtyard as well as parking. Units were of one- and two-bedroom configurations and contained kitchens. There were 12 rental units at the facility.

In 1961 the Biltmore Motel was closed, and the units converted to offices. Today the original buildings still exist and operate as business offices.

Black Diamond Auto Cabins – 1635 Grand Avenue

By 1929 Black Diamond Auto Cabins was renting units to guests. The court was built in the usual cabin court style so prevalent at the time. By 1937 the court was renamed as the Fern Glen Court. By 1954 the Fern Glen was out of business.

Today the area is part of the I-10 easement where it intersects Grand Avenue.

Blue Bonnet Auto Court – 811 South Nineteenth Avenue

The Blue Bonnet Auto Court was in operation by 1929. The facility utilized standard cabin court construction with each cabin being a rental unit. The size of the facility is not known.

In 1939 a guest at the court died from burns sustained in his cabin. He was filling the heater with gasoline when the heater exploded. It appeared, at first, that the burns were not life-threatening as he was able to extinguish them in a nearby irrigation ditch. However, he experienced complications and expired.

The Blue Bonnet was closed by 1961 and quickly demolished. Today the lot is vacant of permanent buildings.

Blue Crown Auto Court – 3401 East Van Buren Street

The Blue Crown Auto Court was in business by 1932. The facility was built in cabin court style with individual buildings rented as units. In 1958 the court was razed to make room for the Caravan Inn East.

Older addresses were not always accurate. While it may not appear so, today the land is located where the New Day Center is situated.

Blue Point Court – 1628 Grand Avenue

By 1931 the Blue Point Court was in business. The court utilized cabins as rental units, which was common of many auto courts during that time. By 1937 the Blue Point became the Court Carol. By 1947 the Grand Avenue Court across the street had closed, and the Court Carol took on that name.

The Grand Avenue Court (formerly Court Carol) was closed by 1971. Today the real estate that once held the Blue Point is part of the I-10 and Grand Avenue interchange easement.

Bobs Motel – See Cross R Motel

Bobs Van Buren Motel as it looks today (Photo by Author 2012)

Bobs Van Buren Motel – 3602 West Van Buren Street

Bobs Van Buren Motel was open by 1947. The facility utilized single-story, strip motel style construction. The building was laid out in a shallow U-shape.

Bobs was closed as a motel by 1987. Today the Bobs Van Buren Motel buildings still exist. They are utilized as part of a car wash business.

Bolin Court – 1002 South Twenty-Ninth Avenue

The Bolin Court was renting rooms by 1955. The buildings were duplex structures and rented both short- and long-term in the beginning. The court operated as apartments only after 1970.

In the late 1990s the buildings were demolished. Today an industrial metal business operates on the property.

Bona Vista Court – 1046 North Thirty-Second Street

The Bona Vista Court was a small, three-unit facility. It was advertised as a court from 1949 to 1956. This was likely to take advantage of the booming transient market. Afterwards, the facility went to long-term rentals only. Today the area is part of the Loop 202 structure.

Bonner Hotel – 27 South Fifth Street

By 1916 the Bonner Hotel was in business. The facility was a 19-room hotel with a restaurant. In 1939 the hotel was purchased by H.H. Rice who also owned the Raymond Hotel. He renovated the hotel and added 11 rooms. Rice's hotels catered exclusively to African Americans.

It is likely that the Bonner Hotel was originally named the Adalade Hotel. The Adalade was opened by 1915 in the same vicinity as the Bonner. It disappears from records in 1916 when the Bonner appears.

The Bonner was closed by 1957. Today the parking garage for Chase Field and the Phoenix Convention Center is on the property.

Borgouist Cabins – See Cummins Court

Bower House – 521 East Monroe Street

The Bower was a rooming house with seven rooms. By the early 1920s it became an apartment house.

The area is a parking garage today.

Box A Motel – See Ford's Motel

Branding Iron Lodge circa 1957 (Author's Collection)

Branding Iron Lodge – 7150 North Seventh Street

The Branding Iron Lodge was in business by 1951. Some of the buildings did exist by 1949 but may not have been rented at the time. When completed, the facility consisted of six rental buildings and an owner's quarters at the street. The rental buildings were built inside an orange grove with ample room around each to provide privacy. The lodge advertised the ability to pick your own fruit for breakfast.

The facility was closed by 1979 and was soon demolished. Today a modern dentist office and residences utilize the real estate.

Bridges Auto Court – 2020 East Van Buren Street

The lodging history of 2020 East Van Buren is interesting. In the late 1920s the property held a short-lived camp listed under the name Cox Auto Camp. By 1930 the camp was gone, and the area was listed as a gas station for many years. During this time the owner, W. H. Bridges, began experimenting with the construction of mobile homes. By 1937 Bridges was producing custom mobile homes and became known as a pioneer in the local mobile home industry.

By 1941 the property was again marketed to tourists under the name Bridges Auto Court. The facility was built in cabin court style. The court made one more name change to Turley Auto Court in 1948. This was short-lived, and by 1951 the property no longer catered to transient guests. Fittingly, the property became a trailer sales business for many years afterwards.

Today the Bridges Auto Court real estate is part of the I-10 easement where it meets Van Buren Street.

Bronco Motel – See Edgerton's Motel

Brown House – See Golden Rule Rooming House

Buckeye Motel – See Circle Inn Court

Buckeye Road Court – See Red Wing Court

Bucks Court – See Bills Cottage Court

The former Bungalow Court managers home, now a barber shop (Photo by Author 2014)

Bungalow Court – 401 North Twenty-Seventh Avenue

The Bungalow Court was a cabin-style facility located on the corner of Twenty-Seventh Avenue and Melvin Street. The facility was in operation by 1948. It included 10 rental units and a two-bedroom, brick-stucco home. The court began operating as apartments by 1963.

The cabins no longer exist as they were demolished in the 1990s. However, the stucco home still stands and is utilized as a barber shop.

Burbank Rooms – 28 South Second Avenue

The Burbank Rooms was in business by 1912 as a downtown rooming house. It became part of the Dorris Hotel by 1939.

Today the area contains the Calvin C. Goode Municipal Building. Second Avenue no longer exists in that area.

Butler's Guest Ranch – 8502 North Central Avenue

Butler's Guest Ranch was in operation by the early 1930s. The ranch was seasonal, being open from October to June, and accepted up to 10 guests. Butler's catered to guests with health problems and preferred they stay the entire season. Guests at the ranch stayed in two-bedroom cottages and utilized on-ranch saddle horses for entertainment. At the time of construction, the ranch was in a rural area north of Phoenix. The area was known as the "Orange District" due to the vast orange groves that covered the area.

By 1969 the Guest Ranch was no longer accepting guests. It was demolished in the early 1980s. Today Butler Drive is the only clue the ranch ever existed. The area is residential housing today.

Byers House – 103 East Jefferson Street (109 South First Street)

The Byers House was built and opened in 1893. Built on the site of the former Plaza Boarding House, the hotel was a two-story brick structure located on the southeast corner of Jefferson and First Streets.

Just like today, Phoenix has always had its share of homeless people on the downtown streets. In January of 1894 a mentally disturbed man was found wandering the streets. He was identified as the son in a wealthy family from Texas. A local benefactor put him up in Phoenix's newest hotel, the Byers House, until the family could retrieve the man.

In 1901 the Byers House became the Phoenix Hotel after a remodel. Around 1947 the hotel began using the 109 South First Street address. By 1955 the Phoenix Hotel was no longer in business. Today the area where the Phoenix Hotel stood is part of the US Airways Center. Due to the relocation of Jefferson Street, it's likely that a small part of the hotel would be in Jefferson Street today.

Byron's Lodge – See Monte Vista Lodge

C & E Motel – See Cross R Motel

The former C & M Motel, now apartments (Photo by Author 2014)

C & M Motel – 2828 West Buckeye Road

By 1951 the Cunningham family opened their motel on the site of their previous grocery store endeavor. Little is known about the motel, but it did contain kitchenettes. A pool hall and café were also located on the property. The name C & M Motel may be a play on words for the last name Cunningham.

By 1961 the facility became the Cunningham Apartments. Today it is still rented as apartments, and the original building still stands.

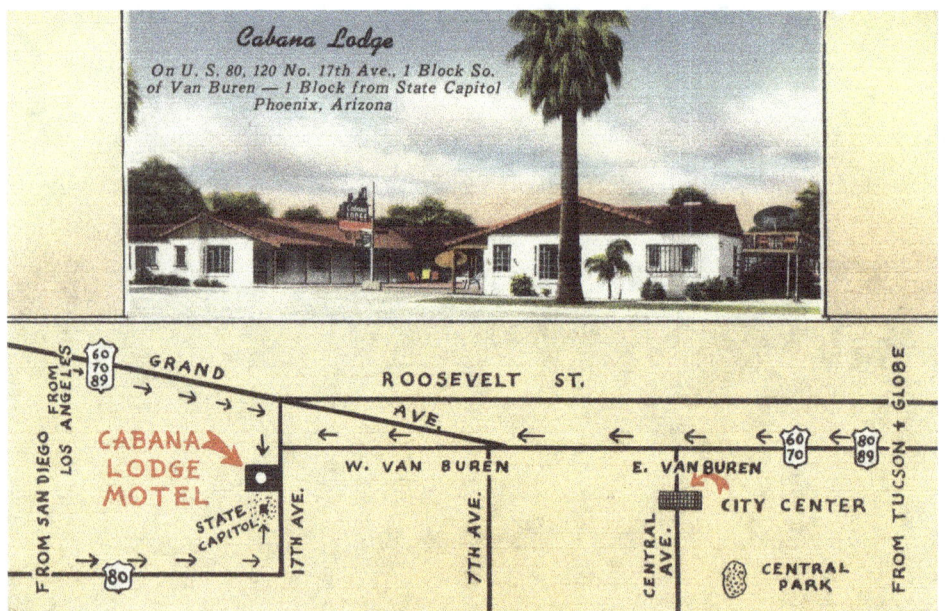

Cabana Lodge circa 1950 (Author's Collection)

Cabana Lodge – 120 North Seventeenth Avenue

The Cabana Lodge was accepting guests by 1949. The style and size of the facility are not known.

By 1975 the Lodge was out of business and demolished. Today the real estate once occupied by the Cabana Lodge is a parking lot.

Cabrera Court – 1738 East Monroe Street

The Cabrera Court was a small cabin court consisting of seven or eight buildings. It was in operation by 1948 but was no longer a court by 1956. Its buildings were demolished in the 1960s to make room for a large apartment complex.

At the time that the new apartments were built, Monroe Street was moved one half block north. This was the former alley on the block between Van Buren Street and the old Monroe Street alignment. This puts the Cabrera Court on the south side of the current Monroe Street.

The area remains an apartment complex today with the 1960s buildings still in use.

Cactus Court – See Stefford's Cottages

Cactus Motel – See Eli Motel

Cactus Rock Lodge – 7645 North Sixteenth Street

By 1952 the Cactus Rock Lodge was accepting guests. The facility was a 14-unit hotel with a swimming pool and stables. It operated as a guest ranch in a very rural and picturesque area at the base of Squaw Peak (Piestewa Peak). The lodge was popular for corporate retreats with companies such as Trans World Airlines in the 1950s and 1960s.

By 1974 the Cactus Rock Lodge was no longer operating. It sat vacant for a few years, and by 1977 the Cactus Rock Lodge building was converted to the Hole-in-the-Wall Restaurant. The Pointe West resort was built around the lodge. The restaurant remains as part of the Pointe Hilton Hotel today in its original building. The preservation of the lodge by the hotel appears to have been a conscious decision.

Calico Cat Court – 3001 East Van Buren Street

By 1938 the Calico Cat Court was accepting guests. The facility was built in cabin court style utilizing individual buildings as units. The court went through a few name changes. For a short time in 1941 it was called the O&E Tourist Court. By 1942 it became the Bellevue Court, and by 1948 the facility became the Hawthorne Court.

In 1939 a couple was robbed at gunpoint in their cabin at the Calico Cat. The culprits blinded the couple with flashlights as they robbed them. The robbers were eventually caught and tried.

By 1960 the Hawthorne Court closed and soon became a trailer sales facility. Today the area is an auto repair facility.

California Inn – See The Ivon

The Camelback Lodge circa 1970 (Author's Collection)

Camelback Lodge – 4222 East Camelback Road

The Camelback Lodge was built in 1954 with 12 rental units. The facility was built in two-story motor inn style and included a pool. The motel was somewhat upscale with wall-to-wall carpeting and date palm landscaping. A second building consisting of rental units was constructed in the 1960s. This utilized the same type of construction used earlier.

In 1974 the lodge was sold and demolished to build a new bank. These buildings still exist today as office buildings.

Camelback View Auto Court – 3543 (3595) East Van Buren Street

The Camelback View Auto Court was in business by 1932. The facility was built in cabin court style with individual buildings rented as units. The facility was also known as Joes Court and Wilkins Court at various times. This is because the property was owned by Joe Wilkins. By 1955 the court was out of business.

Today the land is vacant.

Camp Joy – 2229 East Van Buren Street

Camp Joy was an early auto camp and court. It was opened in 1927 to serve the new motoring season that had developed in the Phoenix area. The facility was built in the early auto court style with individual cabins and camping areas.

Camp Joy closed in 1960. The property is now a car lot.

Camp Phoenix Court – 2220 East Van Buren Street

Camp Phoenix opened in 1930 as an addition to the new camps and courts opening to service the growing auto tourist season. The facility had different accommodations for different types of travelers. Three sections were developed: the court area, the trailer area, and the camping area.

Camp Phoenix closed in 1977. Today the property is undeveloped land.

Camp Seven Up – South Eighteenth Street near Jackson Street

Little is known about Camp Seven Up. It was located on South Eighteenth Street, likely on the west side, near the railroad tracks south of Jackson Street. Aerial photos of the property show a few cabins and what was likely a camping area. The facility was advertised from 1939 to 1947.

Today the area is industrial.

Campbell Motel – See Ford's Motel

Canary Court – 2041 West Van Buren Street

The Gunnel Tourist Camp was established by 1925. It provided camping facilities to the new automobile tourists and utilized the address 221 North Twenty-First Avenue.

By 1930 the tourist camp was replaced by the Canary Court, which utilized cabin court construction. The Canary's cabins included 21 units built in either one- or two-bedroom configurations.

In 1941 the owner of the court was charged with the crime of working female employees more than 48 hours. Apparently one of the motel maids complained about working too many hours at the auto court.

The Canary Court was closed by 1984 and demolished by 1987. Today the real estate which once held the Canary Court holds a gas station.

Capitol Auto Court – 1825–33 West Van Buren Street

By 1929 the Capitol Auto Court was accepting guests. The court was built in cabin court style. In the case of the Capitol, each rental cabin consisted of two rooms.

One morning in 1942 guests at the Capitol woke to find their items missing. During the night thieves had stolen the pants and a handbag from the occupants in three separate cabins.

By 1958 the Capitol Auto Court was out of business. Its cabins were demolished, and a new Jack in the Box fast-food restaurant was built in its place. Today the real estate still holds a Jack in the Box. However, the building is modern.

Capitol Hotel – 242 East Washington Street

By 1894 the Gardiners had demolished the Phoenix Hotel and built the Capitol Hotel in its place. The facility was a two-story structure which included a café. Shops and saloons were located on the ground floor. Within a few years the hotel began to be operated under lease agreements.

In 1943 the hotel experienced some excitement. A man was caught attempting to break into the safe at the nearby Copperstate Bar. The thief attempted to thwart police by disappearing in the Capitol Hotel. He was apprehended on the roof of the building.

In 1958 the hotel was becoming a problem to nearby merchants. The facility had operated without a license for two years, and upon inspection three pages of violations were observed. These included very tight quarters for guests and raw sewage under the porch. Neighboring merchants complained that women could not walk along the north side of Washington Street safely, even during the day. Wine and liquor bottles needed to be cleared from the area each morning. The facility was under lease but still owned by Laurabel Gardiner. Later that year most of the block was demolished, including the hotel, to make a parking lot.

Laurabel Gardiner was 86 at the time of the demolition and was the wife of the original land owner, John Gardiner. They had married in 1875, just a few years after John had built the first hotel in Phoenix. Laurabel had been named the most popular woman in the territory in 1871 and given a piano and silver plaque by the newspaper. In 1871 she was the only Caucasian woman in the town of Phoenix, which had 75 male residents at the time.

Today the Phoenix Symphony Hall is located on the property.

Caravan Inn - East – 3323 (3333) East Van Buren Street

The Caravan Inn on East Van Buren opened in early 1959. It was built on property formerly utilized by the Rancho De Oro and Blue Crown auto courts, which were demolished for the Caravan's construction. The facility included a restaurant and banquet facilities as well as leased offices. Construction was two-story motor hotel style with a central courtyard. Caravan Hotels was a chain which featured racing camel and rider signage capitalizing on the Arabian-themed hotel phenomena.

Several Caravan Hotels were built in western states, including two in Phoenix. The chain was soon operated by Western Hotels, which is now Westin Hotels and Resorts.

Caravan Inn East circa 1960 (Author's Collection)

The New Day Center, formerly the Caravan Inn East, today (Photo by Author 2012)

The Caravan East operated under the Caravan name until 1992. In 1993 it became a Days Inn and remained so until 2007. The facility was purchased along with the adjacent former Bagdad Inn by United Methodist Outreach Ministries (UMOM) in 2007. UMOM renovated the structures for use as homeless housing.

The original buildings utilized in the Caravan Inn East still exist as UMOM's New Day Center.

Caravan Inn - West - 1501 Grand Avenue

The Caravan Inn West opened in late 1959 as the sister property to the Caravan Inn East, located across town. Built on the real estate of the former Evergreen Court, the Caravan Inn West was a full-service motor hotel with an on-site restaurant. The facility was part of the Caravan Inn hotel chain which used an Arabian theme to attract guests. The chain was owned by Western Hotels which has become Westin Hotels and Resorts.

Caravan Inn West circa 1960 (Author's Collection)

Caravan Inn West as it looks today (Photo by Author 2012)

The Caravan Inn West only lasted a couple of years before it became part of the nearby Bali-Hi Motor Hotel. In 1967 the facility was purchased to become part of the Casa Contenda Nursing Home group, which had facilities in southern California. Casa Contenda finally opened in June of 1968 with a grand opening on September 15th. The nursing facility concept was not successful, and by early 1971 the property was converted to the Oasis Motor Hotel.

The motel operated as the Oasis until 2007 but did have some intermittent closures. The complex was purchased in 2007 and promptly closed. A major renovation took place, and in late 2011 the property reopened as the Oasis on Grand. The Oasis on Grand is a mixed income apartment complex which caters to the artist community.

Carlock Auto Court – 3150 (3200) East Washington Street

The Carlock Auto Court was a short-lived cabin court. It was located on the same property as the McNeeley Service Station and started operation about 1944. By 1948 it became a trailer court.

Today a fast-food restaurant is located on the property.

Casa Del Sol Court circa 1945 (Author's Collection)

Casa Del Sol Court – 602 South Seventeenth Avenue

The Casa Del Sol Court was operating by 1939. The facility was a cottage court utilizing duplex buildings with carports between them. One of the eight cottages was utilized as an office. The court was laid out in a U-shape with a central courtyard. Eventually the northern strip of cottages was expanded by converting the carports to living space.

The Vista Palms Apartments, formerly the Casa Del Sol Court, today (Photo by Author 2012)

By 1978 the facility was converted to apartments. Today the Casa Del Sol Court still exists as apartments.

Casa Rosita Motel – See Zila Motel

Casa Siesta Lodge circa 1960 (Author's Collection)

Casa Siesta Lodge – 5100 North Thirty-Sixth Street

By 1952 the Casa Siesta Lodge was in operation. The facility consisted of the lodge and 24 casitas. A popular restaurant was located in the lodge. The rooms were built in single-story strip motel style and featured a 60-foot pool. Other amenities included a putting green, shuffleboard, and riding stable. The lodge was located in a rural area at the time, on six acres in an orange grove.

The Casa Siesta was owned by Lou Thesz for many years. Thesz was the Heavyweight World Wresting Champ three times. He still holds the record for the longest time as the champ.

In 1969 the Casa Siesta experienced a fire and was closed. The owner at the time considered remodeling as the buildings still stood. However, it was sold and redeveloped into a residential area. Today the area is still residential.

The Castella Court, now apartments (Photo by Author 2014)

Castella Court - 2025 West Washington Street

The Castella Court was in operation by 1930. The facility consisted of seven cottages arranged in a U-shape. One of the cottages was utilized as an owner's quarters. By 1938 the facility became known as Jaynes Court.

By 1959 the court converted to an apartment-only business model. It still exists today as apartments. A newer, strip-style building was added about 2001 and given a similar look to the older portion.

Cecil Hotel – See Elmo Rooming House

Central Avenue Hotel – 515 North Central Avenue

The Central Avenue Hotel was renting furnished rooms by early 1910. The size and configuration of the facility is not known. It is likely the rooms were second-floor units similar to most downtown rooming houses at the time. By 1912 the property took on the name Annex Hotel.

The Annex Hotel was demolished to make room for the construction of the Apache Hotel, which opened in 1920. The area is currently part of the Walter Cronkite School of Journalism.

The Central Hotel building still exists (Photo by Author 2012)

Central Hotel – 122 East Washington Street

The Central Hotel was built and opened in 1889. The facility was a two-story structure with 35 sleeping rooms to rent. It also included a restaurant and saloon.

The Central Hotel Saloon was very popular as it was the only bar in town that dispensed beer directly from cold storage vaults. The vaults were located in the cellar and were cooled using pressurized ammonia. Anheiser-Busch, Pabst, and Weiland beers were also bottled in the cellar for sale in the city. The saloon was able to hold and serve imported beers as well due to its cold storage capabilities.

The Central had some deaths occur in the 1890s. In 1891, a New York native, Charles Crandall, committed suicide in room 31. He left a torn suicide note that read, "I am all broke up physically, mentally and morally, so here goes. Goodbye". In 1893 another suicide took place, this time in room 26. The 19-year-old man shot himself in the heart. He sent a letter on Central Hotel stationary to his brother-in-law stating his intentions. Another incident took place that same year. Two men who were sworn enemies became entangled in a fatal argument in front of the hotel. Lee Burton attacked Lee Rine from behind. A pistol was drawn, and Rine was shot. He stumbled into the Central Hotel Saloon where he passed away. Burton was arrested and convicted for his crime.

Joseph Thalheimer, the hotel's owner, was an excellent business owner with strong convictions. In 1893 he allowed himself to be arrested in a protest against the city. The city passed an ordinance that required saloon owners to suspend liquor sales on Election Day. Thalheimer ignored the law and fought it in court rather than paying a small fine.

Through the years the hotel remained, but the saloon was closed. A shoe store utilized most of the ground floor of the building. By 1949 the hotel closed, but the shoe store lasted for decades longer. Today the Central Hotel building still exists and is utilized as a night club.

Central Hotel – 32 South Central Avenue

Rooms had been rented on an apartment basis for years at 32 South Central. By 1961 the rooms became known as the Central Hotel. The hotel was short-lived, and by 1969 it was no longer functioning. Demolition took place in the 1970s to build Patriots Park.

Today the real estate is part of the CityScape complex.

Central Motel – 4220 South Central Avenue

By 1948 the Central Motel was in business. The facility was a cabin-style court with five cabins.

The former Central Motel, now apartments (Photo by Author 2014)

By 1977 the Central Motel began operating as apartments. Today the facility still exists and the cabins are still being used.

Central Park Court – 113 East Tonto Street

The Central Park Court was a small cottage court located just south of Central Park. The facility consisted of four large cottages utilized as rental units. The court was in operation by 1930. By the mid-1950s the facility was closed and the buildings razed.

Today a children's center is located on the property.

Central Plaza Inn circa 1972 (Author's Collection)

Central Plaza Inn – 4321 North Central Avenue

Construction began on the Central Plaza Inn in 1969 with an opening date in January 1970. The facility was a full-service motor hotel built in the standard style with the exception of having three floors. Five of the multi-story buildings were placed in a U-configuration creating a centralized courtyard and pool area. A single-story building at the front of the property served as a lobby and restaurant. The motel was built in modern Mexican style and became a member of the Best Western referral association. The facility was known for its unusual poured concrete pebbled railings.

In 1976 the Central Plaza played a part in the bombing assassination of Don Bolles, an Arizona Republic newspaper investigative reporter. John Adamson, the bomber, stayed at the hotel during and after the killing. He was also paid by an exchange that took place anonymously in one of the Central Plaza's rooms. Adamson was hired by Kemper Marley, a liquor wholesaler, after Bolles had written unflattering articles about Marley. Marley apparently believed these articles played a part in his failure to gain a seat on the Arizona Racing Commission.

The Central Plaza took on the Best Western flag in the mid-1980s. About the same time its name changed to the St. Francis Hotel. By 1993 the facility became a Holiday Inn and began using that name alone. The hotel operated until it was demolished in 2006. Today the property remains vacant.

Cha Kel Court – See Sun Valley Court

Chancewell Manor Lodge – See Redman's Guest Lodge

Charlesann Court – 5602 North Seventh Street

The Charlesann Court was in operation by 1949. The facility consisted of two single-story, strip-style buildings. It was sold mainly as apartments through the years. From 1953 to 1955 the facility was advertised to short-term renters.

The court still existed as apartments until 2014, when it was demolished.

Chicago Rooms – See Thibodo House

Romney Motor Hotel, formerly the Chilton Inn, circa 1970 (Author's Collection)

The former Chilton Inn operating as an Econo Lodge in 2012 (Photo by Author)

Chilton Inn – 3037 East Van Buren Street

The Chilton Inn was open and accepting guests by mid-1964. The new facility replaced the Palm Lane Auto Court which was demolished in 1963. Built in two-story motor hotel style, the 96-unit motel was configured in a long U-shape and included two pools. Other amenities included a lounge, dining room, and coffee shop.

Chilton Inns was a new Phoenix-based motel chain with other locations in Gila Bend and Yuma. The chain was owned by a group led by Paul Chilton and Art Linkletter. Linkletter was a celebrity most noted for hosting the television show "Kids Say the Darnedest Things".

By mid-1965 the Chilton Inns were bought by the Yavapai Hotel Corporation. Yavapai already owned the Gadsen Hotel in Douglas, Arizona, and had a Ramada Inn being built in Prescott, Arizona. The Yavapai released common stock to the public at $3.00 per share. However, soon afterward Wayne Romney purchased the Chilton properties. By 1969 the property was called the Romney Chilton Inn and then just the Romney Motor Hotel. Romney built his own chain of hotels that lives on today as Paragon Hotel Corporation.

The motel changed names again in 1981 to Wards Motor Hotel. By 2004 the facility became known as the Best Inn and finally the Econo Lodge.

Today the Chilton Inn's original buildings are still in use as an Econo Lodge.

Chippewa Motel – See Eli Motel

Circle Inn Court – 1724 West Buckeye Road

The Circle Inn Court was in operation by 1948. The facility consisted of eight cabins used as rentals and a five-room home. Another cabin was added at some point to make nine rental units. By 1956 the court was renamed the Buckeye Motel.

By 1977 the motel was closed and, at some point, demolished. Today an auto repair business is located at the address.

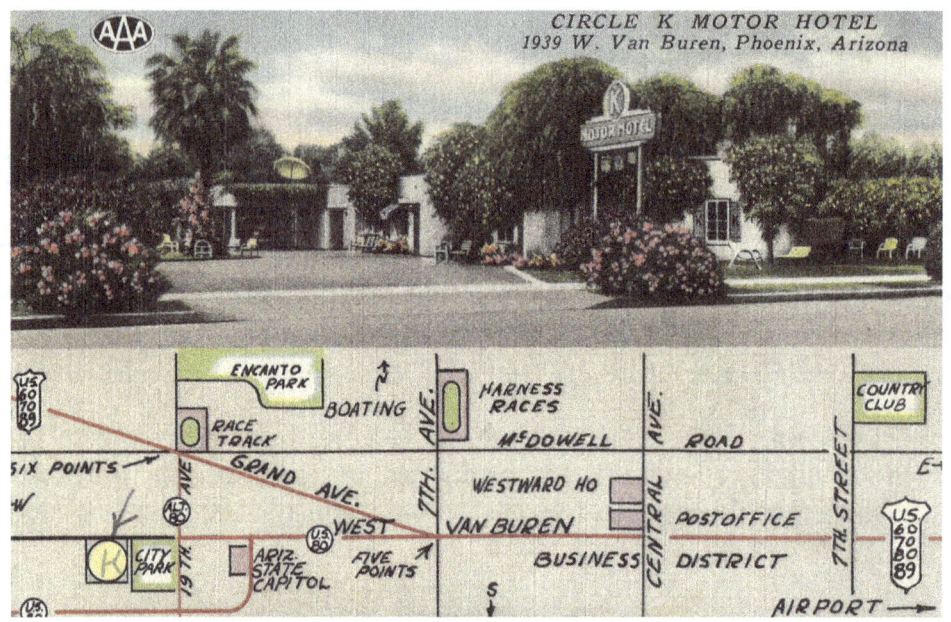

Circle K Motor Hotel circa 1940 (Author's Collection)

Circle K Motor Hotel – 1939 West Van Buren Street

The Circle K Motor Hotel was accepting guests by 1939. The facility featured duplex cottages arranged in a U-shape. The cottages yielded 18 units with carports between each building. At the time of construction, the motel was located next to a city park. The motel utilized this aspect in its advertising.

The Circle K Motel in 2012 (Photo by Author)

As the Circle K aged it became more and more utilized as apartment rentals. By 1996 the entire facility was rented as apartments. The Circle K still exists today and is rented as apartments.

Circle L Motel – 3040 (3800) Grand Avenue

By 1946 the Circle L Motel was renting rooms. The facility was built in cottage court style with cabins arranged in two rows. A trailer court facility was located in the rear. The Circle L and the Santa Fe Motel were under the same ownership and shared a café and the trailer facilities.

By 1968 the Circle L Motel was closed, and the cafe remained open. It's possible that the cabins were utilized by the Santa Fe Motel as units. However, the Circle L cabins were demolished sometime between 1972 and 1975, before the Santa Fe Motel closed.

Today the real estate is utilized by an auto auction company.

Circle Motel – See Zila Motel

City Center Motel circa 1960 (Author's Collection)

City Center Motel as it appears today (Photo by Author 2012)

City Center Motel – 600 West Van Buren Street

The City Center Motel accepted its first guest in 1959. The facility consisted of two buildings built in two-story motor inn style and built on the old Williams Hotel property. Modern styling was featured in the design and utilized an unusual second-story overhang in the front building. This created a covered parking area. The builders utilized two buildings because they could not purchase a small piece of property in the middle of their planned project. Instead of cancelling the project, they simply built around the existing auto shop in the middle. Eventually the property became part of the motel.

The City Center had its share of crime issues. In one incident in 1963, an armed robbery was stopped in process. Police gave chase on foot after the burglar shot a policeman in the face. The perpetrator was cornered and received two fatal gun shots from police. It was soon discovered that the man had robbed the Stone Motel on the previous evening.

In 1965 Raymond and Mabel Murray of New Jersey purchased the City Center Motel. The night following their purchase they were welcomed to the neighborhood by thieves. Two armed men forced their way into the Murrays' room at the City Center and relieved them of fifty dollars.

The City Center became the Best West Inn by 2010. It never lost its original signage and was returned to the City Center Motel in 2014.

Classic Motel – See Pasadena Motel

Clemens Court – See Craft Court

Clinton House – See Grand View Hotel

Clover Motel circa 1960 (Author's Collection)

The Clover Court as it appears today as apartments (Photo by Author 2012)

Clover Court – 911 South Seventeenth Avenue

By 1940 rooms were being rented at 911 South Seventeenth Avenue. Originally named the Fountain Court, by 1941 it had been renamed as the Clover Court. The facility consisted of at least 11 cottages and an owner's home. Spanish theme was dominant with stucco walls and tile roofs. Carport roofs were originally placed between the cottages. These were eventually filled in to create additional rental units.

In 1944 the son of one of the long-term Clover Court residents was reported missing in action. He was a Liberator Bomber pilot. Unfortunately, this was not an unusual occurrence at the time.

By 1984 the Clover had become an apartment building. It still exists as apartments today.

Cocanut Grove Motel circa 1960 (Author's Collection)

Cocanut Grove Motel as it appears today (Photo by Author 2012)

Cocanut Grove Motel – 2012 West Van Buren Street

The Cocanut Grove Motel opened by 1950. The motel utilized a combination of two-story motor hotel and single-story strip motel construction. A quaint looking bungalow served as the office and living quarters. For some time the affiliated Cocanut Grove Restaurant was located at 2006 West Van Buren Street.

Today the facility still functions as the Coconut Grove Motel, with corrected spelling. Changes have been made to the office building and the pool is gone, but most of the buildings remain unchanged.

Coliseum Inn circa 1970 (Author's Collection)

Coliseum Inn – 1560 Grand Avenue

The Coliseum Inn was opened in 1966. The facility utilized single-story, strip motel style construction. Three buildings were constructed and held 50 rooms and a lobby area. The hotel management division of Kelly Inns operated the facility starting in 1967.

The last remnants of the Coliseum Inn buildings demolished in 2013 (Photo by Author 2012)

The Coliseum Inn was closed as a motel by 1991. The last portion of the Coliseum Inn was demolished in 2013. A church utilizes the property today. The distinctive double polygon shaped sign is in use by the church, the last remaining piece of the motel.

Colombo Lodging House – 201 (215) South Seventh Street

The Colombo Lodging House was one of the many rooming houses that sprang up in Phoenix after the year 1900. Phoenix was growing and lodging facilities were opened to meet the need. Most were unnamed facilities, but the larger houses took on a name. The Colombo was in business by 1916 and was able to survive the early auto court and motel boom which closed most of the rooming houses. But by 1959 the Colombo was closed.

In the late 1960s construction began on the expansion of Seventh Street. The street was widened and elevated. The Colombo building was demolished during this construction, and the property became part of the easement.

Colonial Hotel, front and left, circa 1915 (Courtesy McClintock Collection, Arizona Room, Phoenix Public Library)

Colonial Hotel – 135 North First Avenue

By 1911 the Colonial Hotel was in operation. The facility was a three-story building of brick construction which held 52 sleeping rooms. The Colonial became the Reading Hotel by 1919. Its name changed again by 1926 to the State Hotel.

In January of 1954, one of the hotels desk clerks jumped to his death from the roof. William Failey, the desk clerk, told other employees he was going to the roof to get some sun. Observers from nearby buildings saw the man and called police. The fire department set up a net below the man. Failey jumped and was able to avoid the net. He died minutes later.

The State Hotel closed by 1964. Today the US Bank building uses the real estate.

Colony Motel - 3158 West Buckeye Road

The Colony Motel was in business as a trailer court by 1947. The facility soon entered the motel market with a new strip-style motel building. Eventually several buildings containing rental units were built on the property. These included two strip-style motel buildings with 10 rental units, an addition to one strip building which was most likely a garage, a two-story house in the rear, and a gas station and café building at the front of the property. Placed in the center was a two-bedroom home and office. By 1969 the motel became the Cloud Motel.

The Cloud was open for many years, but by 1995 it had closed as a motel. It was demolished in 2010. Today the real estate that held the Colony Motel holds a modern retail building.

Colorado Court – 1617 East Van Buren Street

The Colorado Court began as an early auto camp in 1925. Like most auto camps, the Colorado provided basic needs to automotive travelers who carried camping equipment with them. Soon the Colorado added cabin-style court buildings for transient stays. Upgrades to lodging facilities like this were dictated by competition and had to be performed to remain viable. The buildings were again upgraded to cottages in the 1940s.

In 1948 the Colorado Court changed its name to the Rose Court. The Rose Court operated in similar fashion until 1983. The buildings were demolished just after the facility closed.

Today the Colorado Court property is home to a fast-food restaurant.

Columbia Court – 2501 East Van Buren Street

Columbia Court opened in 1938. It consisted of the usual cabin-style court of the day to serve passing motorists. The facility was in operation until 1951 when it was demolished. In the court's place was built the Flamingo Motor Inn, which opened in 1952.

The property that the Columbia Court once rested on is now a Rodeway Inn. The Rodeway utilizes the Flamingo buildings that replaced the Columbia Court.

Comfort Motel – See Vista Linda Court

Commercial Hotel circa 1915 (Courtesy McClintock Collection, Arizona Room, Phoenix Public Library)

Luhrs Hotel, formerly the Commercial Hotel, circa 1940 (Author's Collection)

Commercial Hotel – 49 South Central Avenue

George Luhrs emigrated from Germany in 1867 at the age of 20. In 1882 Luhrs and his partner Newell Herrick began purchasing land in what would become the downtown area of Phoenix. They built and operated a wagon building business in the area.

Soon they expanded into other business endeavors, including the hotel business. In late 1886 their 20-room Commercial Hotel was opened. The hotel was a two-story wood frame and brick building located near the center of the block. In 1887 the facility was enlarged to include 100 sleeping rooms, a restaurant, and bar and billiard rooms. The new construction was of three stories and covered the corner of Central and Jefferson. Luhrs bought out Herrick in 1890, and most future projects, like the Luhrs building and tower, held the Luhrs name.

In 1909 Luhrs added a third floor to the hotel's older two-story portion. This made it match the newer section and added more rooms to rent. A new wing was added to the hotel in 1912 and utilized the location where the wagon building facilities were formerly located. In 1916 the Commercial Hotel suffered a fire. The fire was not as devastating as the Adams Hotel fire a few years prior, but it did result in much damage. The damage was repaired, and in 1924 the hotel received an exterior upgrade and modernization. At this time the hotel was renamed the Luhrs Hotel. The family operated the property until 1976. The hotel had the distinction of being the oldest business owned by the same family in Arizona. In 1981 the hotel was demolished and the property remained vacant for three decades.

Today the address is once again a hotel site. The Palomar Hotel was built on the site as part of the CityScape project.

Commercial Hotel – 205 East Madison Street

By 1936 the Commercial Hotel was in business. It was a small facility, likely utilizing the second-story. In 1955 the owner, Eileen Doyle, passed away. Shortly afterward the facility was taken over by the Headley family. The Headleys already operated the Headley Hotel at 221 South Second Street. They renamed the Commercial the Headley Hotel. They called the Second Street location the Headley Annex for a couple of years and then the Small Hotel, likely to avoid confusion. The hotels were very close to each other.

By 1973 the hotel was closed. The real estate is part of the US Airways Center complex today.

Commercial Hotel (Second Street) – See Wollpert Hotel

Como Hotel – See Wharton Hotel

Compton Hotel – See Kersting Hotel

Conan Auto Court – 1117 East Monroe Street

The Conan Court was a small cabin facility in operation by 1937. The lot was long and narrow, so cabins were lined along the western property line with access along the east side. The facility quickly started operating on an apartment basis, and by 1948 it was no longer advertised to the tourist trade.

The cabins were demolished in the 1970s, and a modern apartment building is located on the real estate today.

Continental Guest Lodge – See Autopia

Conway Court – See Lincoln Auto Court

Copa Inn – See Desert King Court

Copeland (The) – 368 North Second Avenue

The Copeland was a lodging house that was in business by 1901. It was known as a high-quality house and also operated a dining room. By the mid-1920s the house was no longer accepting short-term renters.

Today a modern printing facility is located on the property.

Copemoar Court – 1114 East Fairmount Avenue

The Copemoar Court was accepting guests by 1931. The facility consisted of six four-room cottages utilized as rental units. By 1937 it was renamed the Seidler Court. This lasted many years, but by 1948 it was renamed the Wells Cottages.

By 1964 it appears the Wells Cottages moved to an apartment-only basis. Today the land which once held the Copemoar Court is undeveloped.

Corbitt's Motel – See Franiva Motor Lodge

Corona Cottage Court – 1604 East Washington Street

By 1930 the Corona Cottage Court was in business. The facility was a cabin-style court with a café located in the front of the lot.

In 1942 one of the cabins was destroyed by fire. A guest in the cabin was heating water on a gas burner. He left the cabin while his water was warming. Upon his return he found the cabin ablaze. Other cabins were damaged as well.

By 1959 the cabins were no longer being rented, but the café remained open. The entire complex was demolished in the 1960s.

Today a modern gas station utilizes the real estate.

Coronado Court – 1803 East Van Buren Street

The Coronado Court was an auto court built in cabin court style. It contained about 10 cabins and 20 units. The facility opened in 1938 and was closed by 1962.

The courts buildings were demolished in the 1960s. Today the area consists of modern apartments.

Coronado Hotel – See Lamb Hotel

Coronet Hotel circa 1965 (Author's Collection)

The former Coronet Hotel, now offices (Photo by Author 2014)

Coronet Hotel – 1001 North Central Avenue

The Coronet Hotel was opened in 1960. It was built on property previously utilized by a drive-in restaurant. The new hotel was a nine-story, full-service facility. It included apartments, a restaurant, coffee shop, and business offices. By 1963 the hotel became part of the Ramada Inn chain and utilized the name Ramada Coronet Hotel.

The facility was no longer a hotel by 1977. Today the Coronet Hotel building still exists. It has undergone a major renovation and looks nothing like it originally did. It is now an office building.

Corral Court – 1618 West Linden Street

The Corral Court was constructed in the late 1930s or early 1940s. It included 24 cottages that were utilized as rentals. By 1953 the name of the court changed to the Linden Court.

Like most of the motels in Phoenix, the Corral Court catered to both transient and long-term renters. In 1947 one of the court residents, Irene Robinson, was discovered by Gene Autry. Mr. Autry, a successful screen actor, purchased an airplane ticket from her and was impressed. He offered her a small role in the upcoming film *The Last Roundup*. Robinson, who was the current Miss Arizona Aviation, left her position at Trans World Airways to pursue an acting career under the name Rane Dennis.

By 1958 the Corral Court switched completely to a long-term rental model. Today industrial buildings are located on the real estate previously utilized by the Corral Court.

Corral Motel – 1214 North Laurel Avenue

By 1950 the Corral Apartments were open. Soon the apartments would be marketed as a motel. The facility was built in single-story strip motel style. It consisted of two U-shaped buildings facing each other. The configuration left a court and parking area in the center of the buildings. By 1957 the Corral became the Kitchenette Motel.

The Kitchenette Motel no longer operated as a motel by 1964. By 2009 the north building was demolished, and the south building was utilized by a church. In 2013 the south building was demolished as well.

Costantinti Court – See Floods Court

Cottage Auto Camp – See US Auto Court

Cottage Court circa 1940 (Courtesy Library of Congress)

Cottage Court – 5218 East Van Buren Street

The Cottage Court was opened in 1939 in what was then a very rural area. The facility consisted of several cabins built in early auto court style. Cottage Court operated until 1950 when the name was changed to the Minnesota Cottage Court. Like most auto courts, the Cottage Court also rented space for trailers.

Unfortunately, in 1941 a cabin was lost to fire due to a gas stove explosion in an adjacent trailer.

After 1963 the Minnesota Cottage Court operated intermittently as apartments, a trailer court, and transient lodging. The facility was last utilized for lodging in 1983 and demolition took place by 1992. The property formerly occupied by the Cottage Court is now part of the Loop 202 Red Mountain Freeway easement where it meets Van Buren Street.

Cottage Grove Court – 1818 East Washington Street

The Cottage Grove was open by 1932. The facility was operated as apartments for a few years before being marketed to travelers. The facility consisted of about eight duplex cottages and in later years also rented trailer space.

By 1983 the Cottage Grove was out of business. It was demolished in short order. A clay item manufacturer uses the property today.

The former Cottonwood Court offices (Photo by Author 2014)

Cottonwood Court – 3138 (4020) Grand Avenue

The Cottonwood Court was in business by 1948. The facility consisted of a 16-unit motel, café, and grocery store. By 1952 the court became the A Motel in a likely attempt to be listed first in the phone book. By 1981 the A Motel units were being rented as apartments.

Today the property is an automotive body shop. The motel lobby still exists today while the cabins were demolished in the 1990s.

Cottonwood Court – 3159 West Buckeye Road

By 1946 the Cottonwood Court was in business. The facility contained kitchenette cabins for rent and a service station. By 1952 the motel became the J&O Court.

By 1959 the court was out of business. Today a modern gas station is located at the address.

Cottonwood Lodge – 2009 (2013) East Monroe Street

The Cottonwood Lodge was in business by 1957. It was a kitchenette court consisting of 14 units.

By 1964 the facility moved to a long-term rental business model. Today the real estate is undeveloped and used for roof tile storage.

Counhan Court – 4418 East Washington Street

When the Counhan Court was opened is not known. It was certainly in business by 1949. The facility was a cottage court consisting of six units. Each cottage contained four rooms. By 1955 the court became the Oasis Motel. By 1959 the motel was no longer in business. It was demolished in short order.

Today a modern hotel is located on the property.

Court Carol – See Blue Point Court

Court Motel – 3648 Grand Avenue

The date the Court Motel opened is unknown. The facility first appears in known records in 1951, but it was likely in business for many years prior. Built in cabin court style, the motel included between 25 and 30 units. It had both kitchenettes and 30 trailer spaces.

The Court Motel was out of business by 1965 and was immediately demolished. Today the address is a parking lot.

Cox Auto Camp – See Bridges Auto Court

Craft Court – 1729 East Van Buren Street

Craft Court was a cabin-style auto court that opened in 1938. By 1948 the facility was no longer renting rooms to travelers, but rather the units were used as apartments. The facility again became an auto court in 1954 under the name Clemens Court. However, by 1957 the court had once again become apartments.

The area is now part of a restaurant complex.

Craus Bungalows – 2118 West Washington Street

By 1928 the Craus Bungalows were in operation. The facility consisted of approximately nine three-room cottages. By 1935 the name was changed to the Yavapai Cottage Court. Around 1951 the facility went to an all-apartment business plan under the name Guess Apartments. However, by 1958 the name was changed to Guess Court, and it was advertised to short-term tenants again.

The motel only lasted a few years. By 1963 it became apartments-only again. Today modern residential housing is located on the property.

Crescent Court – 1001 South Seventeenth Avenue

The Crescent Court was renting rooms by 1944. The court was of unknown construction, but it was likely a cabin court. A name change by 1953 left the court named the Windmill Hotel Motor Inn. The facility again changed names by 1960 becoming the D-Bar-G Motel.

In 1965 a woman was living at the D-Bar-G Motel during a separation from her husband. The estranged couple entered into an argument over his alleged threatening of their children. While he was standing in the doorway to the room, she pointed a gun at him. The man taunted her to shoot. The woman complied by shooting him in the leg and groin. She was promptly arrested.

By 1966 the D-Bar-G Motel was out of business. Today the property is an undeveloped lot.

Crest Lodge circa 1955 (Author's Collection)

Crest Lodge – 3411 East Van Buren Street

The Crest Lodge opened in 1948 with 18 units. The facility was one of the last to utilize cabin-style construction as strip-motels were becoming popular. In 1994 the facility was closed, and it was demolished by 1996.

The area is now a parking lot for a local business.

Crooks Court – 3710 Grand Avenue

When the Crooks Court opened is not known. The first mention of the facility is in 1952 when a man was found dead in one of the cabins. He and three others had been overcome by fumes from an unvented gas heater. The other three men were revived. It is very likely that Crooks Court was built many years prior to this event. The facility consisted of a cabin-style court which consisted of 22 units by 1956. It appears the court declined in size and held only 16 units by 1959. By 1962 some buildings were being rented as store rooms, small businesses, and apartments.

The address is an undeveloped lot today.

Cross R Motel – 2104 East Van Buren Street

The Cross R Motel opened in 1951. The property became the C & E Motel in 1964 and then Bobs Motel in 1965. In 1967 the property was listed as a distress sale in the Arizona Republic newspaper. The motel closed permanently and was demolished in 1983.

The area is now part of the I-10 easement.

Culver Street Court – 1830 West Culver (Walnut) Street

By 1948 the Parker family had a couple of cabins for rent behind their home at 1830 Walnut Street. These appear to have been initially rented as apartments. By 1950 the street name had changed to Culver, and the facility became the Culver Street Court. Eventually about nine cabins were built. By 1952 the facility took on the name Parker Cabin Court.

After 1964 the Parker Cabin Court operated mainly as apartments. By 1983 it stopped accepting short-term renters all together. Industrial buildings are located on the property today.

Cummins Auto Court – 1708 West Yuma Street

The Cummins Auto Court was in business by 1950. The facility was a small cabin court which also included trailer spaces. For a short time, around 1959, it may have been known as Hurley's Court. George Cummins, the owner, passed away in October 1965. Soon after the court was sold and became the Borgouist Cabins.

By 1971 the facility no longer operated as a motel. Today the real estate is occupied by more modern rental units.

Cy-Erna Motel – See Eli Motel

D-Bar-G Motel – See Crescent Court

Dabney Auto Court – 1020 (1002) South Seventh Avenue

The Dabney Auto Court at 1020 South Seventh Avenue was in business by 1928. The facility consisted of seven cottages used as rental units.

By 1936 the facility was closed, and a restaurant operated on the property for a few years. A large housing complex was built on the property and surrounding areas in the 1940s. These apartments were replaced with a modern complex known as the Matthew Henson Apartments.

Dallas Hotel – See Grand View Hotel

Davis Court – 1726 East Washington Street

The Davis Court was operating by the mid-1930s. The facility was a cabin-style court of unknown size. By 1945 the business name changed to Jacks Tourist Court, likely due to new ownership by J. Jackson.

By 1961 the court was out of business. Today the area is a parking lot.

Day Hotel – See Thibodo House

Del Ano Motel – 2125 West Van Buren Street

The Del Ano Motel was in business by 1948. Single-story, strip-motel construction was utilized. This type of construction was very modern when the motel was built, but it would soon become the standard. By 1958 the motel was renamed the Sombrero Motel.

Sombrero Motel, formerly the Del Ano Motel, circa 1965 (Author's Collection)

By 1979 the Sombrero Motel was out of business. Today a used car company utilizes the property where the Sombrero once stood.

The Kinds Court, later Del Camino Lodge, circa 1950 (Author's Collection)

Del Camino Lodge as it appears today (Photo by Doug Truran 2012)

Del Camino Lodge – 2949 East Van Buren Street

The Del Camino Lodge opened in 1949 as the Kinds Hotel Court. The facility utilized individual buildings arranged in the usual U-pattern. Each building in the court contained two rental units. Tile roofs and stucco gave the buildings a Spanish look. By 1953 the court had taken the Del Camino name.

By 1962 the facility had become part of the adjacent Dunes Motel.

The original buildings that comprised the Del Camino Lodge still exist. They are empty and boarded up now.

Del Coosha Court – 2125 East Van Buren Street

The Del Coosha Court was a cabin-style court opened in 1940. The court operated for many years until 1962 when the name was changed to the Valley Motel. This incarnation lasted until 1984 when the motel was closed. By 1990 it was demolished.

Today the area is part of the I-10 easement where it meets Van Buren Street.

Del Ray Hotel – See Stag Hotel

Del Reo Lodge – See Villa Vista Motel

The Delmar Court, now apartments (Photo by Author 2014)

Delmar Court – 1459 East Fillmore Street

The Delmar Court was in operation as apartments by 1930. In the mid-1940s the court took on the Delmar name and started accepting shorter term tenants and tourists. The facility consisted of nine three-room cottages arranged in a U-shape. By 1960 the court no longer catered to short-term renters.

In 1945 one of the Delmar Courts long-term renters, P-40 instructor pilot First Lieutenant William Doughty, crashed in the desert near Tonopah Arizona. He was based out of Luke Field and died upon impact.

Today the Delmar Court's original buildings still operate as apartments.

Delozier Auto Court – 1727 East Van Buren Street

The Delozier Auto Court was a very short-lived court operating from 1934 to 1938. The property was utilized as a tire store by 1939.

The only known occurrence at the court was a curtain fire in one of the units in 1938, caused by a match that had not been extinguished. The property is currently used as a parking lot for a local business.

DeManana Motel – See Pioneer Lodge

Den (The) – 16 North First Street

The Den was a downtown rooming house which utilized the second floor of the building at the northwest corner of Washington and First Streets. The Donofrio ice cream factory was located on the lower level along with their wholesale offices, directly across the street from Korrick's department store. By 1921 The Den was no longer renting rooms, and the facility was in use by the Young Men's Hebrew Club.

Today a modern high rise building occupies the entire block.

Dennis Hotel – 15 North Second Street

The Dennis Hotel opened by 1896. By 1908 the facility became the New Dennis Hotel, likely after a renovation. By 1914 the facility became the Franklin Hotel.

The Franklin operated successfully for many years, but by 1970 it was no longer viable and went out of business. It was demolished within the decade. Today the Phoenix Symphony Hall building is located on the property.

Hotel Denver (the building with the Tovrea sign) circa 1948 (Author's Collection)

Denver Hotel – 14 South Central Avenue

The Oriel Hotel was opened in 1900. The facility was a former theatre building that was remodeled to contain furnished rooms and offices. In 1903 the hotel changed management and became the Denver Hotel.

The Denver Hotel was very long-lived but was closed by 1976. Today the real estate is part of the CityScape complex.

Denver Hotel Annex – See Thibodo House

Deserama Motel – See Red Barn Motel

Desert Breeze Motel circa 1950 (Author's Collection)

Desert Breeze Motel – 1213 North Sixteenth Street

The Desert Breeze Motel was operating by 1947. The facility consisted of two strip-style buildings placed parallel to each other. The motel soon started catering to long-term guests. Its name changed to the Desert Breeze Apartments by 1951.

Today the area is not developed.

Desert Grove Auto Court – 4801 East Roosevelt Street

Little is known about the Desert Grove Auto Court. It was in operation by the late 1940s and was very small with only a few cabins. By 1954 it was no longer in operation.

Today the real estate is utilized by the Balsz School District.

Desert Hills Hotel circa 1957 (Author's Collection)

The Desert Hills as it appeared in 2012 during its demolition (Photo by Author)

Desert Hills Hotel - 2745 East Van Buren Street

The Desert Hills Hotel was opened in 1953 with two-story, motor inn style buildings and 180 rooms. The facility included a coffee shop and dining facility. A major expansion through the purchase and demolition of the adjacent Sea Breeze Motor Inn took place in 1965. This expansion made the Desert Hills a large convention center complex with 206 rooms. For some time the Desert Hills was part of the Best Western referral chain.

The Desert Hills closed in 1985 when it was purchased by the Salvation Army. The original buildings were used by the Salvation Army until 2012 when they were demolished to make room for a new Salvation Army complex.

Desert Inn Motel circa 1965 (Author's Collection)

Desert Inn – 950 West Van Buren Street

The Desert Inn Motel was opened in 1951. The facility was a two-story structure holding 80 rooms built in motor inn style. A restaurant, coffee shop, and lounge were also featured on the property. For some time the property was a member of the Best Western chain. The motel was built by J.K. Orton who was a hotelier from Salt Lake City. The Ortons were involved in many motel projects after their move to Phoenix. They built, owned, or operated properties like the El Rancho, the Mission, the Royal Palms, the Tahiti Inn, the Desert Sun, and the Desert Hills. The family also built properties in other Arizona cities.

The Desert Inn as it appeared in 2012 prior to its demolition (Photo by Author)

The Desert Inn was robbed maliciously a couple of times. In 1967 a robber hit the night auditor in the head with a rock. He beat him about the chest and back and then robbed the motel. The auditor was treated and released. In 1971 the facility was robbed again, this time by two masked and armed men. One robber pushed the night clerk to the ground and in doing so discharged his gun. This resulted in a shoulder injury to the night clerk. He was forced to open the safe and the cash drawer. A silent alarm was triggered, and as the men robbed the motel, police arrived. One of the perpetrators was shot in the abdomen and both were arrested.

By the time the Desert Inn was built it had become mandatory to have a swimming pool on the property. This can be a great draw for guests, but it can also be a liability. The Desert Inn pool experienced at least three different incidents. The first was in 1968 when a desk clerk discovered a fully clothed woman at the bottom of the pool. The woman was pulled from the pool and given artificial respiration by the clerk. When medics arrived they utilized a resuscitator, and the woman responded. She was hospitalized and survived. In 1969 a local six-year-old girl wandered away from a function at University Park next to the motel. She somehow ended up in the Desert Inn pool and was discovered in an unconscious state. An off-duty ambulance driver having dinner at the restaurant utilized mouth to mouth resuscitation on the girl, but it was too late and she passed away. The third incident took place in 1972 and was eerily similar to the 1969 incident. A local four-year-old boy wandered away from University Park and also ended up in the Desert Inn pool. The boy was discovered at the bottom of the pool by a motel guest. The guest utilized mouth-to-mouth resuscitation and received no response. A motel desk clerk then gave the boy a vigorous heart massage during which the boy revived. He was treated and released.

The Desert Inn operated under the original name until the mid-2000s when the facility closed. It was demolished in the summer of 2012.

Copa Inn, formerly Desert King Court, circa 1970 (Author's Collection)

Desert King Court – 2834 East Van Buren Street

By 1946 the Desert King Court was pulling in visitors off Van Buren Street. The facility included 16 units and a manager's quarters laid out in two rows along the property lines. The court operated as the Desert King until 1957 when the name changed to the Keystone Lodge. In 1962 the name changed again to the Copa Inn. The Copa Inn endured as lodging and apartments until its closure and demolition in 2007.

Today the property is a vacant lot.

Desert Pool Motel - See Airways Motor Hotel

Desert Rest Motel – 4131 East Van Buren Street

The Desert Rest Motel was accepting guests by 1948. The facility was both a motel and trailer court. The construction style of the buildings is unknown. In 1951 the motel was renamed the Red Rooster Motel. This only lasted a year, and the facility became the Starlite Motel.

The Starlite Motel became strictly a trailer court by 1982. Today the area is part of the Airport Technology Center.

Desert Rose Motel circa 1965 (Author's Collection)

Desert Rose Motel – 3424 East Van Buren Street

Built on the land regained by the razing of the Parkview Court, the Desert Rose Motel opened in 1957. The two-story facility featured 57 units built in motor inn style and placed in a large U-configuration. A lobby area at the front included a lounge, coffee shop, dining room, and meeting rooms. Built at a cost of $300,000, the motel featured a drive-in registration system. Guests did not need to leave their vehicle to rent a room.

The former Desert Rose Motel operating as apartments today (Photo by Author 2012)

The Desert Rose was a very modern and respectable motel. It had some of the worst luck of all the motels in Phoenix. The motel was robbed at least five times in its first 10 years. In one instance a guest was robbed as well.

In 1967 a 14-year-old girl and 20-year-old man were both found shot in one of the rooms. The girl died shortly after being discovered. She was one of four girls who were freed at gunpoint by the man and an accomplice from the Maricopa County Detention Home, where the girls were incarcerated. The shootings were a result of a suicide pact between the young girl and the man. Under each of them, .38 caliber pistols were found.

In 1969 Harley Kimbro was murdered in room 104. Harley was a local Phoenix resident who was tricked into a meeting with his killer by the possibility of a house sale. His killer, Karl Kummerlowe, murdered him, dismembered his body in the bathtub, and then put him in three ice chests. Kummerlowe was caught by local police when he disposed of evidence in the trash at the Ramada Inn. The officers happened to be on a stake-out at the Ramada Inn and witnessed Kummerlowe's attempt to get rid of the evidence. The police soon discovered the ice chests and their contents. Kimbro was the husband of Kummerlowe's former lover. She would not divorce Kimbro for Kummerlowe. Kummerlowe was sentenced to life in prison in 1973.

The Desert Rose Motel remained in business until 2000 when it became an apartment complex. The original buildings still survive today as apartments.

Desert Sky Hotel circa 1970 (Author's Collection)

The former Desert Sky operating as the Travel Inn in 2012 (Photo by Author)

Desert Sky Hotel – 3541 East Van Buren Street

The Desert Sky Hotel opened in early 1961. It was constructed in two-story motor inn style with exterior entrances even though they called it a hotel. The facility included a pool area, coffee shop, 24-hour switchboard, and a television in each room.

The new motel replaced the former ABC Court facility, which was demolished for the Desert Sky construction. The facility was successful enough to add a new wing in 1965.

The Desert Sky operated until 1973 when it became the Quality Inn. In 1998 it became the Econo Lodge, which only lasted a few years, and by 2002 it was renamed the Economy Inn. By 2005 the facility had become the Rodeway Inn and in 2010 became the Travel Inn. As of 2014 the motel is closed.

Desert Star Motor Hotel circa 1950 (Author's Collection)

Desert Star Motor Hotel – 4120 East Van Buren Street

Located on the northwest corner of Van Buren Street and Forty-First Place, the Desert Star Motor Hotel was accepting guests by 1949. The facility utilized single-story, strip-motel-style construction. An extended roofline and stucco partial walls gave the facility a Spanish look. Tile roofs over 26 rental units completed the theme.

Desert Star Motor Hotel circa 1965 (Author's Collection)

The Desert Star operating as a Howard Johnsons in 2012 (Photo by Author)

In 1964 the Desert Star was rebuilt. A new 55-unit, two-story facility replaced the old building. It was built in motor hotel style with exterior entrances. Each room faced a central courtyard with a pool. The owners obviously knew they needed to rebuild to keep up with the competition.

The Desert Star operated until 1983 when it became a Comfort Inn. By 1997 it converted to a Ramada Limited, and just recently a Howard Johnsons.

Today the Desert Star's 1964 buildings still function as a Howard Johnsons motel.

Desert Sun Hotel circa 1961 (Author's Collection)

The remnants of the Desert Sun Hotel as they appear today (Photo by Author 2012)

Desert Sun Hotel – 1325 Grand Avenue

The Hotel Desert Sun was opened in 1955. It was owned and built by the Orton family who were involved in many motel projects in Phoenix. They also built, owned, or operated the El Rancho, the Mission, the Royal Palms, the Tahiti Inn, the Desert Inn, and the Desert Hills. The Desert Sun was built in two-story motor inn style and had exterior entrances even though it was called a hotel. The original construction included 67 rental units, a single-story lobby building, a coffee shop, and a restaurant. A 40-unit addition was built in 1959. One of the unique aspects of the property was the Tahitian Room which was built using authentic pieces from Tahiti. The Ortons had collected the items during an extended visit to Tahiti where one of their sons resided.

By 1961 the Desert Sun had become the Motel Desert Sun under Manger Hotel chain ownership. Manger Hotels was a long-standing hotel company based in New York. The Manger name didn't last long in Phoenix as the property was bought by the Porter House Motel chain in 1963. After Porter House acquired the facility, it was renamed the Porter House and became the chain's headquarters. By 1966 the motel name was back to the Desert Sun.

Today some of the Desert Suns buildings still exist. A large portion of the room structure was destroyed by fire in 2005.

Desert View Motel – 5130 (5226) East Van Buren Street

By 1952 the Desert View Motel was in business. The type of construction and layout are unknown.

In 1965 the Desert View was robbed, and the crooks were apprehended by Scottsdale police. The police discovered that the car was registered to an Ohio man who was murdered in Indianapolis. The two crooks also had the dead man's identification and credit cards. They admitted to stabbing the man, taking his car, and driving to Phoenix.

The Desert View Motel was closed and demolished by 1989. Today the area is a vacant lot.

Detroiter Tourist Court – 3308 (4404) Grand Avenue

The Detroiter Tourist Court was in business by 1944. The facility included eight cabins, two houses, and a gas station. By 1949 the court became the Illini Motor Court. In 1965 the cabins and houses were sold and moved off property.

Today the real estate holds a used car business.

The Dew Drop Inn operating as apartments in 2012 (Photo by Author)

Dew Drop Inn – 1223 Grand Avenue

By 1928 the Smiths were renting cabins on Grand Avenue on an apartment basis. Around 1946 the cabins were given the name "Dew Drop Inn" and were targeted to the transient market. By 1955 the facility became known as the Rosewood Village Motel. Another name change occurred by 1959, and the court became the Rose Alice Motel. The name changes were sensible since the owner's name was Mrs. Rose Smith and her daughter was named Alice. The Rose Alice consisted of a small cabin court which had grown to eight units by 1969. At some point the original cabins were joined together to create a strip-style motel building. A newer strip-style motel building was also built across from the original cabins.

By 1988 the Rose Alice Motel stopped advertising as a motel and switched to an apartment business model. Today the Rose Alice still exists and is rented as apartments.

Dewitt's Tourist Court – See Forney's Court

Dick's Court, now apartments (Photo by Author 2014)

Dick's Court – 1501-09 West Garfield (Acacia) Street

Dick's Court was built in the late 1920s and rented as apartments. The facility consisted of five large cabins built in a row along what was then Acacia Street. The cabins were connected with gable roofs over the area in between them. This created covered parking. Dick's Court appears to have been advertised to the transient market by 1948.

By 1963 the facility went back to an apartment-only business model. Today the original Dick's Court buildings still exist. They are rented as apartments.

Didit's Court – 1331 Grand Avenue

By 1932 an auto court existed at 1331 Grand Avenue. The original name is not known, but by 1939 it was known as Didit's Court. By 1944 the name disappears, but the property ownership remains the same. It's quite possible that cabin rentals continued for some time.

In 1940 one of the cabins at Didit's Court was destroyed by fire. Inside, a man was found deceased. He had been staying in Phoenix in an attempt to help his tuberculosis symptoms. It was determined that the blaze had begun due to the use of a respiration lamp. The lamp operated using an open flame and created a vapor that the man would breathe in. Fortunately, one of the man's friends questioned if any currency was found with him. None was found even though it was known he had a large sum with him. The people that had helped put the fire out were questioned, and one of them confessed to stealing the money. Apparently he had found the man dead earlier in the night and stolen his money. Later he returned to the cabin and, using an accelerant, set the cabin on fire. He then helped the other guests, and firemen put the fire out. The perpetrator received a 5–10-year prison sentence for his deed.

Eventually the property that once held the Didit's Court was utilized to build the Desert Sun Motel. Today the remnants of that motel still exist.

Dixie Camp – 6600 East Van Buren Street

By 1932 the Dixie Camp was accepting guests. The camp probably started as an auto camp but soon had cabins built. The facility included a tavern, known as Scotties Place, and a gas station as well. By 1942 it appears the gas station was closed, and no mention of the court appears after this time.

Today the property is owned by the city zoo.

Dixie Court – 1310 –18 East Adams Street

The Dixie Court began as a smattering of residential homes with monthly rental cabins. In the early 1940s the Dixie Court started with the buildings at 1318 East Adams Street. Soon after, the court expanded to include the buildings adjacent to it. The court was marketed to both the tourist market and long-term renters. Fourteen units were available for rent.

One of the cottages that would become part of the Dixie Court was the scene of a murder in 1926. George Ford shot a woman in the cottage three times, fatally wounding her. The court found Ford insane, and he was remanded to the state mental hospital on Van Buren Street. Ford escaped from the facility in 1935, but was found in Kansas in 1938.

By 1956 the Dixie Court was no longer operating. It sat vacant for a few years before being split up. The individual buildings operated as apartments again for a short time. The facility was demolished in the 1960s.

Today Adams Street no longer exists at the location. The road was removed to build the Shaw School, which still occupies the real estate.

Dixie Hotel circa 1930, white building on the southwest corner, Washington Street and Fourth Avenue (Courtesy of the Flood Control District of Maricopa County)

Dixie Hotel – 401 West Washington Street

In the 1890s Frank Moss, a local wagon maker, built what came to be known as Moss Hall at his residence on the southwest corner of Fourth Avenue and Washington Street. The hall was used for religious and political gatherings and seminars.

In 1906 the building was completely remodeled and rental rooms added. The facility became known as the Moss Rooming House. By 1915 the building was renamed the Fourth Avenue House. This only lasted a couple of years, and by 1918 the facility became the Dixie Hotel.

In 1967 Joseph Begin was shot and killed in a room at the Dixie. After an argument in the room, Betty Jenkins shot the man. Jenkins was charged with murder but plead guilty to the reduced charge of voluntary manslaughter. She was sentenced to 9–10 years in prison.

The Dixie Hotel was very long-lived, but by 1974 it had closed. The property was used as a parking lot for many years. In 2000 the Sandra Day O'Connor United States Courthouse was opened on the property formerly utilized by the Dixie Hotel.

Dobbs House – See Grand View Hotel

Dobson Court – See San Antonio Court

Dorris Hotel – 32 South Second Avenue

The Dorris Rooming House was open before 1899 as it was remodeled that year. It was a two-story structure with 16 rental rooms. By 1939 the Dorris added the Burbank Rooms in the building adjacent to the hotel. By 1948 the two-building complex became the Beasley Hotel. The hotel took on the name Elgin Hotel by 1958. This was a long-standing name of another hotel on Jefferson Street. In 1963 a hotel on Washington Street took on the Elgin Hotel name, and this location was no longer operated as a hotel.

In 1955 Otis Barnes, a guest at the Elgin Hotel, was allegedly killed by another guest in the ground floor bar at the facility. Arleigh Shackelford was caught by the bartender taking coins from the March of Dimes collection box. Shackelford was asked to leave, and Barnes attempted to help eject him from the bar. A scuffle ensued and Barnes ended up with a knife blade lodged in his brain. Shackelford was tried for murder and acquitted due to a lack of evidence that he was ever in possession of the murder weapon.

Today the area contains the Calvin C. Goode Municipal Building. Second Avenue no longer exists in that area.

Downtown Hotel – 23 East Washington Street

The Ellingson Building was constructed in 1899. The building first held a furniture store and offices. Later it became the "Woodmen of the World" hall. After the hall portion of the building stood vacant for some time, it was converted to a hotel. The hotel was in business by 1945. It was a two-story structure with 60 rental rooms.

By 1963 the hotel was closed, but the building was still utilized for other businesses.

The Ellingson Building (white building, left) in 1899 (Author's Collection)

The Ellingson Building was placed on the National Register of Historic Places in 1985. It was removed from the list in 1988 as it had been demolished. Today the CityScape complex utilizes the real estate.

Downtown Motel – 510 East Adams Street

The Downtown Motel was in operation by 1951. The facility was a converted home and contained six rental units. By 1957 the motel was no longer operating. It was demolished in the 1960s.

The Phoenix Museum of History was located on the property until it was closed in 2009.

The former Drake Motel, now operating as the Spur Apartments (Photo by Author 2014)

Drake Motel – 810 South Seventeenth Avenue

The Drake Motel was in operation by 1961. The facility was constructed in single-story, strip-motel style. Layout was generally in a box shape with two entrances to a central court area. By 1968 the motel's name was changed to the Spur Motel.

In 1969 one of the motel managers was accidently shot in the legs by her husband with a shotgun. The shot was serious and nearly severed her foot. There was no saving her left leg, which was amputated below the knee.

By 1986 the facility switched to renting exclusively as apartments. Today the Spur still exists as apartments.

Drive In Court – 2139 East Van Buren Street

The Drive In Court was a short-lived court opened in 1957. The court was located in the rear of the property behind a secondhand store. By 1960 the court was no longer in business.

The property now holds the El Capri night club.

Drive Inn Auto Court – See Last Chance Auto Court

Dunes Motel – See Hudson Lodge

Duran Hotel – 707 East Jefferson Street

The building at 707 East Jefferson was operated as apartments and furnished rooms since early in the century. About 1930 it became known as the Duran Hotel. It was likely a second-level hotel as was usual at the time for small lodging facilities. A grocery store and café were housed in the lower level for some time.

In 1944 a guest of the hotel was killed as a result of gambling outside the hotel. The man entered into an argument with another man he had been playing craps with. The man struck him and knocked him to the ground. He proceeded to stomp on his head until he was deceased.

The Duran Hotel was closed and demolished by 1969. A modern office building is located on the property today.

The former Dusty Trail Motel, now apartments (Photo by Author 2014)

Dusty Trail Motel – 2146 East Adams Street

By 1950 the East Adams Apartments opened at 2146 East Adams. Many motels in Phoenix varied business models between short-term and long-term renters. In this case, the business began as apartments and turned to a motel model. By 1952 the apartments became the Dusty Trail Motel. The facility was an eight-unit motel utilizing three strip-style buildings. By 1959 the Dusty Trail became the East Adams Motel.

The East Adams became apartments by 1961. Today the facility still exists and is rented as apartments.

Earle Hotel – See Savoy Hotel

Earll Court – 1740 East Earll Drive

The Earll Court started as apartments in place by 1930. By the late 1940s the facility had the original building utilizing cottages under one roof, and a series of separate cabins. Likely due to the huge demand for overnight rooms, the facility began accepting short-term renters about 1951. It returned to apartments only by the end of the 1950s.

The buildings were demolished in the early 1980s. Today a parking lot is located on the property.

East Adams Motel – See Dusty Trail Motel

East Lake Park Auto Camp – East Lake Park (corner Jefferson and Sixteenth Streets)

An auto camp was located at East Lake Park for a short time around 1925. Many auto camps appeared around this time period to service the new automobile travelers. The facility provided camping accommodations to those travelers who carried their own camping equipment. Existing amenities at the park likely made the area a good candidate for an auto camp.

Today East Lake Park still exists. Both the auto camp and lake are long gone.

Eastside Court – 1863 East Van Buren Street

By 1935 the Eastside Court was open and accepting guests. The facility was a standard design cabin-style court.

In November of 1940 a cabin was robbed of $4,500 and the guest beaten. He was admitted to the hospital in critical condition.

In 1947 a Staff Sergeant from Williams Field and a waitress were arrested by the Phoenix vice squad. The man put up a fight and ran naked down Van Buren Street before being apprehended. Most motels in Phoenix experienced visits from the vice squad with arrests based on the city's moral standards code.

The Eastside Court was demolished and replaced by the Pasadena Motel in 1948. Today the motel still exists and has been renamed the Classic Motel.

Eastside Tourist Court – See McLean Auto Court

Eddie Hotel – See Wollpert Hotel

Bronco Motel (Edgerton's) circa 1960 (Author's Collection)

The former Edgerton's Motel operating as apartments in 2012 (Photo by Author)

Edgerton's Motel – 4630 East Van Buren Street

Edgerton's Motel was in operation by 1949 as an addition to an existing restaurant on the property. The facility was a mixture of cabins and strip-style motel units. Most likely the facility started with cabins and added the strip sections later. Eventually the buildings were built together tightly to create a strip out of individual buildings. In 1973 the restaurant was destroyed by fire. It reopened by 1974.

In 1958 a woman was found dead and a man critically injured in one of the cabins. Police speculated it was a murder-suicide attempt. The only witness was the woman's three-year-old daughter who would not talk about it. The man's young son was outside the cabin when the shots were fired.

By 1952 the motel had changed names to the Bronco Motel. The facility closed as a motel and started operating as apartments by 1982.

Today the property, with its mismatched buildings, still exists and is used as apartments.

Egyptian Motor Hotel – 765 Grand Avenue

The Egyptian Motor Hotel was in operation by 1955. The facility was built in two-story motor hotel style and included 51 rooms. A coffee shop was also located on the property. The motel was themed as Arab/Egyptian and utilized Egyptian-inspired designs in its construction. Many themed motels were built in Phoenix in an attempt to compete in the heavily competitive market.

Egyptian Motor Hotel circa 1960 (Author's Collection)

The Egyptian operating as the Las Palmas Inn in 2012 (Photo by Author)

The Egyptian was part of the Ranger Motels chain for some time in the 1960s. It then became part of the Romney Hotels chain under the ownership of Wayne Romney. Both chains were Phoenix-based endeavors.

Robberies occurred at least twice at the Egyptian. In 1961 the motel was robbed of under $100. The pair of robbers were apprehended shortly afterward during another attempted robbery at the Desert Sky Motel. In 1969 the Egyptian was robbed again. This time a guest entered the lobby at the time of the robbery. Both the clerk and the guest were forced to lie face down on the floor during the robbery. As the robber left, he shot the guest on the floor for no apparent reason. The guest died and the robber was apprehended in short order.

The Egyptian became the Oklahoma Hotel by 1984. This lasted a few years and by 1987 the facility took on the Las Palmas Motel name. The property still functions as the Las Palmas today.

Eighteen Sixty-Five Motor Court – See Pasadena Motel

El Cerrito Hotel – 713 North Central Avenue

The El Cerrito Hotel began in the early 1930s as the Luscor Apartments. The facility either utilized the building or was built on the property of a previous boarding house. It took on the name El Cerrito by 1940, but was still operated as apartments. By 1949 the apartments began to be marketed as a hotel.

By 1989 the hotel was closed. A parking lot is on the property today.

El Comanche Motel – 5225 South Central Avenue

The El Comanche Motel began as apartments built in the late 1940s. By 1956 the facility had taken on a motel business structure. The motel consisted of four rental buildings which were likely duplexes. An additional smaller building was located in the rear and may have been an owner's quarters. The main buildings were arranged in two rows of two facing each other. This created a central parking area.

The motel became apartments in the early 1980s and was demolished a few years later. A modern retail mall is located on the property today.

El Cortez Apartment Hotel circa 1965 (Author's Collection)

The former El Cortez Apartment Hotel operating as condominiums (Photo by Author 2014)

El Cortez Apartment Hotel – 3130 North Seventh Avenue

In 1964 the El Cortez Apartments opened. The apartment complex was owned by Chilton Inns, a Phoenix-based hotel chain. The facility was a 165-room, three-story complex built in a rectangle around a central court. The court was a recreational area which included a pool. The El Cortez operated primarily as apartments, but around 1965 it began to be marketed as a hotel.

By the 1980s the El Cortez moved back to an apartment model. Today the facility operates as condominiums.

El Don Motel – See Red Horse Motel

El Estribo Lodge circa 1960 (Author's Collection)

El Estribo Lodge – 4602 North Elsie Avenue

Neil Gates, an architect who moved to the area in 1928, designed and built his home in the Arcadia area near the Jokake Inn. The building he designed was an open space concept utilizing Spanish design. The home was large with five bedrooms and included a solarium. In the 1940's the home was converted to a guest lodge, the El Estribo. The original garage was divided into two guest rooms and a new cottage building was built to hold rental units. The facility was known as one of the better resorts in Phoenix and is said to have lodged many Hollywood stars. Its location among the Arcadia resorts like the Paradise Inn and Jokake Inn helped to solidify its upscale image. The El Estribo was owned by Charles Alberding for a period prior to the 1980's. However, it does not appear to have been advertised as an Alsonett Hotel. In the 1980's the El Estribo Lodge was converted back into a residence and is now listed on the National Register of Historic Places.

The Freeway Motel, formerly the El Lynn Motel (Photo by Author 2014)

El Lynn Motel – 2425 West Buckeye Road

The El Lynn Motel was opened by 1951 under the name Motto Guest Lodge. It became the El Lynn by 1952. The facility consisted of two sections of single-story, strip-motel buildings. They were arranged in an L-shape.

By 1976 the facility became the Freeway Motel and still functions as such today.

El Molino Court circa 1955 (Author's Collection)

El Molino Court as it appears today (Photo by Author 2012)

El Molino Court – 2913 East Van Buren Street

By 1949 the El Molino Court was open for business. The facility consisted of individual buildings each holding two rooms for a total of 12 units. Flat roofs and stucco walls set the style of the facility. By 1959 the El Molino had become part of the adjacent Dunes Motel.

Today the original El Molino buildings still exist but are boarded up and vacant.

The El Oeste Lodge, now a residence (Photo by Author 2014)

El Oeste Lodge – 4649 North Fifty-Sixth Street

The El Oeste Lodge was built in 1924 as a private residence. By 1949 it had become a guest lodge taking in winter vacationers utilizing bungalows as guest units. In the 1990s the facility stopped operating as a guest ranch, and the bungalows became apartment rentals.

The El Oeste Lodge sign still hangs in front of the property. In 2012 the sign was stolen, and the theft made the local television news. The sign was returned soon afterwards.

Today the lodge still exists as a residence, and the bungalows operate as apartments.

El Ranchito Motel circa 1950 (Author's Collection)

El Ranchito operating as apartments in 2012 (Photo by Author)

El Ranchito Motel – 3060 (3850) Grand Avenue

The El Ranchito was accepting guests by 1946. The facility utilized single-story, strip motel style construction. Early on the motel also utilized cabins. In 1968 the motel became the Godsoe Motel. The new name was short-lived as by 1969 the facility became the Delmar Motel. By 1976 the motel took back its original El Ranchito name.

By 1984 the El Ranchito was converted to apartments and remains so today.

El Rancho Annex – See Phoenix Motor Lodge

El Rancho Motor Hotel circa 1960 (Author's Collection)

El Rancho Motor Hotel – 1300 West Van Buren Street

The El Rancho Motor Hotel was selling rooms by 1946. Unusual for the timeframe and location, the El Rancho consisted of multiple two-story buildings built in hotel-style. The facility utilized a Spanish motif with stucco walls and tile roofs. Guests could choose from 90 units, 39 of which had kitchenettes installed.

The property appears to have had few issues over the years. In 1955 the hotel night clerk was robbed at gun point and told to lie on the floor. The thief took the cash from the drawer and left.

By 1991 the El Rancho was closed, and it was demolished by 1992. Today a modern apartment complex resides on the real estate the El Rancho existed on.

El Ray Motel – See Ohio Motel

El Rita Motel – 3513 East Van Buren Street

The El Rita Motel was in operation by 1947. Little is known of the size or configuration of the motel. The El Rita was out of business by 1971. The buildings were demolished in the 1970s and 1980s.

Today a storage facility is on the property.

El Rokay Lodge circa 1955 (Author's Collection)

El Rokay Lodge – 5049 North Seventh Street

The El Rokay Lodge was operating by 1951. The facility included 15 rental units and a three-bedroom owner's quarters. The obligatory swimming pool was also included.

The El Rokay was closed in the mid-1980s and demolished by the late 1990s. An automotive repair business is now located on the property.

El Royale Court circa 1935 (Author's Collection)

El Royale Motor Court – 106 North Seventeenth Avenue

The El Royale Motor Court was an early Seventeenth Avenue court opened by 1931. The facility was a cabin court of unknown size. Its proximity to the Arizona capitol building made the court popular with politicians and government workers.

In 1968 Vladko Denev arrived from his native Bulgaria and stayed at the El Royale. He became fast friends with the Assistant Attorney General, Carl Waag, who also lived at the court. Denev overstayed his visa and was in danger of being deported. The Bulgarian was in fear of being classified as a political enemy and executed if he was returned to his home country. With the help of the Waag family, Denev's case was brought to congress. The issue dragged on for years, and in 1973 Denev was allowed to stay in the United States.

The court was out of business by 1969 and demolished in short order. Today the El Royale's address is a parking lot.

Eldorado Hotel – See Parker House

Eldorado Motel – See Sun Court

Elena Court – 3514 Grand Avenue

The Elena Court was operating by 1930. The business utilized cabin court design and had at least 27 units. One of the cabins was destroyed in 1953 when a car crashed into it.

By 1959 the court was out of business. Today the area is in the easement area where the Indian School Road bridge and ramp system connects with Grand Avenue and Thirty-Fifth Avenue.

Elgin Hotel (Second Avenue) – See Dorris Hotel

Elgin Hotel (Washington Street) – See Ambassador Hotel

Elgin Hotel – 32 West Jefferson Street

By 1942 the Elgin Hotel was accepting guests. The hotel was located in the Kempner Building. By 1958 the hotel became the Pearson Hotel, and then the Miller Hotel by 1959. The Beasley Hotel on Second Avenue took on the Elgin Hotel name at the time.

The Miller Hotel was closed by 1971 and was eventually razed. Today a comedy club is located on the property.

The former Eli Motel, now used as an auto repair facility (Photo by Author 2014)

Eli Motel – 2519 West Van Buren Street

By 1948 the Eli Motel was open. The facility was a small, eight-unit motel of apartment-style construction. The motel went through a bewildering array of name changes. By 1951 the property had become the Chippewa Motel. By 1955 it was the Cy-Erna Motel. By 1957 it was the Whites Motel. By 1958 it became the Townsend Motel. By 1960 it was the Terry Ann Motel. By 1963 it was the Western Motel. By 1964 it became the Lo-Ra Motel. Finally, by 1967 it became the Cactus Motel.

The Cactus Motel was closed by 1983. An auto repair shop now resides on the property. The office utilizes one of the original buildings.

Elite Hotel – See Holmes Rooming House

Elmo Rooming House - 438 West Washington Street

By 1921 the Elmo Rooming House was in business. The fraternal organizations the Odd Fellows and Moose both had their club rooms in the building during the early 1920s. By 1925 the facility became the Globe Hotel. By 1929 the name changed to the Cecil Hotel. New management along with a renovation took place in 1935. The building became the Utah Hotel that year. The hotel endured until 1970.

Today the Comerica Theatre is located on the real estate.

Elvas Motel – 2105 East Adams Street

Elvas Motel was in operation by 1953. The facility was small, and its configuration is not known. It was sold in 1957 and became the Williams Court. By 1960 it began operating under an apartment business plan.

Today the property is in the I-10 easement.

The former Embassy Square Hotel operating as condominiums (Photo by Author 2014)

Embassy Square Hotel – 805 North Fourth Avenue

The Embassy Square Hotel was opened in 1964 as an apartment building. The building was a large, 11-story building with 80 apartments. Each apartment featured a private balcony. An outdoor pool was oddly placed on top of the building's carport with access from the third floor. Other amenities included a coffee shop and laundry facilities. Over two million dollars was spent on construction.

Shortly after opening, the facility became known as the Embassy Square Hotel, and transient guests were welcomed. This was likely a business decision based on lack of apartment occupancy. It was advertised as "Where Every Room is an Apartment". The building slowly reverted back to an apartment-only facility.

Today the building still exists as the Embassy Condominiums.

Emerald Pool Lodge – 1502 North Forty-Sixth Street

The Emerald Pool Lodge was in business by 1949. It was built on a 3½ acre orange grove. A long driveway led to an oval drive with the namesake pool in the center. Buildings were placed in a semicircle around the drive. The original build consisted of eight kitchenette units and a three-bedroom home. Later additions resulted in 14 total units. The facility actively promoted the use of its pool for rent as an additional source of revenue.

The lodge no longer accepted guests after 1969. The buildings were demolished in 2003. It remains a vacant lot today.

Emerick Hotel – 362 North Third Avenue

By 1948 the Emerick Hotel was open on North Third Avenue. The facility consisted of about 15 units. By 1958 the facility was renamed as Long's Guest Lodge. The lodge soon converted to an apartment business model. It was razed by 1969.

Today a modern law office is located at the address.

The former Ernie's Cabins office (Photo by Author 2014)

Ernie's Cabins – 109 North Thirty-Second Place

Ernie's Cabins was a small collection of cabins and trailers. The facility was mostly sold apartment-style. For a few years, around 1966, the cabins were marketed to the transient market. They eventually went back to the apartment model. The cabins still exist today and are rented as apartments.

Espana Hotel – See Jefferson Rooms

Espanol Hotel – 222 East Jefferson Street

Anselmo de Miguel, a Spanish immigrant and Flagstaff innkeeper, moved to Phoenix and opened the Espanol Hotel by 1925. It was a two-story building in the middle of the block. By 1932 de Miguel expanded the complex and changed the name to the Paris Hotel. The expanded hotel utilized the 226 East Jefferson address while the restaurant remained at 222 East Jefferson. It's unknown if the rooms were actually moved or just readdressed.

In 1943 de Miguel was shot by Lucio Arribas, a Spanish merchant marine. The dispute was over money Arribas claimed he was owed. Arribas was remanded to the state mental hospital before sentencing. While at a hospital movie, Arribas escaped from the facility. He called de Miguel and asked if he could stay at the hotel as he was tired of the hospital. Arribas was soon apprehended. De Miguel continued to operate his hotel and lived until 1960 when he was killed in an automobile accident.

In 1968 Irvin Thompson was sitting outside the Paris Hotel rolling cigarettes with some friends. Charles Dixon, a hotel guest, exited the hotel and demanded Thompson give up one of his cigarettes. When Thompson refused, Dixon accosted him and shot him in the head. Thompson was killed and Dixon was apprehended and punished.

By 1982 the Paris Hotel was no longer in business. Today the real estate is used by the Collier Center.

Evergreen Court (Buckeye) – See Tamarack Inn

Evergreen Court – 1509 Grand Avenue

By 1928 the Evergreen Court was in business. The court utilized cabin court construction consisting of individual cabins used as rental units.

A mystery occurred at the Evergreen in 1939. A young girl whose family lived at the court raised both a cat and a rat as pets. After a brief skirmish, Squeeky the rat and Tootsie the cat became good friends and lived in harmony together. The unusual pair and their owner made it into the newspaper.

By 1958 the Evergreen Court had closed. The facility was demolished, and the property used to build the Caravan Inn.

Ewing's Tourist Court – 1212 East Hatcher (Wabash) Road

There was a short-lived court located at 1212 East Wabash in the 1950s. The size and configuration of the facility is not known. By 1959 the court was no longer operating.

Today the real estate is part of a park.

The EZ In still operates today (Photo by Author 2012)

EZ In Motel – 2450 Grand Avenue

The EZ In opened as a trailer court with a few cabins by 1954. Eventually the cabins were replaced by a multiple building complex built in single-story motel style. In the early 1980s a two-story motor hotel style building was added to the facility.

Today the EZ In continues to operate as a motel. The trailer court portion operates under a different name today.

Fain's Court – See Tamarack Inn

Fairmont Hotel – See Grand View Hotel

Far West Auto Court – 1950 Grand Avenue

The Far West Auto Court was open by 1930. The facility utilized the cabin court style, which was the prevalent style of the time. About 16 buildings of various configurations were used as rentals. By 1952 the facility was no longer renting cabins to transient guests and began operating as apartments.

The buildings were demolished in the early 1980s. Today the area is not developed.

Farley House – 618 West Washington Street

The Farley House was in operation by 1893. The facility was a two-story wooden structure and included a restaurant on the ground floor. After operating the old Lemon Hotel as the first Mills House, the Mills family bought the Farley House and renamed it the New Mills House. The name change took effect in the spring of 1896. In 1903 the New Mills was sold. After a thorough renovation the hotel was renamed the Union Hotel.

By 1937 the hotel was no longer in business. Today the Phoenix Police Headquarters is located on the property.

Fenix Auto Camp – 1723 East Van Buren Street

The Fenix Auto Camp was a short-lived auto camp that opened in 1931. By 1935 the facility had become vacant. 1931 was late to open an auto camp in Phoenix as most locations had already added cabin court facilities. Without cabins or trailer facilities the business could not have been viable.

The real estate the Fenix once occupied now holds an electric supply and service business.

Fern Glen Court – See Black Diamond Auto Cabins

The Fifth Avenue Court, operates as apartments today (Photo by Author 2014)

Fifth Avenue Court – 618 North Fifth Avenue

The Fifth Avenue Court was accepting guests by 1931. The facility was built in single-story strip construction in Spanish style. It operated mainly as apartments from the beginning, but did accept transient business for many years. It gradually became all apartments.

Today the Fifth Avenue Court still operates under its original name as apartments.

Fifty-Nine Trees Court – See Air Line Modern Cottage Court

Fillion Motel – See Ford's Motel

Flamingo Hotel circa 1960 (Author's Collection)

The Flamingo Hotel operating as the Skyline Motel in 2012 (Photo by Author)

Flamingo Hotel - 2501 East Van Buren Street

The Flamingo Hotel opened in 1952. It was a two-story motor inn style facility and unusual in that it had rooms located on both sides of Twenty-Fifth Street. The property also included a cafe and the mandatory pool. The Flamingo was part of the Flamingo Hotel chain, which had hotels throughout the southwest.

The motel retained its Flamingo name through the years with additions such as the Flamingo Economy Inn and the Flamingo Airporter Inn. In 2010 the Flamingo name was dropped in favor of the Skyline Inn.

The Flamingo still exists, has undergone a renovation, and became a Rodeway Inn in 2012. Soon after, the facility was split into two motels. The section east of Twenty-Fifth Street remained the Rodeway Inn while the section west of the street became a Knights Inn.

Flint Motel circa 1950 (Author's Collection)

Flint Motel – 4140 East Van Buren Street

The Flint Motel was operating by 1948. The facility was built in cottage court style with two units per cottage. Twelve rental units were available and a house on the property doubled as the office. The motel became the Silver Spur Motel by 1958.

The Silver Spur was closed and demolished by 1986. Today the real estate is part of the Phoenix Gateway Center.

Floods Court – 1709 East Van Buren Street

By 1947 a small cabin court was built on the property of an existing grocery store at 1709 East Van Buren Street. The court was initially known as Floods Court. The ownership of both the court and grocery store changed by 1948, and the facility became known as Costantinti Court. Soon the court stopped accepting transient guests and by 1951 the area was marketed only as JC Market.

Today the address is a used car lot.

Ford Hotel circa 1940 (Courtesy Library of Congress)

Ford Hotel – 11 North Second Avenue

On November 1, 1895, the Ford Hotel opened on the northeast corner of Washington Street and Second Avenue. The building was a three-story structure with fifty feet along Washington and 137.5 feet along Second Avenue. The first floor was utilized for three storefronts, the hotel lobby, and the restaurant and bar. The upper two floors were fitted with 40 hotel rooms. The Ford Hotel was one of the premier hotels in Phoenix for many years. It featured large sleeping porches, which were covered to aid in comfort. The hotel also operated an annex at 205 West Jefferson in the early 1910s.

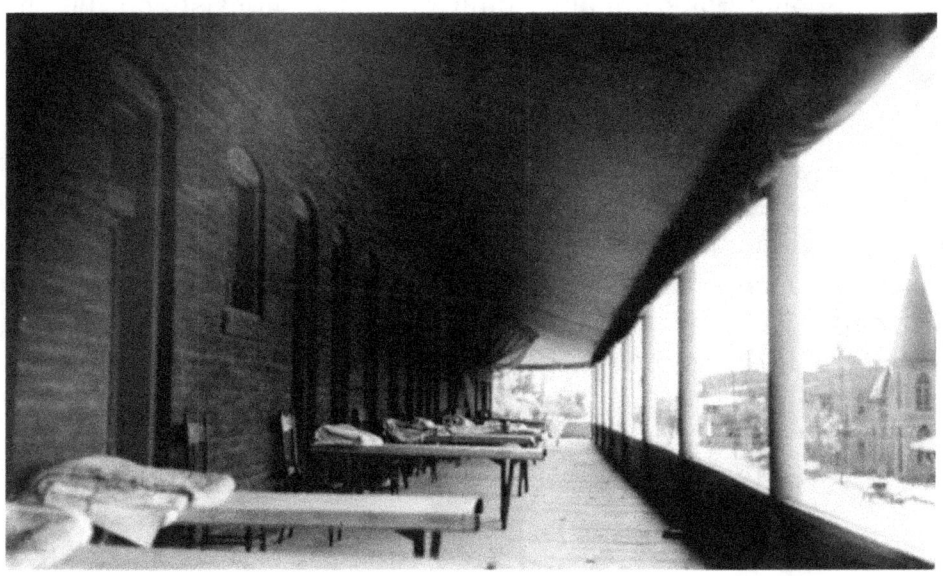

Ford Hotel Sleeping Porch circa 1920 (Courtesy Arizona State Library, Archives and Public Records, History and Archives Division, Phoenix, #97-2146*)*

In December of 1900 Phoenix hosted the "Cowboy and Indian Carnival". It utilized Washington Street in the downtown area as the midway. The carnival held one of the first rodeos in the area. Carnival attractions lined the street, and the event began when a telegram from President McKinley was received. It stated, in part, that "the largest American flag ever unfurled in the territory" was to be seen at the carnival. One end of the flag was attached to the Ford Hotel.

George Hunt, Arizona's first Governor, utilized the Ford Hotel as his headquarters. When Arizona gained statehood on February 14, 1912, the Governor and a group of his political friends walked to the Capitol from the Ford Hotel. The 15-block walk was much more difficult at the time as the streets were not paved.

The hotel ceased to operate as a hotel in 1953. It was remodeled inside to hold offices, and many were utilized for the county courts. The exterior was modernized, and the large sleeping porches were removed by building them in.

In 1965 the First National Bank purchased the hotel building. This completed the purchase of the entire half block. The bank continued to lease space in the building until 1970 when it broke ground for its headquarters building. The last business to be demolished was a bar as the owner had the longest lease in the building.

Today the First National Bank building, built in 1970, still exists on the site. It is now the Wells Fargo Building.

Ford's Motel -2933 West Buckeye Road

Ford's Motel was operating by 1948. The facility included eight one- or two-bedroom units and nine trailer spaces. An owner's home was also located on the property. The motel went through many name changes. By 1957 it was called Fillion Motel, and by 1959 it became the Box A Motel. It quickly became the Campbell Motel by 1958 and then the Tally-Ho Lodge by 1963.

By 1965 the motel was no longer in business. Today the property is an undeveloped lot.

Forney's Court – 1867 East Van Buren Street

Many early business owners made attempts to maximize the income created by their properties. One way was to add a camp or court as they were relatively inexpensive to build and supply. This was what happened with Forney's Court. The property in this case was originally a grocery store. In the early 1930s an auto camp was set up next to the store and operated under the name Midway Auto Camp. By that time auto camps were disappearing, and it seems the Midway did not last long. By 1940 the grocery store owner had built a series of cabins next to the store. The facility operated under Dewitt's Tourist Court for a couple years until the name changed to Forney's Court.

We know the facility was in full operation in 1943. Records show a domestic dispute in cabin number four resulted in a man being hospitalized that year.

By 1948 the court ceased operation, but the grocery store remained. Today the property still functions as a grocery store.

Fortune Cottages – 5021 East Van Buren Street

In 1943 cabin rentals became available at 5021 East Van Buren on an apartment basis. By 1947 the cabins began to be offered to transient guests under the name Fortune Cottages. In 1957 the cabins were sold and moved off the property.

Today the property is the parking lot for the Tovrea Castle.

Fosters Court Verde – See Verde Motel

Fountain Court – See Clover Court

Fourth Avenue Hotel – See Stenlake Rooming House

Fourth Avenue House – See Dixie Hotel

Francis – See Steinegger Lodging House

Franciscan Motel circa 1950 (Author's Collection)

Franciscan Lodge – 2900 East Van Buren Street

The Franciscan Lodge was opened in 1946. The facility featured a late use of the cabin court design with individual cottages. The cottages were laid out in the usual U-pattern with a central courtyard and parking area. The Franciscan Lodge became the Tahiti Inn Huts in 1959. See Tahiti Inn for more information.

Today the area once occupied by the Franciscan Lodge is a steel company.

Franiva Motor Lodge circa 1955 (Author's Collection)

Franiva Motor Lodge – 4229 North Seventh Street

The Franiva Motor Lodge was open by 1949 across the street from where the Veterans Administration Hospital was soon to be built. The name was a combination of the owner's names, Francis and Iva Daly. The Dalys were active in the motel associations with Francis being the Vice President of the Arizona Motor Hotel Association for some time. The motel was built in motor inn style and consisted of three buildings containing 18 rental units. Eventually a fourth building and pool were added. By 1956 Iva had passed away, and the motel changed hands. The facility's name was changed to the Corbitt's Motel.

The facility became a residence and offices by 1971. It was demolished in the 1990s. Today a parking lot utilizes the real estate.

Franklin Court – 1416 North Seventeenth Avenue

The Franklin Court was in business by 1940. The facility was a cabin court with nine rental units.

By 1962 the Franklin Court was out of business. Today the area is a parking lot.

Franklin Hotel – See Dennis Hotel

Fredley's Motel – See Aldridge Court

French Rooming House - 431 West Washington Street

As early as 1902 the Frenches were renting rooms on Washington Street. The facility was used off and on through the years. By 1941 it became known as Norms Hotel and Smith's Hotel by 1942. It became the Bell Hotel by 1947. All the while the Phoenix Trunk Factories showroom was located in the building.

By 1967 the facility no longer functioned as a hotel. Today the Sandra Day O'Connor Courthouse is located on the property.

Part of the former Fresno Guest Ranch, now operates as a church (Photo by Author 2014)

Fresno Guest Ranch – 6630 North Central Avenue

The Fresno Guest Ranch was opened in early 1952. Situated on three acres, the facility contained a 14-room house and 12 rental units. The meeting lodge could hold up to 600 people.

In 1953 the First Christian Church purchased the facility. The meeting area was converted to hold church services and functions. The guest rooms continued to be rented for a few years. It is likely they were eventually converted to classrooms.

Today the church is still located on the property. A new church was built, but the lodge building still exists.

Frontier Lodge circa 1950 (Author's Collection)

Frontier Lodge – 2823 East Van Buren Street

The Frontier Lodge was in operation by 1946 on Van Buren's motel row. The facility started with cottage-type units with covered parking. Subsequent construction was single-story strip motel style. Eventually the cottage units were incorporated into a strip style. By 1968 there were 42 single-story, strip-style units.

The Frontier went through the usual name changes for modernization and ended up using the Frontier Motor Hotel name. The facility was closed by 1991, and demolition took place by 1995.

Today the property where the Frontier once stood is a vacant lot.

Fuller Cottages – See Stefford's Cottages

Fulton Hotel – 216 West Washington Street

The Fulton Hotel was open by 1963 in the old Arizona Showman's Association Building. The building was a two-story brick building.

The Fulton was closed by 1972. Today the Phoenix City Hall is on the real estate.

Gardner's Hotel – 1229 East Washington Street

The Gardner family operated the Phoenix Costume House on Washington Street. About 1939 they started offering rooms for rent. Some of the rooms were in the costume building, and at least one cabin was for rent at the rear of the property.

In 1942 a 58-year-old pastor from California was found dead in a rear cabin. He had hung himself from a rope in the building. It was later discovered that he had previously attempted suicide by cutting his throat and wrists.

By 1950 the hotel was no longer advertised. The cabin in the rear was rented on an apartment basis. Today the Arizona Bridge to Independent Living building is on the property.

Gardner's Motel – 2921 East Broadway Road

Gardner's Motel was in business by 1953. The size and configuration of the facility is not known. By 1963 the facility became the Pueblo Motel. The motel operated a six-unit annex at 3825 South Thirtieth Street for a short while.

The Pueblo was out of business by 1984. Today an industrial building is located on the property.

Gardner's Motel Annex – 3825 South Thirtieth Street

Gardner's Motel Annex was a small six-unit apartment building. It was utilized for a short time as the motel's annex. This was from approximately 1957 to 1960. The facility became apartments afterwards. Today the area is industrial.

Garland Smith Court – 1113 East Apache Street

The Garland Smith Court was in operation by 1955. The facility was a small cabin court with six rental units. It operated as both apartments and an auto court through the years.

The facility was short-lived and was out of business by 1960. It was demolished within the decade. Today the real estate is vacant.

Gary Auto Court – 3024 West Van Buren Street

Court Gary was in business by 1931. The facility featured a cabin-style court as well as a trailer court.

In 1944 a woman was found screaming for help in one of the cabins. She had been tied to the bed with a scarf and had a wire placed around her neck. The woman claimed her accoster attempted to make her sign paperwork that was stolen from her family home eleven years earlier. The paperwork had to do with Texas oil endeavors.

By 1969 all of the cabins were demolished, and the facility welcomed trailers only. A small mall is located at the address today.

Part of the Gateway Court still exists (Photo by Author 2012)

Gateway Court – 3706 East Van Buren Street

The Gateway Court was opened in 1939 with 12 units. The facility was built in cabin court style with individual cottages arranged in a U-shape. The Gateway operated until 1982 when it became apartments.

Today most of the Gateway Court still exists. One row of cabins has been razed. What remains is a good example of a simple, early cabin court.

Gavin Court – See Westward Ho Court

Gaylord Motel circa 1970 (Author's Collection)

The Gaylord Motel operating as the Best Inn in 2012 (Photo by Author)

Gaylord Motel – 3547 East Van Buren Street

The Gaylord Apartment Motel was opened in 1965. The motel was built on property formerly occupied by the Trails End Court. The Gaylord was built in two-story motor hotel style. Each of the rooms included a full kitchen, bedroom, and living room. The facility operated as the Gaylord until 1986 when it became the Parkview Inn. By 2004 the facility was operating as apartments-only. Recently, the motel has taken on the name Best Inn and Suites and is accepting transient guests again.

Gel Mar Court – 2146 East Monroe Street

The Gel Mar Court was a small motel located at the corner of Monroe and Twenty-Second Streets. It consisted of four cottages and a single-story strip motel building. The facility was in operation by 1948.

In 1964 the motel manager observed a man on fire running behind the motel. The manager obtained a quilt and put the flames out, saving the man's life. The man had been attempting to start his car by putting gasoline in the carburetor. He became covered in gasoline and soon after caught fire.

The court stopped functioning by 1986, and the building was demolished soon afterwards. Today the real estate is a parking lot.

Gilbert House – 221 West Adams Street

By 1888, and likely even earlier, the Gilbert House was in business. The facility was one of the many smaller hotels located in the city. A renovation of the hotel was performed in 1893.

In 1899, George Trook, the 12-year-old son of the hotel owners, died from eating mulberries. This is unusual as mulberries are not poisonous. Since the berries had been eaten off the ground, there was speculation that they were rotten or had picked up some pesticides. From a twenty-first century perspective, it seems likely that the boy died from some other cause.

A crying baby boy was found on the steps of the Gilbert in 1906. He was brought into the hotel, and authorities were summoned. A note was found on the baby that read, "Please take this baby to either the orphans' home or the convent, and there will be clothes and money sent to him each month. I want him to have the best of care and I will pay whoever takes him well. So give him the best of care. Will want to see him in a good home". It was signed simply, "Bob".

By 1917 the Gilbert House was no longer renting rooms. The real estate was likely used in the construction of the Orpheum Theatre, which broke ground in 1927. The Orpheum still exists today.

Gilberts Motel – 221 North Ninth Street

The large house at 221 North Ninth Street was being rented by the month by 1910. It was a seven-room home and individual rooms were rented as apartments through the years. Around 1958 the home was marketed as Gilberts Motel and rooms were rented nightly as well. By 1960 the motel was closed.

Today a modern apartment complex utilizes the property.

Gillis Tourist Home – 716 East Van Buren Street

For a few years in the 1950s S.P. Gillis opened his home to transient guests. The facility would most likely be listed as a bed and breakfast today. A tourist home is simply a private home where rooms are rented as furnished units. Today a University of Arizona building is on this property.

Gingham Dog Court – 3000 East Washington Street

By 1938 the Gingham Dog Court was in operation. The court was a cabin-style court utilizing cabins as rental units. The cabins were aligned along the property lines in two rows leaving a courtyard in the center. By 1948 the facility became the Sky Harbor Court. After a few years the name was shortened to the S&H Court.

By 1971 the court was no longer accepting guests and was demolished within the decade. Today the Phoenix Ale Brewery building is on the property.

Glenwood Lodging House– 245 East Monroe Street

By 1900 there were rooms being rented at 245 East Monroe. The facility started as a private boarding house. It was described as a large residence and featured both suites and single rooms for rent. The business became known as the St. Elmo Lodging House. By 1913 the facility was operating under the name The Glenwood and advertised apartments and rooms.

By 1941 The Glenwood was no longer operating. The West Building of the Phoenix Convention Center now stands on the property.

Globe Hotel – See Elmo Rooming House

The Glow Court operating as apartments in 2012 (Photo by Author)

Glow Court – 1545 West Roosevelt Street

The Glow Court was in operation by 1948 under the ownership of William Glowacki. It utilized six duplex buildings to create 12 rental units. The Glow Court was utilized as apartments from the beginning, but was also advertised to the traveling public until the mid-1950s.

The Glow Courts original buildings still exist and are rented as apartments.

Godsoe Motel - El Ranchito Motel

Gold Hotel circa 1910 (Courtesy Library of Congress)

Gold Hotel – 309 East Washington Street

The old Lemon Hotel was purchased and demolished by Anton Gold in about 1906. The new Gold Hotel was built in its place and was open by 1907. Mr. Gold had an entrepreneurial spirit and had previously owned the Roma Saloon in town. The facility included a restaurant as well as offices for other businesses.

The Gold Hotel was demolished in December of 1919, and a new motion picture theatre was constructed. Today the area is part of the Phoenix Convention Center.

Gold Spot Inn Tourist Court – 2222 West Van Buren Street

The Gold Spot Inn was accepting guests by 1926. This facility was one of the early auto courts and featured both cabin and camping facilities. Cottages were built in two- or three-room configurations.

The Gold Spot was closed by 1963 and demolished shortly afterwards to build Interstate 17.

Golden Rule Court – 709 West Buckeye Road

Little is known about the Golden Rule Court. It was open by 1934 and closed by 1948. It included an auto court of unknown size and style, and a café.

Today a modern mini-mall is on the property.

Golden Rule Rooming House – Southwest Corner Jefferson and Third Streets

The Golden Rule Rooming House was located at the Southwest corner of Jefferson and Third Streets. The facility was in business by 1896 and disappears from records by 1906. It is likely that the facility was known as the Brown House prior to becoming the Golden Rule. The historical record describes the two facilities at very similar locations.

Today the Bank of America Tower is utilizes the real estate.

Golden Rule Tourist Camp – 1110 South Seventh Avenue

The Golden Rule Tourist Camp only appears in the historical record from 1930 to 1932. However, it likely opened earlier and may have stayed open after 1932. Aerial photos from 1949 show the cabins were demolished by that time. The facility was substantial with around 20 rental cabins in 1930.

Today a shopping mall is located on the property.

Golden West Hotel – See Steinegger Lodging House

Golden West Lodge - 4150 East Van Buren Street

The Golden West Lodge was in business by 1948. The construction and configuration of the motel is not known. The property was small and included kitchenettes. For many years the motel property doubled as a used car lot under the name J&T Motors.

The Golden West closed by 1983 and was demolished by 1984. Today the property is part of the Phoenix Gateway Center.

Good Luck Auto Court – 1608 East Washington Street

By 1931 the Good Luck Auto Court was accepting guests. It was built in cabin court style with each cabin being a rental unit.

In 1938 the owner was charged with working a female employee longer than 48 hours in one week. This was a crime at the time. He was found not guilty.

By 1959 the Good Luck was no longer in business. The area was cleared of its buildings in the 1960s. Today a modern gas station utilizes the real estate.

Gordon Rooming House - 427 West Jefferson Street

By 1916 the Gordon House was accepting guests. Very little is known about the facility. It changed names by 1919 to the Palms Rooming House. By 1923 the name changed again to the Attaway House. By 1929 the facility was closed.

The Maricopa County Facilities Management building is now on the property.

Graham Place – 3547 (3597) East Van Buren Street

The Graham Place was operating by 1932. The facility utilized individual cabins as rental units. In 1947 the court's name was changed to the Trails End Court. By 1957 the court was closed and became a trailer sales business. Eventually the land would be used for the Gaylord Motel.

Today the land holds the Best Inn and Suites, the former Gaylord Motel.

Grand Avenue Court – 1625 Grand Avenue

The Grand Avenue Court was renting cabins by 1930. It contained 14 cabins for rent. As trailers became popular the court added trailer and pad rentals to its business model. By 1945 the facility became a trailer court and cabins began to be eliminated. The name of the business was changed by 1947 to reflect the business model change. However, the Grand Avenue Court name lived on when the Court Carol took on the name now that it was not in use.

See the Court Carol listing for more information.

Grand Avenue Court – 2830 (3500) Grand Avenue

By 1939 the Grand Avenue Court was renting rooms. The facility included several cabins and a gas station. Sources show between 12 and 25 cabins on the property at various times. By 1949 the court had been renamed the Alhambra Court. This was obviously a reference to the area of town in which the court was situated. In the late

1950s the court was purchased by the owner of a decorative rock company. He added the rock company to the motel property using a couple of cabins as offices. The cabins were faced with decorative rock, and by 1963 the court became the Rock Center Motel.

In 1947 a man who lived at the court was shot and killed on the property near the gas station. He was accidently shot by his friend in a scuffle with a third man. The friends had apprehended the man after he had sold one of them a car with a counterfeit title. The incident was deemed an accident, and the shooter was not punished.

In 1971 a woman shot a motel resident and another woman in an apparent argument over money. The shooter then shot herself. The shooter and the man were taken to the hospital. The woman was only slightly injured.

The Rock Center survived until 1998 when the motel was closed. The real estate was eventually used as part of the easement in building the Grand Avenue Bridge over Twenty-Seventh Avenue.

Grand Canyon Hotel – 143 South Third Street

What would become the Grand Canyon Hotel began as a rooming house. The facility was a two-story structure which existed by 1899 and likely earlier. It was operated as a rooming house for many years and took on the name Grand Canyon Hotel by 1921.

By 1932 it was no longer in business. The Produce Hotel was built on the real estate some years later. Today the Phoenix Convention Center utilizes the property.

Grand Hotel – 502 East Washington Street

The Grand Hotel was in business by 1923. The facility was a three-story building that included rooms, a café, and several other leased business offices. Even an auto top business was located in the building.

By 1973 the Grand Hotel was out of business. It was quickly demolished and became the Civic Plaza parking lot. The Arizona Science Center is located at the address today.

Grand View Hotel (far right) circa 1908; part of the Ford Hotel can be seen to the left (Courtesy Library of Congress)

Grand View Hotel – 122 West Washington Street

By 1899 the Grand View Hotel was renting rooms. The facility was a two-story structure located on the north side of Washington Street a few doors down from the Ford Hotel. The hotel went through many name changes beginning with the Fairmont Hotel by 1909. It became the Dobbs House by 1913 and the Palgrave House by 1916. In 1918 the facility was renamed as the Park Hotel. By 1930 it was the Dallas Hotel. It became the Clinton House for a time in the 1930s. By 1939 it became the Strand Hotel.

By 1948 the hotel was no longer renting sleeping rooms. Today the Wells Fargo building stands on the property.

The former Graystone Court, now operates as offices (Photo by Author 2014)

Graystone Court – 645-49 North Fourth Avenue

The buildings at 645 and 649 North Fourth Avenue were built in 1920. They were obviously built together with the same brickwork and style. Both are elegant, two-story buildings. The northern building is about twice the size of the other. Originally the buildings appear to have been residences and offices. About 1931 the southern building became apartments and the northern building became the Graystone Court. The Graystone was always principally an apartment building. They did accept short-term renters early on. About 1947 the two buildings together became Graystone Court. By the 1950s the court stabilized with an apartment business plan.

Today the original Graystone Court buildings still exist as professional offices.

Green Glen Motel – See Royal View Motel

The Wrangler Motel, formerly the Green Parrot, circa 1960 (Author's Collection)

Green Parrot Auto Court – 2360 East Van Buren Street

The Green Parrot Auto Court opened in 1928. The facility was built using individual cabins surrounding a central court similar to most auto courts at the time. The facility made it convenient for travelers as it also contained a cafe and grocery store.

The Green Parrot operated until 1954 when its name was changed to the Jay Hawk Motel. The facility again changed names in 1957 when it became the Wrangler Motel. The Wrangler operated until 1975 when it was closed permanently. Demolition took place by 1977.

The property where the Green Parrot stood is now vacant.

Greenhaw Auto Court – 801 West Buckeye Road

Little is known about the Greenhaw Auto Court. It was in business by 1932 and closed by 1948. The property became a salvage yard immediately after the court closed. Today it is a vacant lot.

Green's Motel – 1741–45 West Van Buren Street

Green's Motel began as a series of cottages and cabins that were rented as apartments. By 1949 the buildings were brought together and marketed as the Green's Motel. There were eight cottages and a home on the property. The cottages were all rented as apartments by 1961.

Some of the buildings were demolished in the 1960s, and the rest were razed in the early 1980s. A restaurant is located on the property now.

The Greenway Manor Court's original buildings still operate as the State Motor Lodge (Photo by Author 2012)

Greenway Manor Court – 3810 East Van Buren Street

The Greenway Manor Court was built in 1947. Construction consisted of multiple buildings arranged in a U-shape facing a central parking area. The Greenway only kept its original name until 1951 when it took on the name Spiral Motel. The name was again changed in 1954 to the State Motor Lodge.

The State Motor Lodge still exists with its original buildings and has operated under the same name since 1954.

Greenway Motor Hotel circa 1965 (Author's Collection)

Greenway Motor Hotel – 1208 West Van Buren Street

The Greenway Terrace Court opened in 1942. The new auto court was a 36-unit, cottage-type court which featured painted brick walls, tile roofs, and a coffee shop. Both one- and two-bedroom units were available, some with kitchenettes. Built at a cost of $120,000, the Greenway was Andy Womack's fourth auto court construction project. Other courts included the Mayfair Motor Hotel and the Palomine Inn. Many investors and contractors built lodging facilities to sell them instead of operate them. Womack was one of these contractors.

Property for the Greenway was procured from Isabella Greenway King, the widow of General John C. Greenway. The Greenways were very influential in Arizona with many commercial enterprises. Isabella was an Arizona Congresswoman for some time. Isabella had purchased the property to build an American Legion home in the memory of her former husband. This never came to fruition and Andy Womack was able to purchase the real estate in 1940. Womack decided to name the motel the Greenway after John and Isabella Greenway.

Eventually the Greenway was renamed the Greenway Motor Hotel. A new office addition was constructed in a further attempt at modernization. An additional 14 units were also added through the years.

The Greenway was closed by 1990 and demolished by 1996. Today the real estate that once held the Greenway now holds a modern apartment complex.

Gregory House – 225 East Washington Street

The Gregory House was built in 1885 by J. M. Gregory. Since the hotel was built before Phoenix had rail service, all lumber and materials had to be hauled in as freight. This was more easily accomplished because Mr. Gregory was involved in both the lumber and freight businesses. The building was a 30 by 70 foot, two-story facility which included 40 rental rooms. A restaurant was housed in an adjoining single-story building.

The Gregory House had a good reputation as one of the better lodging houses in Phoenix. It was used as the election location for the 1891 election of delegates to the Territorial Constitutional Convention for precinct 2. The purpose of the convention was to frame a state constitution decades before Arizona became a state. Gregory kept up his facility with regular cleanings and a major renovation in 1893. This included new furniture, carpet, wallpaper, and paint.

In April of 1911 the Gregory House burned beyond repair. Only the shell remained, and it was quickly removed from the site. Barney Kersting, owner of the Gregory since 1906, built the new Alturas Hotel near the site. Today the real estate is part of the Collier Center complex.

Guess Court – See Craus Bungalows

Gunnel Auto Camp – See Canary Court

H & R Auto Court – 2364 East Van Buren Street

The H & R Auto Court was a cabin-style court located on the northwest corner of Twenty-Fourth Avenue and Van Buren Street. The court was built in 1928 and was somewhat different from other Van Buren courts as it utilized art deco styling more heavily than most.

The H & R Auto Court was demolished in 1961 to make room for the flamboyant Kon Tiki Motel. Today the property is a vacant used car lot.

Halls Court – See Howards Court

Halls Motel – 1925 East Van Buren Street

After a change of ownership in 1949, the Palace Auto Court was renamed the Halls Auto Court. Soon thereafter the cabin court was converted to a strip-style motel. It's unknown whether this was all new construction or whether the cabins were incorporated into the new buildings. In any event, Halls Court was renamed Halls Motel by 1952.

The Halls Motel retained its name throughout but was closed as a motel by 1984. It was demolished by 2007. Today the area is an undeveloped lot.

Hammons Rooms – 1022 East Washington Street

Cabins owned and rented by George Hammons existed by 1948. The cabins were only intermittently rented on a short-term basis.

In 1960 an unemployed truck driver was found dead in one of the Hammons cabins. He had been there about a week as the cabin was locked from the outside with a padlock. The man had suffered a bullet wound to the head, and an obscene note was left in the cabin. It was an obvious homicide.

The Hammons Rooms were no longer rented after 1960. Today a bridal center is located on the property.

Happy Home Hotel – 31 South First Avenue

The Steinegger Building was constructed before the year 1900. It was owned by one of the original founding Phoenix residents. The family also owned the Steinegger lodging house. The building was used as offices for decades. It appears the change to a hotel was in the works as early as 1960. Office tenants were leaving the building and by 1963 the Happy Home Hotel was utilizing the building.

By 1967 the building was no longer functioning as a hotel. A few years later the entire block was demolished to create Patriots Square Park. Today the CityScape complex utilizes the property.

Happy Place Cottages – 1701 Grand Avenue

By 1932 the Happy Place Cottages was renting cabins. The facility utilized cottage court construction and had 15 buildings. By 1948 the Happy Place became the Penn Court, which was a second location for the Penn Court at 745 Grand Avenue. By 1955 the Happy Place was no longer renting to transient guests.

The buildings were razed, and today there is a locksmith located at the address.

Hardwick Hotel – 24 West Jackson Street

The Hardwick Hotel was built in 1894 following the construction of the Santa Fe train terminal. Business was so good for the facility that 16 rooms were added in 1896. This resulted in 30 rental units. In 1911 it was again announced that the Hardwick would get a major renovation. This one was to include the addition of two extra stories. It is unknown whether that renovation actually took place.

In February 1901 the famous baseball player Tom O'Brien died at the Hardwick. O'Brien was an outfielder in the major leagues with such teams as the Orioles, Pirates, and Giants. He died at the age of 27. Newspaper articles describe his death as due to pneumonia. However, the legend says he died from drinking too much salt water to remedy sea sickness. It does seem odd he would suffer from sea sickness in Phoenix.

The Hardwick closed about 1925. This was likely due to the closure of the Santa Fe Railroad passenger terminal which was located adjacent. In 1923 the new Union Station was opened a couple of blocks away. Also, by 1925 automobile travel was becoming a major factor in the tourist and professional travel market.

Today the area is a parking lot.

Harmony House Motel - 2133 East Monroe Street

The Harmony House began as the Bolt Apartments and was a cottage-style court. It began operating as a motel by 1964. The facility became the Sunrise Motel around 1980 and was closed permanently in the mid-1980s.

The original buildings were demolished in 2001. Today the area is a parking lot.

Harris Court – See Sutton Court

Harvard Motor Court circa 1940 (Author's Collection)

Harvard Motor Court – 1552 West Van Buren Street

In 1936 the Harvard Motor Court was opened. The court utilized seven duplex cottage buildings and a single unit to create 15 rental units. Units varied between one- and two-room units, some with kitchenettes.

The Harvard was closed by 1981 and demolished shortly afterward. Today the real estate once used by the Harvard holds a dollar store.

Hawthorne Court – Calico Cat Court

Hayes Rooms – 335 East Jefferson Street

The Hayes Rooms was a rooming house in operation by 1914. By the 1940s the facility had become a house of prostitution. The facilities owner, Florence Davis, was arrested twice on charges of operating a brothel. Both arrests were the result of sting operations by the city vice squad. After the second arrest in 1947, the facility no longer used the Hayes name. It did rent furnished rooms, on an apartment basis, for many years afterward.

The rerouting of Jefferson Street put the location of the Hayes Rooms on the north side of modern Jefferson Street. Originally it was on the south side. Today a parking structure is on the property.

Headley Annex – See Headley Hotel

Headley Hotel (Madison Street) – See Commercial Hotel (Madison Street)

Headley Hotel – 221 South Second Street

What would become the Headley Hotel was accepting guests by 1914. It operated as a small rooming house for many years under no official name. In the mid-1940s the facility took on the Headley Hotel name. In 1955 the Headleys began operating the Commercial Hotel at 205 East Madison. They renamed that facility the Headley Hotel. The existing Headley Hotel on Second Street became the Headley Annex for a couple of years. It was then renamed the Small Hotel. The hotels were very close to each other.

By 1966 the motel ceased to function. Today the real estate is part of the US Airways Center complex.

Helen's Cottages – See Lucille's Motel

Henderson Court – 1809 West Van Buren Street

The Henderson Court was in business by 1945. Three- and four-room duplex apartments had been rented by the Hendersons at the location for some time before 1945. However, by 1945 they decided to rent to the transient market as well. The facility consisted of six rental apartment units in duplex form.

By 1963 the court was no longer renting units. It was razed in the 1960s. An automotive collision center is now located at the address.

The Hi-Chi Court; no longer operating in 2012 (Photo by Author)

Hi-Chi Motel – 3430 West Buckeye Road

By 1951 the Hi-Chi Motel was operating. The facility was a single-story strip motel with 11 units.

The Hi-Chi became apartments by 1976. Today the motel still exists but is fenced up and closed.

Hialeah Court – 2502 East Washington Street

By 1945 the Hialeah Court was accepting guests. The facility utilized three larger buildings with rental units in apartment style. By 1950 the name of the facility changed to the Round Up Ranch. By 1958 the facility was out of business.

The buildings were demolished in the 1960s. Today a modern office building is at the address.

Hide Away Court – 4027 North Central Avenue

The Hide Away Court was an approximately 12-unit cottage court. The facility was built as cottage-style apartments and utilized the name Bungalow Apartments. By 1955 the apartments began to be marketed to the transient market, and its name was changed to the Hide Away Court. By 1958 the buildings were demolished, and a new commercial building was placed on the property.

Today the area is a vacant lot.

Hide Away Motel – 2125 East Monroe Street

The Hide Away Motel was a small motel consisting of two-room cabins. The buildings were constructed in the late 1940s, but the facility was not advertised as a motel until the mid-1950s.

In 1955 part of the facility was destroyed by fire. A couple staying in a rental unit was intoxicated and smoking. This caused a fire in which the husband was killed. His wife, who left the room when the fire started, was located at a local tavern. It appeared the husband was looking for his wife when he was overcome, not knowing she had already fled the unit.

The motel moved to an apartment business plan in the early 1960s. The buildings were demolished in 2001. Today the area is a parking lot.

Hilltop Court circa 1940 (Courtesy Library of Congress)

Hilltop Court – 5147 East Van Buren Street

Hilltop court was opened in 1939 as a cabin-style court. The facility also featured a service station and curio shop. The court afforded a great view of Tovrea Castle as it was located very close by. Two of the cabins were destroyed by fire in 1965 with the cause attributed to children playing with matches. The Hilltop Court was closed in 1974 and used as residences for some time afterward. It was demolished by 1980.

The property utilized by Hilltop Court is now undeveloped.

Hitching Post Court – 1924 East Van Buren Street

The Hitching Post Court was a short-lived court of which little is known. The facility was operating by 1947 and closed by 1951 when a pharmacy was opened on the property.

The location is now a used car lot.

Hiway House circa 1960 (Author's Collection)

The last remaining portion of the Hiway House, the Star Theatre (Photo by Author 2012)

Hiway House - 3148 East Van Buren Street

The Hiway House opened in early 1957 as part of the Hiway House hotel chain. The chain was created by the owners of the Flamingo Hotel chain and Del E. Webb. The East Van Buren location also served as the chain's headquarters. The hotel was built as a resort and convention center with colonial motor inn style construction. The property also boasted a miniature train for guests' enjoyment and transportation to the property's 250 rooms.

The chain operated as the Flamingo-Hiway House chain until April 1958 when the chain was split, and the Del E. Webb Company became the sole owner of the Hiway House brand. In 1961 the hotel was sold, along with some of the other properties, to a group of investors under a new corporation, Hiway House Hotels, Inc. This company failed in 1964 and Webb repossessed the assets, including the Hiway House on East Van Buren. The principals of the failed corporation were indicted for stock fraud in Hiway House Hotels and some were convicted. Unfortunately, the Hotel remained insolvent and was put into receivership in 1966. By late 1967 the hotel had changed hands and became the Phoenix Airport Travelodge.

In 1979 the facility was leased to the Arizona Department of Corrections for use as a women's prison called the Arizona Center for Women. The state soon after purchased the property. The facility was utilized until 2001 when the inmates were transferred to other facilities, and the buildings remained empty. The property was sold to private ownership, and the buildings were demolished in 2006 to make room for a residential development. As of 2014 the property remains vacant.

Part of the Hiway House convention center originally known as the Phoenix Star Theatre still exists. It is now the Celebrity Theatre and is located just north of where the rest of the facility once stood.

Hiway Inn – 1735 Grand Avenue

The Hiway Inn was opened in early 1959 as part of the Hiway House chain under Del E. Webb's ownership. The facility was named Hiway Inn to eliminate any confusion with the Hiway House located on East Van Buren. The Hiway Inn was constructed in colonial motor hotel style with two-story buildings on the property of the former Standard Motel.

The facility was sold to the new corporation Hiway House Hotels, Inc. in 1961. This lasted until 1964 when the Del E. Webb Company repossessed the facility due to a default situation.

Hiway Inn circa 1965 (Author's Collection)

The Hiway Inn operating as the Horace Steele Commons in 2012 (Photo by Author)

The motel became known as the Hiway Inn Coliseum in 1973. The facility closed in 1986 and became the Horace Steele Commons in 1998.

The original Hiway Inn buildings still exist as the Horace Steele Commons. The facility is used as apartment residences for homeless adults re-entering society.

Hodges Court – 3776 Grand Avenue

The first mention of Hodges Court in historical records is in 1952. The newspaper reported that a couple living at the court were sentenced to ninety days in jail for child neglect. Police had found the mother intoxicated at the bar and the father intoxicated in bed. The children were hungry and told police they had been at the bar to retrieve their mother several times to no avail. It is a certainty that the Hodges Court was in business for several years before this first mention, but its opening date is unknown.

The court was built in unknown style, but it was likely a cabin court and included a tavern on the premises. By 1958 the court had been renamed as Rita's Court. Both the court and the tavern became the Red Mug by 1960.

By 1964 the facility was no longer in business. Today the address is an undeveloped lot.

Dr. Stroud and his new building (Hoffman House) in 1901 (Courtesy Library of Congress)

Hoffman House – 27 North Central Avenue

The Stroud Building on North Center (Central) Avenue was built in 1900. The building was a Queen Anne style, two-story building. The upper floor was rented as sleeping rooms for some period of time. It was advertised as such from 1912 to 1917, but was likely utilized for much longer. It's possible they were used as long-term rentals much of the time. The rooms were sold under the name Hoffman House and sometimes under the name The Stroud Rooms. The lower floor held many businesses over the years, including a saloon and a camera store. Originally, a bowling alley was located in the basement.

Today the large modern "One North Central Building" resides on the real estate.

The Holiday Inn operating as apartments in 2012 (Photo by Author)

Holiday Inn – 702 South Seventeenth Avenue

The Holiday Inn was accepting guests by 1950. The facility was built in single-story, strip motel style and laid out in a U-pattern. It was small and held only 11 kitchenette units. The motel was likely named after the 1942 Bing Crosby movie of the same name. The Holiday Inn was not part of the national chain and predated the franchise by a few years. For this reason the motel was able to retain its name even after the Holiday Inn chain locations entered the Phoenix market.

The Holiday Inn became the Holiday Apartments by 1976. Today the Holiday Inn still stands with its weathered sign intact. It is still rented as apartments.

Holiday Inn circa 1970 (Author's Collection)

The Holiday Inn stripped to concrete in 2012 (Photo by Author)

The Holiday Inn operates as apartments today (Photo by Author 2014)

Holiday Inn – 2247 East Van Buren Street

The Holiday Inn on Van Buren was opened in early 1964. This Holiday Inn was the first in the chain to be built in Phoenix. The earlier Holiday Inn on Seventeenth Avenue was not part of the national chain. The facility was built using concrete pours to produce a four-story tower. The building had 170 guest rooms and was built at a cost of two million dollars. A modern look is what the builder was striving for, and it was achieved through the use of window glass covering most of the front of the building. The facility was built as a convention center with banquet and meeting room space, as well as a restaurant and bar.

The Holiday Inn operated until 1982 when its name was changed to the Airport Central Hotel. It was closed in 1996 and eventually stripped down to its main concrete structure. The empty shell sat dormant for many years. In 2014 the facility was rebuilt into apartments.

Holiday Inn – 2201 South Twenty-Fourth Street

The Holiday Inn on Twenty-Fourth Street was the hotel that should never have been built. The city did issue a building permit for the hotel project. However, about halfway through the construction the city realized that the facility was being built on land needed for airport expansion. In July of 1968 construction was ordered to be stopped. The City of Phoenix attempted to pay the developer for costs incurred, but the price was too high. The city council decided to let the construction continue.

The hotel went on to be completed and opened in 1969. The facility remained a Holiday Inn until 1992 when it was converted to a Knights Inn. It was closed permanently in 1996 and demolished by 1997. The property was utilized as part of an airport expansion project.

Holland Court – See Mohave Court

Holland House – 301 North First Avenue

The Holland House was opened in 1911 on the corner of Van Buren Street and First Avenue. Little is known of the facility as it is rarely mentioned in the historical records. The last mention was in 1935 when permission was given to move the facility back from Van Buren Street. The city was in the process of widening the road.

Today the area is open space and a light rail terminal.

The Hollywood Court, vacant in 2012 (Photo by Author)

Hollywood Court – 2138 West Washington Street

The Hollywood Court was open by 1929. The facility consisted of six brick cottages and an owner's quarters in the rear. It appears the Hollywood was built as part of a three-court complex including the San Antonio and Washington Courts. It's likely the same developer built them to sell separately. By 1932 the Washington and Hollywood Courts were combined to create the Palmdale Court.

The Hollywood Court became apartments by 1964. Today the Hollywood Court's original buildings still stand but are vacant.

Hollywood Guest Manor – 4710 North Central Avenue

The Hollywood Guest Manor was a rental home located across the street from Brophy College. As early as 1942 the home was being rented to seasonal visitors. By 1948 the Hollywood name appeared, and the home was marketed to short-term visitors.

By 1952 the manor was no longer renting its rooms. Today the property is an undeveloped lot.

Hollywood Hotel – See Virginia Hotel

Holmes Rooming House – 40 North First Avenue

By 1904 the Holmes Apartments was in operation. The facility soon was operating as a rooming house renting both rooms and suites. By 1912 it was operating under the name Elite Hotel. By 1928 the hotel was no longer in operation.

Today the Wells Fargo complex is on the property.

Home (The) – See Polk House

Home Court (Van Buren Street) – See Stallings Auto Camp

Home Court – 11 North Twentieth Street

The Home Court on Twentieth Street was in business by 1942. This was just a couple years after the Home Court on Van Buren and Seventeenth Streets closed. Any association between the two is not known. The court was a cabin-style court arranged in two rows along the property lines. A single roof was placed on each row of cabins to create a covered parking area.

The court became apartments by 1962 and was demolished in the 1970s. Today the Performance Radiator building is on the real estate.

The Homedale Court operates as an auto repair facility today (Photo by Author 2014)

Homedale Court – 3926 West Buckeye Road

By 1952 the Homedale Court was renting rooms. The facility was a single-story, strip-style motel with seven units. There were also two- and three-room apartments, and trailer space rentals.

By 1964 the facility became apartments. The buildings still exist and are utilized as part of an automotive repair business.

HoMotel Court – 1837 West Van Buren Street

Little is known about the HoMotel Court. It was in business by 1948 next to the Capitol Auto Court. By 1952 a gas station was located at the address, and no further mention of the HoMotel can be found.

Today the real estate is vacant.

Horse Shoe Auto Court – 1507 West Buckeye Road

By 1930 the Horse Shoe Auto Court was in business. The court utilized 17 cabins as rental units. A small restaurant was also located on the property. The facility survived for many years, but by 1948 it was closed and demolished.

Today the real estate is partially vacant and partially residential.

Horseshoe Motel circa 1970 (Author's Collection)

Horseshoe Motel – 4250 Grand Avenue

The Horseshoe Motel was in operation by 1953. The facility utilized single-story, strip-motel construction. The buildings were laid out in a U-shape and included 27 units.

By 2003 the motel had been demolished. The land was used in the easement for the Grand Avenue Bridge over Forty-Third Avenue.

Hotel Court Motel – See Wings Motor Court

Howards Court – 3100 West Van Buren

By 1931 Howards Court was in operation. The facility was a cabin court of unknown size. By 1938 the business had been renamed as Halls Court. Halls Court had two locations for some time. The other location was on East Van Buren.

Halls Court was out of business by 1972. A grocery store now stands on the property.

The Dunes Motor Hotel, formerly the Hudson Lodge, circa 1965 (Author's Collection)

The Hudson Lodge buildings in disrepair in 2012 (Photo by Doug Truran)

Hudson Lodge – 2915 East Van Buren Street

The Hudson Lodge opened in 1946. The facility consisted of individual buildings with two units in each. A standard U-shape arrangement was chosen. The Hudson Lodge operated until 1959 when the court was renamed the Dunes Motel. The Dunes featured a gable-style roof with a large, steep eave over the lobby. This was obviously an upgrade to make the property appear to be more modern.

About the same time, in 1959, the El Molino Court was absorbed into the Dunes Motel. By 1962 the Del Camino Court was also added to the Dunes Motel. At some point new roofs were added to the El Molino and Del Camino to make them match the Dunes.

In 1961 the Dunes made the news when one of the managers led the police to a robber. In the early morning hours a man attempted to procure a room at the Dunes. The manager only opened the door slightly, decided the man didn't look safe, and refused him service. Shortly afterwards, the Tahiti Inn nearby was robbed at knifepoint using a red-handled fishing knife. Sometime later the manager at the Dunes spotted the robber, and he was followed to a local cafe. He was apprehended at the cafe with a red-handled fishing knife. He later confessed to the crime.

By 2000 the Dunes was no longer a motel, although it still catered to the housing market as apartments.

Today the original buildings of the Hudson Lodge, El Molino, and Del Camino still exist. They are boarded up and vacant. The huge eave above the Dunes office has been shortened, probably for the same reason it was built: modernization. At least two fires in the vacant buildings have made them unusable for future use.

Hughes Rooms – 2723 West Buckeye Road

The Hughes Rooms was a large, sixteen-room brick home located on the corner of Buckeye Road and Twenty-Seventh Avenue. It was a modern rooming house built in the 1950s. By 1957 it was accepting guests. The facility likely catered mostly to longer term tenants.

The business was demolished in the 1970s. Today a gas station is located on the property.

Hunky Dory Auto Court – 923 (987) South Nineteenth Avenue

The Hunky Dory Auto Court was in business by 1929. It was a series of seven cottages of varying size built along the northern property line. By 1934 it had become the New Hunky Dory Court. The facility became part of the Maricopa Auto Court around 1948. The two courts had been competitors in the same block for many years. See the Maricopa Auto Court listing for additional information.

Today the area is vacant of buildings.

Hurds Court – 2216 East Lincoln Street

By 1952 the Hurds Court and Grocery was in business. The court consisted of four or five cottages. They were likely duplex buildings resulting in eight to ten rental units. By 1955 the court became the Ortiz Court. The court was no longer in business by 1959. However, the buildings did exist for many years and were likely used as apartments.

The buildings were demolished in the 1970s, and the area became part of the airport car rental strip. Today the car rentals are in a different area, but the real estate is still part of the airport complex.

Hurley's Court – See Cummins Court

Hutch Motel – 909 West Madison Street

By 1948 the Hutch Apartments were in business. The facility quickly changed to a motel business model. By 1960 it was renamed the Pink Palace Motel, and by 1963 it became the Alamo Motel.

By 1973 the facility took on the name Lahoma Lodge and moved to a rest home business model. Today the facility is partially undeveloped and partially a parking lot.

Hyatt Chalet – 938 East Van Buren Street

The Hyatt Chalet Motel opened in the spring of 1963. The facility was built in two-story motor hotel style and included 40 units. It was built utilizing an A-frame roof structure and Swiss chalet styling. An International House of Pancakes restaurant was built as part of the facility.

The motel was built by Hyatt Chalet Motels Incorporated, which was headquartered in California. The chain utilized a co-ownership business model enlisting managers that invested one-quarter or one-half ownership.

By 1975 the motel became known as just the Chalet Lodge. By 1989 the name had changed again to the Super 6 Motel. Oddly, the name changed to the Super 7 Motel in 1992. This name lasted until the motel was demolished in 2007.

Today the property is an undeveloped lot.

Ideal Auto Court – 1801 Grand Avenue

By 1930 the Ideal Auto Court was accepting guests. The facility utilized cabin court style construction with 20 cabins arranged in a J-shape.

The Ideal Auto Court was closed to guests by 1971 and demolished in the early 1980s. Today the address is an auto mechanic shop.

Illini Motor Court – See Detroiter Tourist Court

Illinois Court – 2209 East Washington Street

By 1930 there were a few rental cabins behind the residence at 2209 East Washington. The apartments grew and took on the name Illinois Court by 1948. The facility consisted of the owner's home, nine rental cabins, and several trailer spaces.

In the summer of 1967 the buildings were removed from the property. Today a van rental business is on the property.

Imperial 400 Downtown circa 1965 (Author's Collection)

Imperial 400 - Downtown – 201 North Seventh Avenue

The Imperial 400 at five points was opened in early 1962. Construction utilized motor inn type design with a pair of two-story buildings facing each other. The 71-unit facility was located on property leased for 99 years from the Halstead Lumber Company, which was formerly located on the site. The owner's capitalized on the Five Points location (the intersection of Van Buren and Seventh Avenue) by including a five-pointed pool. The pool was less than lucky for one guest from Oklahoma who did not survive a 1968 swim.

The Imperial 400 Downtown operating as the Friendship Inn in 2012 (Photo by Author)

Construction of the motel was part of a large building spree of Imperial 400s across the United States. The chain used standard and recognizable building design, which made them very consistent throughout the country. The chain utilized a co-ownership program in which the motel managers made an investment in the facility. The slogan "Aye, Royal Accommodations at Thr-rifty Rates" was used to target its value-minded consumer. In 1963 the co-owner of the motel filed a 1.5 million dollar lawsuit against Imperial 400 claiming false statements were made during the purchase.

The motel was operated as the Imperial 400 until 1972 when it became the Friendship Inn. In 1986 the name was changed again to the Travel Inn. By 2004 the name had been changed back to the Friendship Inn. The original Imperial 400 buildings still exist and are operated as the Friendship Inn today.

Imperial 400 - East – 3830 East Van Buren Street

The Imperial 400 East was opened in early 1961 at a cost of $350,000. Construction of the motel was part of a large building spree of Imperial 400s across the United States. The chain used standard and recognizable building design, which made the chain very consistent throughout the country. This included two-story, motor inn style construction where the offices received a distinctive roof design. The East Van Buren location included 42 rooms.

La Casa Real Motel, formerly the Imperial 400 East, circa 1970 (Author's Collection)

The chain utilized a co-ownership program in which the motel managers made an investment in the facility. The hotel chain used the slogan "Aye, Royal Accommodations at Thr-rifty Rates" to target its value-minded consumer.

The motel operated as Imperial 400 until 1969 when it became the La Casa Real Motel. In 1977 the facility closed, and the location is now a parking lot.

Imperial Room/Hotel – See Jefferson Rooming House

Ingleside Inn – 6121 East Indian School Road

The Ingleside Inn was the first winter resort built in the Phoenix area. William Murphy opened the facility in 1909 and utilized oiled sand golf course greens. Murphy was the builder of the Arizona Canal which delivered water to the Glendale area. In 1923 William Murphy died, and his son Ralph took over the property. Many improvements were made starting in 1923 with a stock sale for improvements, including a new grass golf course built on adjacent property. New sleeping areas were added, taking the occupancy from 40 to nearly 200. Eight cottages were added outside of the main buildings. In 1932, during the Great Depression, financial difficulties overcame the

Ingleside, and it was lost to creditors. At least one owner, Malcolm Little, operated the facility after the failure. In 1941 the resort was sold to California innkeeper Nat Head who immediately renovated the facility. Head purchased 10 acres and all the buildings, but leased the golf course. At this time the facility offered stable riding, golf, swimming, dining, and a recreation hall. In 1945 the facility was again sold. This time the facility was converted and became the Brownmoor School for Girls. The golf course became the Arizona Golf Club the following year. The Brownmoor operated for some time, but the property was again sold. The real estate was eventually developed into a residential area and the original buildings demolished.

Ingleside Inn circa 1925 (Author's Collection)

Today the area is still a mix of residential construction, business offices, and the Arizona Golf Club.

Note: The area in which the original Ingleside Inn buildings were constructed is now within the city of Scottsdale. The author included this listing due to the golf course portion of the property residing within Phoenix city limits and the historical significance of the inn.

Irish Motel – See RV Motel

Irving House – 530 West Washington Street

The Irving House was in business by 1900 and likely even before. The facility contained 12 rental rooms. By 1919 the facility became the Irving Apartments and catered only to long-term guests.

Today the Fox Television building is on the property.

The Ivon, now a residence (Photo by Author 2014)

Ivon (The) – 650 North Sixth Avenue

The Ivon was built and began operating in 1911. It was a three-story building and contained about 25 rooms. The facility contained a cafeteria-style kitchen and served meals to more than just guests. Through the years the business added a heated pool, pool table, ping pong, horse shoes, and a sun deck. By 1918 the facility took on the name California Inn. This name was long-lived, but was finally replaced in 1958. At this time the inn was dubbed the Whitehouse Lodge. The term "lodge" was gaining popularity at the time.

In May 1923 W. E. Remington was shot and killed in the California Inn. He was shot by his girlfriend, Lealah Crandall. The two had experienced a whirlwind romance in which they spent much time riding in Remington's automobile. Remington had proposed marriage and it was accepted. At Crandall's trial she claimed that her suitor made several advances on her virtues. She told the jurors that Remington had taken advantage of her one night after she fainted. She woke, to her surprise, in his bed. When Remington was confronted, he apparently attacked Crandall and she shot him with a borrowed gun. She also attempted to kill herself in the same manner. The jury believed her story and acquitted Crandall of murder in October 1923.

In the mid-1960s the hotel was converted to an alcohol recovery facility. Today the building, which began as The Ivon, still exists. It is now a residence.

Ivory Palaces Motor Lodge circa 1950 (Author's Collection)

Ivory Palaces Motor Lodge – 3601 North Central Avenue

By 1948 the Ivory Palaces Motor Lodge was in business. The facility consisted of 21 one-bedroom units. The facility featured an unusual architecture and was a cross between a strip motel and cottages. While built as a strip motel in a U-shape, the entrances projected, creating a cottage look. The Ivory Palaces became the North Central Motor Lodge in 1962. It was completely remodeled and upgraded at that time. Modern looking privacy walls built near the entrance gave the facility a contemporary appeal from the road.

North Central Motel, formerly Ivory Palaces Motor Lodge, circa 1970 (Author's Collection)

The North Central was out of business by 1976. Demolition occurred in short order. Today the real estate is undeveloped.

J and R Motel – See Tangier Apartment Motel

J&O Court – See Cottonwood Court

Jacks Tourist Court – See Davis Court

Jackson Motor Court – 1822 West Jackson Street

Apartments were available at 1822 West Jackson by the late 1930s. They began to be advertised as a motor court by 1952. This only lasted a few years and by 1960 they were again rented as apartments. The facility was a cabin court with six units.

In 1942 Sargent Henry Gottil, a long-term renter at the facility, was a turret gunner in World War II. During a bombing raid in Germany he had a bad feeling and asked the pilot if he could leave the turret temporarily. Immediately after leaving the turret a piece of flak entered the turret and would have certainly injured or killed him.

The facility was demolished in the 1960s. Today the area is vacant.

The last cabin left from Jackson's Court (Photo by Author 2012)

Jackson's Court - 3125 West Buckeye Road

By 1947, and probably much earlier, there was an auto court at 3125 West Buckeye. The facility included a cabin court utilizing 12 small cabins as units. It also held a trailer space rental area, a liquor store, and a gas station. A two-bedroom home was built for the owners.

By 1955 the cabins were no longer rented as motel units. Today, one run-down cabin still exists on the property. The liquor store is still in operation.

Jaime's Motor Inn Cottages – See Motor Inn Auto Court

Jay Hawk Motel – See Green Parrot Auto Court

Jaynes Court – See Castella Court

JB Court – 1517 North Seventeenth Drive

The JB Court was a residential home surrounded by several outbuildings. Seven rentals were available on the property and sold as apartments. In the late 1950s the units began being marketed to tourists under the JB Court name.

By 1970 the property had been demolished. Today the area holds a restaurant and an abandoned used car lot.

Jefferson Hotel circa 1925 (Author's Collection)

Jefferson Hotel in 2012 (Photo by Author)

Jefferson Hotel – 109 South Central Avenue

The Jefferson Hotel was opened in July of 1915 in the heart of downtown Phoenix. The facility was a six-story brick structure with 125 rooms. The complex included a roof garden, sample rooms, coffee shop, and other shop space for lease. Eventually a restaurant was added to the location. The building was thoroughly modern and well-built. It replaced earlier adobe structures, including a mercantile building formerly located on the corner. The hotel utilized the term "fire-proof" in its advertising, probably because it was built just a few years after the Adams Hotel burned nearby.

When a fire did start in the hotel basement, it was extinguished before guests even knew it. Roofing tar was being heated in the basement and caught fire. Smoke was pulled from the area using a device built by the Phoenix Fire Department called the "smoke extractor". Fire fighters soon were able to extinguish the fire with minimal damage.

Prostitution in Phoenix hotels took place regularly, as it did in most large towns. In 1943 three bellboys at the Jefferson were arrested and convicted of monetary gain from prostitution. The bellhops were essentially pimps, and the police had received many complaints which resulted in a raid.

In 1951 Sam Ackel, the hotel owner, passed away. Shortly before his death he gave the hotel, along with other holdings, to his heirs as gifts. In 1957 the federal government sued the family for taxes due. They claimed that the gifts were intended to circumvent estate taxes that would have to be paid.

In 1958 a woman was seen hanging from a fourth floor window ledge. Police and Firemen were able to pull her back into the room. She was charged with drunkenness and fined thirty dollars.

The Jefferson Hotel was made famous in 1960 when the movie *Psycho* was released. In the opening shots Sam and Marion share their lunch break at a hotel. The exterior shots were of the Jefferson Hotel. Marion was supposed to be a Phoenix resident.

The Jefferson closed as a hotel by 1976. It was renovated to become the Barrister Place office building. For some time it held the Phoenix Police Museum. Today the building still exists as the Barrister Place, but appears empty.

Jefferson Rooming House – 319 East Jefferson Street

By 1906 the Jefferson Rooming House was renting rooms. By 1921 the facility became the Alexander Hotel. It took on the name the Imperial Rooms about 1941. By 1957 the hotel became the Mission House Hotel, and by 1960 it became the Imperial Hotel. The size and configuration of the facility is not known.

By 1971 the facility was closed.

Jefferson Street has been rerouted in recent years. The original location of 319 East Jefferson is actually north of the street, and possibly into the street. The Jefferson Rooming House was located on the grounds of the Phoenix Convention Center on the north side of Jefferson.

Jefferson Rooms – 219 East Jefferson Street

By 1920 rooms were being rented at 219 East Jefferson. Rental rooms were located on the second floor of the two-story building. Within a few years the facility became known as the Jefferson Rooms. In 1933 the rooming house became the Espana Hotel. By 1943 the Espana became the Annex Hotel.

In November of 1937 the Espana Hotel was ordered to cease operations by the Maricopa County Court. It was alleged the hotel was a nuisance and being operated as a brothel or house of prostitution. Ten days later the court dismissed the case. The owners of the hotel convinced the judge that prostitution would no longer take place in the facility.

In 1967 a man was shot and killed as he left the Annex Hotel. Police had been summoned from the street due to a disturbance at the hotel. As the policeman approached the facility, two men carrying knives exited the building. The men were ordered to drop their weapons. One man complied and the other lunged toward the officer. The officer shot him. One of the men had been stabbed by the other during an argument in the hotel's television room.

By 1985 the facility was no longer renting rooms.

Today the area where the Jefferson Rooms was located has changed. Jefferson Street has been rerouted south of its original alignment. While originally on the south side of the road, it would now be placed about where the Hard Rock Café is, and into Jefferson Street.

Jo Lyn Motel – See Way West Motel

Jody's Court – 513 South Nineteenth Avenue

Jody's Court was a small cabin court located at the southeast corner of Buchanan Street and Nineteenth Avenue. Originally, a service station, grocery store, and restaurant were located on the property. By the mid-1930s five brick cabins were added, and it operated as a sanitarium. By 1939 the facility became known as Jody's Court and began operating as a tourist court. The court's name soon changed to the Bachelor Court. Eventually eight cabins were erected along the rear and southern property lines. The main store building remained at the front of the lot.

By 1960 the court was vacant and no longer operating. The area had been becoming more and more industrial through the years with steel companies across the street. The cabins were demolished in the 1960s to expand the steel companies. Today the area remains industrial with the Schuff Steel building located on the property.

Joes Court – See Camelback View Auto Court

Johns Court – See Ulloa Rooms

Johnsons Court – 2203 East Monroe Street

By 1941 the Howe Apartments were in operation. In November of 1942 the apartments were sold to the Johnson family. Soon the Johnsons started marketing the facility as an auto court under the name Johnsons Court. The facility was a cottage-type court that included 12 cottages. Each cottage included a living area, kitchen, bedroom, and bath room. By 1950 the court became the Shir-Mar Court.

The facility no longer operated as a motel by 1971. Today the area is undeveloped.

Jokake Inn circa 1960 (Author's Collection)

The Jokake Inn, now at the Phoenician Resort (Photo by Author 2014)

Jokake Inn – 6000 East Camelback Road

The Jokake Inn opened for its first season in 1925. It was a small facility that operated as a tea house. All of the original buildings were constructed of adobe, thereby receiving the name "Jokake" which is Hopi Indian for "mud house". The facility was expanded to become a resort location and guest ranch. In 1935 the Jokake's signature main building and entranceway was constructed. It was built of concrete and adobe, and connected the older buildings together. The Jokake operated successfully throughout the years until it became part of the Phoenician Hotel. It was part of the Alsonette Hotel chain for many years starting in 1951.

In 1973 the Jokake was unwittingly part of a fraud attempt. A man showed up at the facility and began functioning as the resort's new manager. He utilized the position for three weeks in an effort to gain financially though dishonest activity. He was discovered and sentenced to one year in jail.

The Jokake's 1935 expansion entrance building still exists today as part of the Phoenician resort. The older buildings have been demolished.

Joyland – 3515 East Van Buren Street

The Joyland Amusement Park opened in 1923 on the property of the former Maricopa Country Club. The Marion Concession Company of Ohio created and operated the facility. The complex included fair-type rides and also offered entertainment such as concerts. Customers received some extra excitement in 1936 when a small airplane crashed nearby killing four prominent Phoenix businessmen.

In the mid-1930s the facility started offering lodging, camping, and trailer parking to guests. Joyland Park started to decline, and by the late 1940s it was no longer in business. Some parts of the park lived on for some time such as the trailer park and the swimming pool.

The area is now a large warehouse facility.

Ka Dee Modern Court – see Lewis Court

Katherine Court – 210 North Eighth Street

The Katherine Court located behind Monroe school was normally rented as apartments. Rooms were rented on a long-term basis at the address as early as the 1930s. However, by 1957 the facility took on the name Katherine Court and advertised to short-term renters. In 1959 about half the rooms were rented to the transient trade. By 1960 the facility was selling on an apartment-only basis again. The buildings were demolished in the 1970s.

Today the area is a residential development.

Kelly Inn – See Rodeway Inn

Kelso House – See Alhambra Rooming House

Kemp Hotel – 702 East Jefferson Street

The building at the northeast corner of Seventh and Jefferson Streets was renting rooms in an apartment fashion since around 1900. About 1928 it became the Kemp Apartments and soon afterward the Kemp Hotel. The hotel stopped renting rooms by 1962. It was demolished in the 1970s.

Today a modern office building is located on the real estate.

Kennedy (The) – 230 East Monroe Street

The Kennedy was a large, two-story home built in 1896. The residence accepted guests for a time in the 1910s. The house was quite elaborate and upscale. In 1964 the home was demolished to create downtown parking.

Today the Herberger Theater utilizes the space.

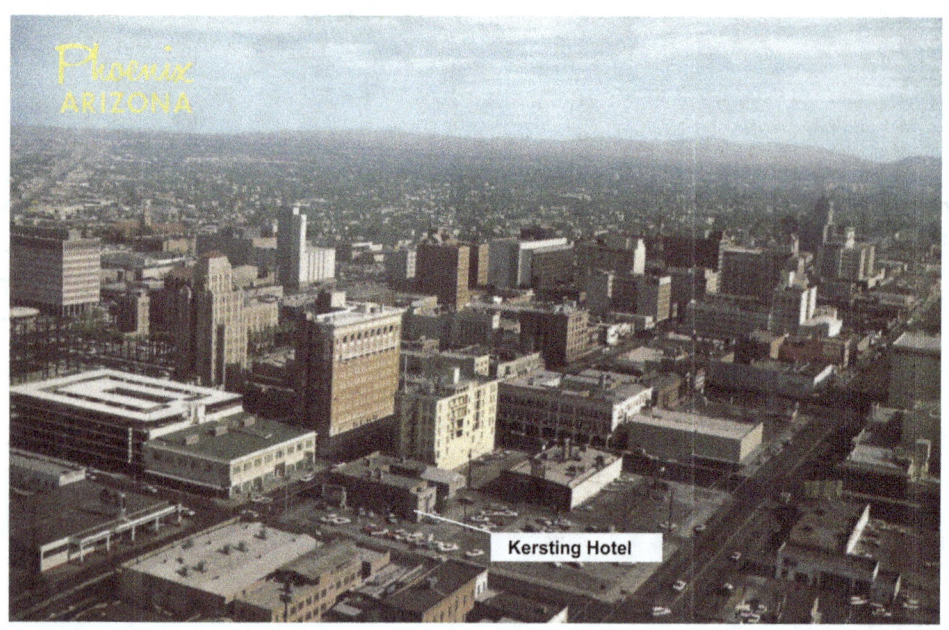

The Kersting Hotel (Morrison at the time) circa 1960 (Author's Collection)

Kersting Hotel – 135 South Central Avenue

The Kersting Hotel was in business by 1909. It was a two-story brick structure located next to the Jefferson Hotel and included food service. By 1944 the Kersting became the Compton Hotel. This only lasted a few years, and by 1948 the facility was named the Morrison Hotel.

Desk clerks at the hotel were not so lucky through the years. In 1919 Ferdinand Roessler, a night clerk, was shot and killed while standing behind the front desk. The assailant escaped. In 1959 Marcus Gleason, another night clerk, was found dead in a vacant room. His hands and feet were bound, his mouth gagged, and he was beaten to death. $30 was missing from the hotel cash register.

When automobiles became a prevalent form of travel, the Kersting began offering parking. The area between the hotel and Madison Street was called the Kersting Auto Park. It may have offered services to auto travelers. More importantly, it gave the hotel an edge on other downtown hotels. Most hotels did not have any parking available as they were built for train and stage travelers.

By 1978 the hotel was closed. Today the area is a parking lot.

Keystone Lodge – See Desert King Court

Kidd's Auto Court – 3553 (3599) East Van Buren Street

Kidd's Auto Court was opened by 1947. It was a standard cabin court with buildings placed in a single row. About a dozen cabins were placed on a long narrow lot. The facility changed its name to the Kings Motel in 1957. Kings Refrigeration was also operated from the location. By 1971 Kings Motel was no longer accepting guests, and the buildings were demolished.

Today the real estate has a welding business on it.

Kilp's Kourt – 4330 North Fifteenth Avenue

Kilp's Kourt was a small, four-building facility opened by 1958. The facility was always marketed more as an apartment building than a motel. However, they did accept transient guests in the early years. By the mid-1960s it was strictly operated as apartments.

Kilp's Kourt still exists today as apartments.

Kimball Hotel – 1656 West Washington Street

By 1930 the Kimball Hotel was in business directly across the street from the State Capital. It was a two-story facility with both the hotel and other businesses in the building. In 1958 the State of Arizona purchased the Kimball. The building was modified to hold various state agencies.

In 1966 the old Kimball Hotel building was condemned. It was soon demolished. Today the Korean War Memorial is located on the property.

Kimber House – 330 South First Avenue

The Kimber was opened in 1897 and named for its owner and operator, Cora Kimber. The facility was a two-story structure located just north of the railroad tracks on South First Avenue. Cora operated the rooming house successfully until 1941. It was closed by

1947 and became a wholesale goods company. In the early 1950s the building was demolished and replaced by a larger building.

Today the Kimber's replacement building still exists, but is not in use.

Kinds Hotel Court – See Del Camino Lodge

Kings Land Lodge – See Phoenix Motor Lodge

Kings Motel – See Kidd's Auto Court

Kings Rest Motel circa 1940 (Author's Collection)

The Kings Rest Court operates as assisted living today (Photo by Author 2012)

Kings Rest Motor Court – 801 South Seventeenth Avenue

The Kings Rest Motor Court was opened in 1937. The facility was built using cottage court style and arranged in rows. Covered carports were located between the cottages. A Spanish theme was utilized with stucco walls and tile roofs. A tile roofed tower was located near the front on each side to add to the facilities design. The office and owner's quarters were located at the front center of the property. Twenty-six units were available for rent.

The Kings Rest was robbed many times over the years. One robbery in 1939 relieved a guest of $275 and a watch. These were taken from under the man's pillow while he was sleeping. Another robbery took place in 1947 at the motel. In this case the robber utilized a stapler as a simulated gun to gain access to the cash register.

By 1981 the Kings Rest became the Oakridge Professional Resident Care facility. The complex provided assisted living housing to seniors.

The Kings Rest is listed on the National Register of Historic Places. The facility's historical importance helped procure funds under the City of Phoenix Low-Income Historic Housing Rehabilitation Program and the Neighborhood Services Department Rental Rehabilitation Program. Through these programs the facility was rebuilt and converted to 26 housing units in the mid-2000s. It remains in use as such today.

The former Kirby's Motel, now operating as apartments (Photo by Author 2014)

Kirby's Motel – 1605 West Magnolia Avenue (Latham Avenue)

Kirby's Motel was built in 1945 on what was then Magnolia Avenue. The facility consisted of three buildings with 14 rental units and a store. The buildings were of single-story, strip-motel construction. By 1952 the motel became the Phoenix Motel.

The motel became apartments by 1986 and still operates as such today. The store front is still operating as well.

Kitchenette Court – See Royal Crest Lodge

Kitchenette Motel – See Corral Motel

Klose Inn Auto Court – 965 East Van Buren Street

By 1928 the Klose Inn Auto Court was in operation. The facility was built as a cabin court with individual cabins being used as units. It appears that the Klose Inn was one of the larger courts in Phoenix with the highest cabin number found in the historical record at number 98.

The Klose Inn experienced some excitement one early morning in 1942. After an accident occurred at the intersection of Eleventh Street and Van Buren, an out of control truck entered the court. The truck hit one of the cabins pushing in the wall and stopping at the bed. A sleeping man was pushed from his bed and found unconscious. The man was hospitalized, and only minor injuries were found.

By 1957 the Klose Inn was closed. A few years later the property was used to build the Phoenix East TraveLodge.

The property which once held the Klose Inn still has the buildings used by the Phoenix East TraveLodge. They are currently a Super 8 motel.

Kon Tiki Motel circa 1965 (Author's Collection)

Kon Tiki – 2364 East Van Buren Street

The Kon Tiki Motel opened in 1962 and utilized two- and three-story construction. The facility was arguably one of the most flamboyant motels in the city. It was heavily Polynesian themed with grass roofs and exposed wood using a South Pacific architectural style. The Kon Tiki also had a popular tiki bar and was a member of the Best Western referral chain. Property used for the complex was formerly used by the H&R Auto Court, which was demolished to make room for the Kon Tiki. The Kon Tiki was demolished in 1997, being closed since 1993. Today the area is a vacant former car lot.

Robberies of lodging facilities were somewhat common in Phoenix through the years; however, the one that took place at the Kon Tiki in 1969 went very wrong. The desk clerk and the robber became involved in a shootout. Both men were killed in the incident. The driver of the car was a former Phoenix police officer and was charged with murder. He was later acquitted as he claimed to have had no knowledge of the robbery. He just dropped the robber off.

Korner Court – 1940 East Van Buren Street

Obviously located on the north corner of Van Buren and Twentieth Street, the Korner Court was open by 1939. The court was a standard cabin-style court utilizing multiple small buildings. By 1948 the court was no longer in business. The buildings were demolished in the 1950s.

The land that once held the Korner Court is now a used car lot.

Kozy Kourt – 4401 East Washington Street

The Kozy Kourt was a cabin court located on what was then the far outskirts of town. The date of construction is not known, but it certainly was in business by 1930. It consisted of about 20 cabins arranged mostly in a U-pattern. In 1936 the court was renovated and a gas station added to the property. The court's name changed to the Seaside Court at the time. By 1938 the court was renamed again to the Pueblo Grande Court. This was obviously due to its proximity to the Pueblo Grande ruins.

By 1971 the Pueblo Grande Court was out of business and was razed. Today the real estate is part of the Pueblo Grande Museum.

La Casa Real – See Imperial 400 East

La Fiesta Motor Court circa 1945 (Author's Collection)

La Fiesta Bungalow Court – 2250 Grand Avenue

The La Fiesta Bungalow Court opened in late 1938. The facility featured an early use of single-story, strip-motel construction. The buildings held 32 units and faced each other to create a courtyard in between. A café, bar, and steam bath were also located on the property. A swimming pool was installed, and for a short while the La Fiesta could claim it was the only motor court in Arizona with a pool.

In 1943 the motel manager was charged with a shooting. While dropping off a guest some people were asked to leave the property. While driving away from the property, the manager shot a woman in the car.

The La Fiesta was closed by 1973 and quickly demolished. Today the property once used by the La Fiesta is an industrial strip mall.

La Fonda Motor Hotel circa 1935 (Author's Collection)

La Fonda Court – 206 North Seventeenth Avenue

The La Fonda Court was one of the early Seventeenth Avenue lodging facilities. It was in operation by 1931. The facility was a cabin court utilizing Spanish styling with stucco walls and tile roofs.

In 1940 the La Fonda became the United States location for the Empressa Turistica de Sonora Mexican tourism bureau. The location provided maps and aid to travelers going to Mexico. Another office in Hermosillo Sonora Mexico aided travelers entering the United States.

The facility was closed and demolished by 1975. Today the La Fonda Court's real estate holds the Arizona Health Services Department building.

Lamb Hotel - 807 North First Street

The Lamb Hotel was operating by 1930 and owned by the Lamb family. The structure was a two-story brick building with interior corridors. By 1934 the business was renamed the Coronado Hotel.

The Coronado Hotel, formerly the Lamb Hotel, still operates as a hotel (Photo by Author 2014)

A second building, constructed in the 1960s, was connected to, and directly in front of, the original building. The new building utilized two-story motor inn construction with exterior entrances.

Both of the Coronado's Hotels original buildings still exist and still function as a hotel.

Lampliter Motel operating as the Lamplighter Place in 2012 (Photo by Author)

Lampliter Motel – 1945 West Van Buren Street

By 1949 the Lampliter Motel was in business. The facility was built on the old Clark Monumental Works property and utilized duplex cottage construction. Two of the cottages included a second level. Two-story cottages were unusual but helped maximize space.

By 1984 the motel had switched to an apartment business model. The Lampliter Motel's original buildings still exist as the Lamplighter Place, a United Methodist Outreach Ministries homeless shelter.

Lane Court – 2401 East Monroe Street

The Lane Court was a small cabin court with seven buildings and nine rental units. The facility was in business by 1949. It operated mainly as apartments, but accepted transients from about 1951 to 1957. The cabins were demolished in the 1970s.

Today a fast-food restaurant is located on the property.

Lanny's Court – 2212 West Buckeye Road

The opening date for Lanny's Court is not known. The facility is first found in records in 1947. However, it is advertised as remodeled at that time. It consisted of 10 rental units and a three-room apartment for the manager. By 1950 the court became known as the Phoenixona Motor Lodge.

The Phoenixona was closed by 1962 and demolished in short order. Today a concrete company is located at the address.

Lantana Auto Court – 1102 East Buckeye Road

The Lantana Auto Court was in operation by 1942. The facility was a cabin court with cottages of two- and three-bedroom floor plans. By 1953 the cabins were rented on an apartment basis rather than to the transient market. It operated as such into the 1970s when it was demolished.

Today the Joe Eddie Lopez Plaza, a modern building, is located on the location.

Lariat Lodge – 5339 East Van Buren Street

The Lariat Lodge was opened in 1952 on the site of what was a local church. The facility consisted of a two-bedroom home, six transient rental units, and one apartment. There was also a woodworking shop on the premises.

In 1965 two women from Texas arrived at the Lariat Lodge. After checking in they proceeded across Van Buren on foot to use the telephone. After assuring friends they had arrived in Phoenix without incident, they started back to the Lodge. Both women were struck by a car and killed as they jaywalked across Van Buren Street. The man who hit them was not charged.

The Lariat Lodge was closed by 1971. It was demolished shortly afterward. Today the area is part of the Riverwalk Condominium complex.

Las Casitas Auto Court – See Silver Arrow Court

Last Chance Auto Court – 1819 East Washington Street

The Last Chance Auto Court was open by 1930. The facility was built in cabin court style and included thirteen cabins. By 1940 the cabin count had increased to fourteen. After 1942 the court became the Drive Inn Auto Court. Some sources, however, list it as the Last Chance for many years after.

In 1943 Karl Myer, the court's owner, was fined for the failure to keep a register of guests. Most cities had laws requiring auto courts to keep a register of guests by the early 1940s. Law enforcement had new difficulties with the advent of motels. It gave criminals new venues in which to hide with relative anonymity. J. Edgar Hoover even wrote an article degrading auto camps and courts titled "Camps of Crime". Myer paid his fifteen dollar fine and likely started keeping a register.

The court was closed by 1961 and soon demolished. Today the area is industrial, and the cabins are gone.

Lazy A Motel circa 1955 (Author's Collection)

Lazy A Court – 2635 East Van Buren Street

The Lazy A Court was opened in 1941 between the existing Rose Bowl and Arizona Motels. The Rose Bowl and Lazy A were affiliated by the same ownership. The Lazy A was a cabin-style court utilizing many separate buildings. Each cottage was finished in stucco and was made to appear Spanish in design.

The facility changed its name to the Lazy A Motel, as most courts did, to remain modern sounding. In 1967 the Lazy A address became the same as the Rose Bowl Motel's address. Both were still under the same ownership. The motels were operated with their individual identities intact until 1984. At that time the Lazy A name was eliminated, and both properties functioned as the Rose Bowl afterward. The facility was closed by 1991 and the buildings demolished by 1998.

Today the property is part of the Salvation Army complex on East Van Buren Street.

Lazy S Lodge – 2511 West Van Buren Street

By 1949 the Lazy S Lodge was accepting guests. The facility contained twelve rental units contained in cottages. The buildings were arranged in the usual U-layout creating a center court. By 1953 the motel changed its name to the Plaza Motel Apartments.

The Plaza Motel Apartments were closed by 1993 and demolished in 2002. An auto repair business is now located at the address.

L-Bar-K Motel – See Antry's Auto Court

Leap Sampson Auto Camp - 1601 East Jefferson Street

By 1926 the Leap Sampson Auto Camp was catering to motorists next to East Lake Park. Auto camps were the earliest lodging facilities to cater directly to the automobile traveler. They provided a place for motorists to camp and usually provided limited amenities like water and sewer service. The Leap Sampson was out of business by 1931. By 1931 auto camps had lost favor. Auto camp owners who wanted to continue in business had to build cabin courts or some sort of permanent shelter for guests. It is likely that the owners decided not to invest in the property.

Today there is a body shop at the location.

Lebanon Hotel – See Parker House

Leland House – 29 East Adams Street

The Leland House was operating by 1902 across the street from the Adams Hotel. It was renovated in 1906 and fitted with new furnishings. By 1910 it was no longer in business.

Today the area is a parking lot.

Lemon Hotel – 309 East Washington Street

The Lemon was one of the early hotels in Phoenix. It was in business by 1883 on the Southeast corner of Washington and Third Streets. Between 1888 and 1891 the facility took on the name the Mills House. The property was owned and operated by E.A. Mills at the time. Mills renovated the property while he owned it. In 1893 the hotel briefly became the Arcade Hotel before taking back its original Lemon Hotel name by the end of that year. The facility was bought by Anton Gold, and the hotel was demolished around 1906 to build the Gold Hotel in its place.

The size and construction of the Lemon are unknown. However, it's likely the facility was wood frame, or wood frame and brick or adobe, due to its construction era and longevity. The facility was advertised as "All Rooms Ground Floor", so it was likely a single-story structure. It did include dining facilities as well.

The area utilized by the Lemon Hotel is now part of the Phoenix Convention Center.

Lena's Cabins – See West Buckeye Court

Les De Lane Court – See Weber Court

Lettuce Inn – Lateral 15 ½ and Grand Avenue

The Lettuce Inn was in business by 1933. The complex included twenty-two cabins, a restaurant, tavern, and service station. An obvious play on words, the Lettuce Inn had a deeper meaning. Most of the Alhambra area along Grand Avenue consisted of lettuce farms at the time. Early addresses along this road were described by the lateral, in this case fifteen and one half. However, they were also described in advertising as "near" or "across from" a certain lettuce shed. Numbered lettuce sheds were located all along Grand between Phoenix and Glendale.

In 1944 there was a fire at the Lettuce Inn that destroyed two cabins. During the fire a group of helpful bystanders and guests moved cabins away from the blaze. An electrical wire from one of the cabins ended up lying across a wire fence. One of the helpers grabbed the fence wire and was electrocuted. He was the only casualty of the fire.

An exact address for the Lettuce Inn is elusive. It was located between Thirty-Fifth and Forty-Third Avenues. The last mention that can be found is in the newspaper in January of 1947. The court could have closed or it may have been renamed. This is about the same time as the addresses on Grand Avenue were changed, so it's difficult to know.

Lewis Court – See Wilberta Court

Lewis Court - 2333 East Washington Street

By 1935 G.W. Lewis was renting rooms on his property on Washington Street. The facility consisted of six cabins and three cottages with three rooms each. Around 1948 the court became the Ka Dee Modern Court.

In August of 1943 one of the long-term guests at the Lewis Court was killed. Lawrence Smith was also a co-owner of a nearby gas station. Willard Blackwood, a local man, pulled into Smith's station and began pumping his gas. When Smith approached him he put the cap back on the car and reset the pump. Smith accused him of stealing gas, and an argument ensued. Blackwood asked for credit but Smith refused. Blackwood drove off and stopped at a friend's house to borrow a gun. He told the friend he was going to shoot a dog. Blackwood then found Smith, who was looking for him, and shot him from about 75 feet away. The gun was then returned, and Blackwood surrendered himself to police.

By 1971 the court was no longer in business. It was demolished in the early 1980s. Today the area is an undeveloped lot.

Lewis Courts Hotel – 417 South Seventh Avenue

The large brick building located just south of the railroad tracks on South Seventh Avenue was utilized as a rooming house from at least the 1920s. It became apartments for a time and then in the mid-1950s became the Lewis Courts Hotel.

The facility was demolished in 1965 and remains a vacant lot today.

The Lewis Hotel as it looks today (Photo by Author 2014)

Lewis Hotel – 362 North Second Avenue

The Lewis hotel began as a private residence built in 1897 by Charles Pugh. It was a two-story brick home built in Queen Anne style. The house was operated as a small inn by Ella May King by the 1930s. The facility began to be operated by E. F. Lewis in the early 1940s. It became known as the Lewis Hotel by 1950. By 1972 the facility was returned to a private residence.

Today the Lewis Hotel still exists but is boarded up and vacant.

Liberty Motel – 1903 East Van Buren Street

By 1930 a cabin-style auto court had been built at 1903 East Van Buren. The court took the name Marino Auto Court until 1932 when it was renamed the Liberty Auto Court. At some time during the 1950s the court added a strip-style motel along the eastern property line and was renamed the Liberty Motel.

The Liberty Motel made the news a couple of times. In 1963 a bank robber was apprehended at the facility. He had robbed banks all over the United States. In 1965 the motel was sued due to a pool injury. A nineteen-year-old man dove in and hit his head against the bottom.

The Liberty remained with the same name until it was closed, around 1995. It was demolished by 2004. Today the real estate is undeveloped.

Lincoln Auto Court – 2107 West Lincoln Street

The Lincoln Auto Court was in operation by 1949. The facility was a cabin court with sixteen cabins. The size and configuration of the facility is not known. After 1955 the court started to change names frequently. It became the Yellow Rose of Texas Court followed by the Willmoth Court. By 1960 the facility was called the Conway Court.

By 1963 the motel was no longer in business. It was soon razed. Today a floor tile company is located at the address.

Linden Court – See Corral Court

Lindsey Auto Court – 123 North Thirtieth Street

The Lindsey Auto Court was operating by 1948. The facility consisted of six buildings placed along the property lines and an owner's home at the rear. The configuration of the buildings are unknown, but were advertised as "apartments and cabins". Trailers were also rented in later years.

By the mid-1960s the Lindsay Auto Court started operating as apartments-only. The court was demolished in the 1970s. Today the area is industrial.

Little Harlem Hotel – 717 East Jefferson Street

The building at 717 East Jefferson Street became the Little Harlem Hotel by 1961. It held other businesses in previous years, including a restaurant that still operated as part of the hotel. Six rental units were available at the hotel which catered to African-Americans.

The Little Harlem stopped operating by 1977. It was demolished in the early 1980s. Today a modern office building is located on the property.

Lo Lo Mai Lodge – 4935 East Thomas Road

By 1949 the Lo Lo Mai Lodge was operating. It was built in the center of a large orange tree grove. The facility consisted of three buildings for lodge activities and sleeping. Units were one- or two-bedroom floor plans. A pool was placed to the southeast of the main buildings. The area was very spacious and rural. As with most lodges, the facility attempted to attract weekly renters as their winter guests. Summers were filled in any manner possible. The lodge appears to have moved to an apartment business plan in the 1960s. By 1969 the buildings and groves were demolished, and residential apartments were built.

Today the area still operates as an apartment complex.

Lo-Ra Motel – See Eli Motel

Log Cabin Court circa 1940 (Author's Collection)

Log Cabin Motel circa 1955 (Author's Collection)

Log Cabin Auto Court – 2515 East Van Buren Street

The Log Cabin was a long-standing cabin court opened in 1939. The facility utilized simulated log siding on the cabins to give them the look of an actual log cabin. Upgrades were made to the property through the years in an effort to stay competitive. The mandatory swimming pool was installed, a gift shop opened, an eighteen-hole putting green, and even a working water wheel was built. The motel served food for a time as well.

The Log Cabin made it through the Van Buren Street decline period. It was finally closed in 2009 and demolished in 2010. Like most Van Buren motels that survived, the Log Cabin became run-down and even operated on an hourly-rate basis for some time.

The Log Cabin's sign hung around until 2012. Today the property is vacant.

Lola's Court – 1550 North Seventeenth Avenue

By 1942 there were cabins for rent at Lola's Court. The facility likely rented as apartments in the early years. Eventually the court started catering to transient guests.

The facility was built in cabin court style and consisted of six buildings. By 1970 Lola's Court was converted to apartments.

Lola's Court buildings were demolished in 2007. Today the area is a parking lot.

Loma Alta Court operating as a shelter in 2012 (Photo by Author)

Loma Alta Court – 3030 West Van Buren Street

The Loma Alta Court was open by 1932. The facility consisted of several cottages utilized as rentals. Spanish architecture with stucco walls and tile accents were featured. By 1948 the court had been renamed the Westwood Court. The court became the Circle Inn by 1985.

In the 1960s a member of what the police dubbed the "Bailout Gang" lived at the Westwood Court. It was a normal business aspect of Phoenix motels to rent to long-term renters as well as to transients. The gang protected its members by committing crimes to collect bail money if one of its members was arrested. Augustine Tisnado, the gang member living at the Westwood, was arrested many times and finally convicted. For his crimes he received six to nine years for robbery, ten to forty years for narcotic charges, and two consecutive five-year sentences for bank robbery.

By 1999 the facility switched to an apartment business model. Today the Loma Alta's buildings still exist and are used as a homeless shelter.

Lone Star Motel circa 1960 (Author's Collection)

Lone Star Lodge – 3707 East Van Buren Street

By 1947 the Lone Star Lodge was accepting guests. The facility was constructed using six buildings plus a lobby and manager's quarters. The lobby building was located in the rear. It's likely that each building housed two or three rental units.

The Lone Star was closed by 2002 and became apartments. The facility was demolished in 2008.

Today the property is a vacant lot with a single palm as the only remnant of the motel.

Lone Tree Motel – 712-14 North Twentieth Place

The Lone Tree Motel was a small, five-unit property, which was originally marketed as apartments. During the late 1950s the facility took on the motel name and started accepting tourist trade. This was short-lived as the motel was located in the future I-10 easement. By 1966 the facility was closed. Today I-10 uses the property.

Long Rest Motel – 3020 West Van Buren Street

The Long Rest Motel was in operation by 1948. The facility consisted of four or five cottages. In the 1970s the motel added a trailer court to its amenities. The Long Rest moved to an apartment business model by 1992.

By 1995 the Long Rest had been demolished. Today the location is an undeveloped lot.

Long's Guest Lodge – See Emerick Hotel

Lorena Auto Court – 2045 East Van Buren Street

By 1938 the Lorena Court was accepting guests. The new business was built using cabin court style construction. The complex also included a restaurant.

In 1943 the facility dug a new cesspool on the property. A man fell into the hole, and suffered a collar bone injury.

In 1947 the property was renamed the Van Buren Motel. This lasted until 1950 when the facility was again renamed to the Steering Wheel Motel.

By 1965 the Steering Wheel Motel closed, and it was demolished by 1975. Today the property is part of the I-10 easement.

Lorena's Motel – 2217 West Grant Street

Lorena Sowers was operating her motel by 1958. The configuration of the facility is not known. By 1966 it no longer accepted guests.

Today the area is industrial.

Los Flores Motor Court – See Motel Inn

The former Los Olivos Lodge operating as the Quality Inn and Suites (Photo by Author 2014)

Los Olivos Lodge – 202 East McDowell Road

The Los Olivos Lodge was built in 1948. It consisted of a large parcel of land with seventeen large cottage buildings. A pool was placed in the center with green area all around. It was an upscale cottage court. In 1956 the facility was rebuilt with a large, new, two-story building which included rooms, banquet facilities, a restaurant, a coffee shop, and a soda fountain. Apartments, studios, and bungalows were now available. All rooms had full kitchens. In the 1960s the remaining original buildings were demolished. Additional new buildings were built, including a new three-story main building with new rooms and a lobby.

The hotel operated as the Los Olivos for many years. About 2004 it became an EconoLodge. By 2009 the hotel changed flags and became a Quality Inn and Suites. It operates as such today.

Lucille's Motel – 2021 East Van Buren Street

Originally opened as Helen's Cottages, Lucille's Motel was operating by 1942. The property assumed the Lucille's name by 1945. Lucille's was built in the individual cabin court style with separate cottages. This was unusual as this type of construction was losing favor to the strip-style motel by the forties.

Virtually all early courts and motels catered to both transient and long-term guests. One such long-term couple was Zelda and Charles Daugherty. In April of 1945 Zelda was presented the Air Medal with two Oak Clusters for her husband. Charles was a Staff Sargent in the Air Corps and was a prisoner of war at the time.

By 1972 Lucille's Motel was no longer operating. It was demolished soon afterward. Today the property is part of the I-10 easement where it meets Van Buren Street.

Luhrs Hotel – See Commercial Hotel

M & P Motel – 4417 East Washington Street

The M & P Motel was a small cabin court located on the far outskirts of town. It was opened by 1948 and likely earlier. By 1961 the facility became the Val Villa Lodge.

By 1963 the Val Villa became apartments-only. It was demolished in the early 1980s. Today the area is part of the Pueblo Grande Museum property.

The Madison Hotel shortly before demolition in 2012 (Photo by Author)

Madison Hotel – 35 East Madison Street

The Madison Hotel was opened in 1909. The facility was a two-story brick building which at some point received a stucco coating, most likely as a modernizing effort. The hotel included an adjoining bar named the Madison Bar and a restaurant called the Madison Cafe. The hotel served downtown Phoenix for many years as a moderately priced facility. As the property aged, it gradually catered to the lower end of the market. The hotel closed by 2005 and was purchased by the owners of the Phoenix Suns basketball franchise. It was located very close to the US Airways Center in which the Suns play. In October 2012 the Madison was demolished to create more parking for the US Airways Center. At the time it was one of the oldest hotel properties still standing in the City of Phoenix.

Main Hotel – See Porter Hotel

Majestic Hotel – See Anheuser Hotel

Mar-Di-Kay Motel – 2400 West Buckeye Road

By 1947 the Mar-Di-Kay Motel was accepting guests. The facility was a cabin court utilizing individual cabins as rental units. Cabins at the Mar-Di-Kay were kitchenettes. The location also had a grocery store.

In 1956 a long-term renter eloped out of state with his girlfriend. The man was 42-years-old and the girl was 16. A marriage license was refused to the couple not due to her age, but to their race. On the marriage license application she was listed as Caucasian and he as Filipino. At the time Arizona had a law against mixed race marriages.

By 1960 the facility became the Parkway Motel. By 1984 the facility was closed as a motel, and it was demolished by 1995. The area is a parking lot today.

Mareci's Court – See Pauline's Court

Maria Motel – 2412 West Buckeye Road

The Maria Motel was accepting guests by 1947. The facility was a twenty-five unit motel with kitchenettes.

In 1971 a seven–year-old boy was kidnapped from school by a family friend. She brought the boy from Tempe to Phoenix, stopped for groceries, and bought the boy a milk shake. They ended up at the Maria Motel where she rented a room. The woman tied the boy up and left the room. He quickly untied himself and gained help from motel management. The boy and his family were re-united.

The Maria Motel was long-lived, but by 1984 it had closed as a motel. It was demolished by 1995, and today the area is a parking lot.

Maricopa Auto Court – 903-23 South Nineteenth Avenue

The Maricopa Auto Court was accepting guests by 1929. The facility was a standard cabin court with fourteen cabins and an owner's residence. It was laid out in a U-shape with a courtyard in the center. By 1948 the court had annexed the adjacent Hunky Dory Auto Court. This expanded the court to the entire block along Nineteenth Avenue. A café was also operated on the property in the 1960s.

The court was closed by 1969 and demolished a few years later. Today the property is void of any structures.

Maricopa Motel – 518 North Twenty-Fourth Street

By 1948 the Maricopa Motel was in operation. The facility was a mix of four cottages with three rooms and seven cabins. It also offered trailer space and a café on the premises. By 1961 the facility became the Twin Wheels Motel. A discotheque was opened on the property in 1965.

By 1973 the motel was closed. The restaurant continued to operate. Today the area is a parking lot.

Marino Auto Court – See Liberty Motel

Market Motel – 3025 East Washington Street

The Market Motel was operating by 1952. It included two strip-style motel buildings. The buildings held thirteen units. By 1955 the Market became Al's Apartment Motel.

By 1963 the facility became apartments only. It was demolished shortly after. Today an industrial testing facility is located on the property.

Marks Hotel – See Stenlake Rooming House

Martin's Tourists – 116 North Eighteenth Avenue

The apartments at Eighteenth Avenue and Adams Street were marketed to tourists starting about 1956. The endeavor did not last long, and the facility became apartments again by 1963.

The apartments were demolished in the 1970s. Today the real estate is utilized by a parking lot.

MaryBill Auto Court – 3000 West Van Buren Street

By 1931 the MaryBill Auto Court was open. The facility was a cabin-style court with trailer facilities. Eventually the court added a small café as well. By 1948 the MaryBill had become Angelo's Court. By 1955 the facility had become mostly trailers and was renamed the Ranch Trailer Park. It was closed by 1963 and demolished in short order.

Today the area is a parking lot.

Marx Palace Hotel – See Stag Hotel

Mary's Cottage Court – 1612 East Washington Street

Mary's Cottage Court was operating by 1943. The facility consisted of cottage type rentals and a grocery store. Five cottages were built in a tight row behind the grocery store.

In 1944 the 48-year-old owner, Joe Mitchell, committed suicide. He shot himself in the head at the court.

By the mid-1950s the court started operating as apartments. It was demolished about 1990. Today a modern gas station is located on the property.

Mary's Motel – See Sun Court

Mascot Hotel – 720 East Washington Street

The Mascot Hotel was in operation by 1928. The size and configuration of the facility is not known. By 1945 the name was modernized to the Mascot Tourist Court. Advertising at the time mentions "modern" rooms. It's possible the facility was rebuilt or just remodeled.

In 1946 Benjamin Goetz, the owner, was fined by the Office of Price Administration in the amount of fifty dollars. The fine was imposed due to overcharging for rooms during governmental price controls. During World War II the government imposed price restrictions on businesses and strict controls on new construction. Apparently the Mascot violated the restrictions.

By 1964 the facility had started utilizing an apartment business model. Today a modern apartment complex utilizes the real estate.

Maxwell House – 446 East Washington Street

The Maxwell House was a rooming house located on the corner of Fifth and Washington Streets. In old aerial photographs it appears to be a small facility, likely a family home. The facility surely accepted guests from 1919 to 1930 and likely during a wider timeframe.

Today the area is part of the Phoenix Convention Center.

Maybern Court – 71 West Watkins Road

By 1940 there were rental cabins at what would become the Maybern Court. It took on the name by 1950. The facility was a small cabin court with five rental units.

By 1962 the court was no longer in business and was soon demolished. Today the real estate is vacant.

Mayes Hotel – 242 West Washington Street

The Mayes Hotel was operating by 1939 in the former Korrick Building. Charles Korrick constructed the building in the early 1920s as an office building. It housed many businesses, including the Phoenix Auto Supply and the United States Office of Veteran Affairs. The facility was a four-story building utilizing concrete construction. It was a strong enough building to be listed as an emergency shelter.

In May 1959 a young woman, Jean Mangum, was found dead in the closet of one of the rooms at the Mayes. She had been beaten and strangled. William Loftis was convicted of manslaughter due to his part in the incident. Loftis, the operator of a nearby bar, took the intoxicated woman to the hotel and checked into one of the rooms. It was argued that the woman was killed in an attempt to fight off Loftis' advances. Loftis received nine to ten years in prison for the crime.

The Mayes Hotel was well known for its flamboyant shoe shine "boy". The stand was located under the front steps and run by Stan Layman. Layman was stationed in the South Pacific during World War II and was a shipfitter with the Seabees (Naval Construction Battalion). He later became a middleweight boxer and had the scars to prove it. Layman gave character to the job and the Mayes Hotel through his strong personality. The signs he put in his window became popular with the use of witty sayings and humorous slogans.

By 1971 the City of Phoenix had purchased the entire block, including the Mayes Hotel. The buildings were demolished, and a parking lot was constructed on the property. In 1992 construction began on the new Phoenix City Hall, which remains on the property today.

Mayfair Motor Hotel circa 1940 (Author's Collection)

Mayfair Motor Hotel – 1537 West Van Buren Street

The Mayfair Motor Hotel opened in 1938. Utilizing cottage court construction, the Mayfair made use of flat roofs in a distinctly art deco style. The facility consisted of fourteen units with attached garages. Two of the units were designed with two bedrooms. The Mayfair was constructed by Andy Womack, a contractor who built both homes and auto courts to resell.

The owners of the Mayfair had some difficulty during the 1940s. First their son, Staff Sargent Gordon Scarlett, was reported as a German prisoner of war in early 1944. A few months later, the infant son of one of the guests was electrocuted in one of the units. A $12,500 lawsuit brought by the parents of the infant claimed his death was a result of known faulty wiring in a floor lamp. These events, plus possible rumors, must have frustrated the owner. In January of 1945 she placed an ad in the newspaper stating that the Mayfair Motor Hotel was most certainly not for sale.

The Mayfair was closed by 1984 and demolished by 1989. Today the area is a vacant lot.

The former Mayflower Motel operates as apartments today (Photo by Author 2012)

Mayflower Motel – 3710 East Van Buren Street

The Mayflower Motel was built and renting rooms by 1941. The facility utilized multiple gable-roofed buildings placed along the east and west property lines. The usual central courtyard was not included. Instead, an office and manager's quarters were built in the center. The buildings utilized a setback where older motels would have placed covered parking. The facility also operated a cafe on the property.

The Mayflower became apartments by 1991 and still exists today.

McCoy's Motor Court circa 1960 (Author's Collection)

McCoy's Motor Lodge operating as apartments in 2012 (Photo by Author)

McCoy's Motor Court – 1930 West Van Buren Street

By 1926 the McCoy's Motor Court was in operation. The facility was built in cabin court style with cabins aligned in rows. This placement allowed for covered parking to be built between the cabins. The facility had a Spanish appearance due to white stucco and certain design elements.

In 1961 one of the cabins was destroyed by fire. Two persons were inside at the time, and both were killed in the fire. A bystander pulled one of the victims from the fire but it was too late.

In 1973 the court made the papers for raising the rent. As with most early motels in Phoenix, the McCoy's rented rooms to long-term guests as well as transients. One such renter was a decorated World War I veteran who lived at the court for thirteen years. When new ownership took over the court his rent was raised from fifteen dollars per week to thirty-five dollars. The tenant publicly voiced his opposition to the newspaper, and an article appeared in the news. Soon after, the man was evicted for complaining publicly. This decision resulted in a follow-up news column in which public opinion was shown to be against the owner.

By 1977 the court had been renamed the Casa Royale Guest Home. Its name was changed again by 1979 to the Royale Rest Motel. By 1984 the facility moved to an apartment business model.

The McCoy's original buildings still exist as the Las Casitas Apartments.

McLean Auto Court – 5139 (6500) East Van Buren Street

The McLean Auto Court was operating by 1935. The facility was very far out of town at the time. It was on the northeast corner of the Tovrea Castle property. The court consisted of several cabins and a home. By 1947 the facility became the Eastside Tourist Court.

By 1959 the court was no longer in business, and the cabins were demolished in the 1960s. Today the real estate is undeveloped.

Meeks Court – 4433 East Van Buren Street

The Meeks Court was built in 1948 utilizing single-story, strip-motel construction. The court became the Travelers Lodge in 1950. By 1957 the facility was closed, and the area became a trailer sales business.

The building was razed about 1990. Today a bank utilizes the property.

Melville Guest Lodge – 84 West Moreland Street

The large home at 84 West Moreland Street was utilized as a rooming house for many years. In the early 1950s it became known as the Melville Guest Lodge, or simply The Melville. The facility provided furnished rooms and board. Most renters were long-term.

The facility was demolished in the 1960s, and the real estate became part of Hance Park. This property is located directly above the Deck Park Tunnel today.

Menear's Court – 2033 East Monroe Street

By 1948 Menear's Court was in business. The facility included units of both single- and two-room floor plans. A community area with a television room and shuffleboard was also included. By 1952 the name of the facility became the Palm Circle Court.

By 1968 the facility became apartments and was utilized as housing for women. Today the real estate is used in the I-10 easement.

Meremac Hotel Court – 2021 East Monroe Street

The Meremac Hotel Court was in business by 1947. The facility consisted of fourteen units with two rooms each. Each was fitted with a kitchenette.

By 1969 the facility no longer accepted guests. Today the I-10 easement utilizes the property.

Mesquite Court – 1747 East Madison Street

The Mesquite Court was opened in 1912 as the Mesquite Camp Sanatorium. The facility was owned and operated by the Williams family. Mrs. Williams formerly operated the Alhambra Hotel in Mesa, Arizona, and was experienced in the lodging industry. The Mesquite Camp catered to those suffering from tuberculosis. The camp operated as a sanitarium many years longer than other health resorts before switching to a regular tourist court. By 1938 the facility had made the change. However, by 1942 the court was no longer operating. A contributing factor was likely the death of Mrs. Williams in 1939. Mr. Williams had passed previously in 1923.

The area is industrial today.

Mexico Cafe Auto Court – 1735 East Van Buren Street

The Mexico Cafe Auto Court was a cabin court which opened in 1940. The facility operated a few doors down from its namesake, the Mexico Cafe. By 1948 the Mexico Cafe Auto Court was no longer renting rooms.

The property now holds an abandoned building, which was built after the Mexico Cafe Auto Court closed.

Michiana Motel – 2117 East Monroe Street

The Michiana Motel was in operation by 1948 and still under construction. Early 1949 aerial photos show four buildings were complete. The facility consisted of five duplex, cottage-style buildings built in a U-configuration. A small center courtyard was built. Eventually a pool was installed at the southwest corner of the property.

By 1960 the facility began operating as the Michiana Apartments and stopped advertising as a motel. A sixth cottage was built in the 1980s at the southeast corner of the property. The facility was demolished in 2003.

Today a parking lot is located on the property.

Midway Auto Camp – See Forney's Court

Midway Court – 3604 Grand Avenue

The Midway Court was in operation by 1930. The facility was of cabin court design utilizing eight cabins. At some point a gas station was added to the property as well.

In 1952 a man was found dead in one of the cabins in an apparent suicide. The man was a laid-off miner from Bumble Bee, Arizona. He ingested a bottle of sleeping pills and left a post card. The card claimed that he was out of money, unemployed, and going to Hell.

The Midway Court was out of business by 1965 and quickly demolished. Today a storage facility exists on the property.

Midway Court – 4216 (4202) East Washington Street

The Midway Court was a cabin court operating by 1941. The facility included approximately sixteen cabins arranged in two rows. This left a court area in the center.

By 1971 the Midway was out of business, but its buildings were not razed until the early 1980s. A modern industrial area is located on the real estate today.

Miller Auto Court – See Alameda Court

Miller Auto Camp – 1755 Villa Avenue

The Miller Auto Camp was located at the southwest corner of Villa Avenue and Eighteenth Street. The facility was a grocery store with a few cabin rentals. It was an early camp and first appears in records in 1926. It was likely in operation a couple of years prior. By 1928 the facility was no longer in business.

Today Eighteenth Street no longer continues south from Villa Avenue. The area is utilized by St. Luke's Hospital now.

Millers Auto Court – 2010 East Buckeye Road

By 1947 Karl Miller had built at least some apartments on the property of the former Henshaw Auto Wrecking facility. Soon he had a ten-unit auto court on the property and was renting to both long-term renters and tourists. The facility consisted of multiple buildings.

By 1963 the facility was renamed Millers Court Apartments and moved to an apartment business model. It functioned as such into the 1980s. By 1986 it was demolished, and the land is part of the I-10 easement where it meets Buckeye Road today.

Miller Hotel – See Elgin Hotel (Jefferson Street)

Millers Court – See Tamarisk Court

Millers Motel – 415 East Polk Street

For a very short time in the 1950s the apartments at 415 East Polk were advertised as the Millers Motel. It was a two-story building with apartments on both floors.

The entire block was demolished, and the Arizona Center occupies the space today.

Milner Hotel – See Savoy Hotel

Mills House – See Lemon Hotel or New Mills Hotel

Minnesota Cottage Court – See Cottage Court

Minnie's Court – 1826 Grand Avenue

Minnie's Court was in operation by 1938. The facility consisted of eight individual cabins used as rental rooms.

The court was closed by 1981 and quickly demolished. Today the real estate is an undeveloped lot.

Mission House Hotel – See Jefferson Rooming House

Mission Motel circa 1960 (Author's Collection)

The Mission Motel operating as the Paradise Motel in 2012 (Photo by Author)

Mission Motel – 2433 East Van Buren Street

The Mission Motel was built in 1945. It utilized the new strip-style motel construction organized in a U-shape with a central courtyard. The facility used a southwestern mission theme in the construction of twenty-nine units. The building was stucco with tile roofs. A simulated mission bell was located above the office entrance and later above the sign. The motel was known for its use of imported colored tiles throughout the facility's exterior.

In 1992 the Mission Motel closed, and it appears to have remained closed for quite some time. In 2010 the motel reopened as the Paradise Motel.

The Mission Motel still exists today as the Paradise Motel.

Modern Court – Weber Court

The former Moeller Hotel, now operates as apartments (Photo by Author 2014)

Moeller Hotel – 387 North Second Avenue

The Moeller Hotel was built as the Rincon Apartment Hotel about 1930. The facility was a three-story hotel with apartment amenities. The building had a distinctive stepped art deco shape, which set it apart from other buildings in the area. By 1935 the facility became the Moeller Apartment Hotel. It was operated as both a hotel and apartments through the years. By 1969 it began operating as apartments only.

Today the original building has been modernized and still operates as an apartment building.

Mohave Court – 231 East Mohave Street

The Mohave Court was in business by 1948. It consisted of several small cottages built in one-room and two-room configurations. The facility also operated a lunch counter. By 1955 the Mohave became the Holland Court.

By 1964 the facility started operating as apartments only. In the 1990s it was demolished. Today modern apartments are located on the property.

Mokan Motel – 3744 Grand Avenue

The Mokan Motel was in operation by 1930. The facility was a cabin court starting with about fifteen cabins. More cabins were added through the years. By 1963 the address became a trailer sales business and was cleared of its cabins.

Today the area is a trailer court.

Mona Lisa Rooms – 227 West Monroe Street

By 1921 the old Woman's Christian Temperance Union hall was converted into a restaurant with rooms for rent. The facility eventually became known as the Mona Lisa Rooms. By 1932 the facility was converted to a beauty salon and rooms appear to be no longer rented.

Today the AT&T Building is located on the property.

Monroe Court – 948 East Monroe Street

Monroe Court was a large cabin court in operation by 1934. The facility contained at least forty rental cabins arranged in five rows. Monroe Court catered predominately to African-American clientele with long-term rentals. The facility was also advertised as an auto court throughout its existence.

By the mid-1950s the court was closed and demolished. Today the area is residential housing.

Monroe Rooming House – 148 East Monroe Street

The Monroe Rooming House opened on the corner of Monroe and Second Streets before the year 1900. It was certainly open by 1898 and likely even earlier. The building was a two-story structure. By 1938 the building was closed and demolished. It was replaced immediately by a parking lot.

Today a modern parking structure is located on the real estate.

Monte Vista Court – 214 East Broadway Road

The Monte Vista Court was accepting guests by 1949. The facility was a lush cabin court with plenty of trees and shade. It consisted of several three-room cottages and a home. The Monte Vista moved to an apartment-only basis in the mid-1960s. It was demolished in the 1970s. Today the area is industrialized.

Monte Vista Lodge - 325 North Seventh Street

The Monte Vista Lodge was a large home that rented rooms to both short-term and long-term guests. The facility was renting rooms by 1912 under the ownership of the Stewart family. It operated for many years without a name, but by 1950 the facility was being advertised under the Monte Vista Lodge name. By 1953 the name was changed to Byron's Lodge. Another change occurred by 1962 when the name became Wright's Lodge.

The lodge became a residence by 1969. It was eventually demolished in the early 1990s. Today the area is a vacant lot.

Monterey Lodge circa 1950 (Author's Collection)

Monterey Court operating as apartments in 2012 (Photo by Author)

Monterey Court – 901 South Seventeenth Avenue

The Monterey Court opened for business in 1940. Eight cottages were built in two rows around a central courtyard. The cottages were built in duplex-style with some having connecting doors to allow for a larger rental unit. Construction included concrete masonry walls and shingle roof covering. The owner's quarters and office were located in the front and center of the property. The facility grew to at least twenty-five units over the years. For some time in the 1960s the facility also included a tavern.

Like other large cities in the 1960s, Phoenix experienced race riots. Most rioting took place between Nineteenth Avenue and Twentieth Street, and was bounded by Van Buren Street and Buckeye Street. In July of 1967, police were called to the Monterey Court for race related violence. A large group of juveniles were found with fire bombs. Damage appeared to be minimal.

In 1969 two men rang the doorbell at the Monterey Lodge office. It was not unusual for motels at the time to have limited office hours. Late arrivals would ring the doorbell, and the innkeeper would get out of bed to service the guest. In this case, the owner let the men inside expecting a room rental. Instead, the owner was robbed, and after a short struggle was shot in the leg. One of the robbers was apprehended. He was a sixteen-year-old Phoenix juvenile who had been arrested twenty times prior. He had been sent to the juvenile detention center three times prior as well. The judge found no choice but to send him to prison for two to three years. The boy joined two of his brothers already serving time in the prison system.

Today the Monterey Court buildings still exist and have been utilized as apartments since 1984.

Montezuma Motel – See Montezuma Place

Winter Garden, formally part of Montezuma Place, circa 1945 (Author's Collection)

Montezuma Place - 1850-90 East Van Buren Street

By 1909 the Montezuma Place had been established in what was then a rural area of Tempe Road (Van Buren Street). The facility was a health resort, or sanitarium, which were popular at the time. Guests with health issues would spend the winter, or part of it, at Montezuma Place in an attempt to feel better. The warm winters in Arizona made the area ideal for this type of business. Of course the facility included lodging for its guests.

Montezuma Place was the earliest auto camp and court in Phoenix because it already had the facilities needed in place when the auto camps and auto courts became popular. In the 1920s the facility changed its name to Camp Montezuma in keeping with this trend.

Montezuma Motel circa 1965 (Author's Collection)

Early in the 1940s the property was split into the Winter Garden Auto Camp and the Montezuma Auto Court. Winter Garden kept the 1850 East Van Buren address and the Montezuma Auto Court was assigned 1890 East Van Buren. Both facilities offered cabins, camping, and trailer parking. By 1958 the Montezuma Auto Court cabins were replaced by a new single-story, strip-style motel. The new facility was called the Montezuma Motel. The motel built a new addition in the same style in 1963, resulting in a U-shaped complex.

In 1975 Winter Garden was closed and demolished. The Montezuma Motel followed suit in 1976. By 1978 the St. Luke's Hospital, which was located just north of the Montezuma block, had taken over the entire block.

The property once home to the Montezuma Place is now the Van Buren frontage of the St. Luke's Medical Center.

Moon Kist Court – 4638 East Van Buren Street

The Moon Kist Court was accepting guests by 1948. The facility utilized cement block construction. This was a very small motel with a five-room apartment and five transient rental units. One of the five units was a kitchenette. The Moon Kist was short-lived, and by 1953 it was gone.

Today the property is part of the Hohokam Expressway easement.

Morgan Court – See Wilberta Court

Morreale Hotel – See Town House Hotel

Morris Court – See Tamarisk Court

Morrison Hotel – See Kersting Hotel

Moss Rooming House – See Dixie Hotel

Motel 6 circa 1971 (Author's Collection)

The Motel 6 still operates today (Photo by Author 2014)

Motel 6 – 5315 East Van Buren Street

The Motel 6 was built in 1965 and opened in December of that year. Built at a cost of $300,000, the facility was built in two-story motor inn style. The property was the first Motel 6 to open in Phoenix. Motel 6 had started in California and was expanding through the western states at the time.

Today the location is still a Motel 6.

Motel Inn – 1617 West Van Buren Street

The Jennings family had their auto court operating by 1930 under the Ritz Tourist Court name. The facility was constructed in cabin court style and included twenty-three units. Each cabin included a carport and kitchen facilities. Apparently the Jennings family had some difficulty naming the court. By 1931 the court's name became the Auto Rest Court. They favored the Los Flores Motor Court name by 1934, and finally settled on the Motel Inn by 1938. In 1959 the name again changed to the West Siesta Motel.

The Motel Inn had a couple of minor fires. In 1939 a trash can caught fire and left one cabin wall and a car damaged. In 1945 a guest was hospitalized after his pants caught fire in his cabin. He apparently was standing too close to the heater.

The West Siesta was closed and demolished by 1987. Today, a parking facility is built on the real estate the Motel Inn once occupied.

Motor Inn Auto Court – 3301 East Van Buren Street

By 1930 the Motor Inn Auto Court was accepting guests. The facility was a cabin-style court arranged in the familiar U-layout. In this case several cabins were also placed in the center courtyard making a total of 26 units. By 1945 the owners changed the name to Whittles Motor Court. The name was changed again by 1955. The final name, Jaime's Motor Inn Cottages, would only last until 1959 when the court closed and was demolished. Immediately afterwards the property became a trailer sales business. Today the property is utilized for an automotive repair business.

Motto Guest Lodge – See El Lynn Motel

Mountain View Auto Court – 2224 East Washington Street

The Mountain View Auto Court was a cabin-style court open by 1929. The facility consisted of approximately twenty cabins arranged in a U-pattern along the property lines. When it was built, it was the only structure on the north side of Washington on that block.

In 1942 a 43-year-old man, Roy Rolland, was found dead in his cabin. His suicide included filling the room with gas from a space heater. His throat and wrists were slashed, and he was hung from a bathroom shelf hanger. Rolland left a suicide note claiming he was being blackmailed by a man and a woman. It said they had broken his jaw. Rolland's jaw was indeed shattered, and the two were questioned. They admitted to the scuffle but claimed no part in Rolland's death.

By 1967 the Mountain View was closed and demolished. The area became a manufacturing location for house trailers. Today the property is vacant.

Mountain View Motel – See Perma Rest Motel

Mutt and Jeff Camp – 1736 East Van Buren Street

The Mutt and Jeff Camp was an early auto camp that was in business by 1926. It was located on the property of the existing Showelter gas station. The camp catered to the new auto tourist camping business. It provided basic comforts to the guests in a camping setting. The facility never converted to a cabin court as most auto camps did. By 1933 the camp was gone, and the Mutt and Jeff Gas Station continued.

Today the property is used by the Southwest Autism Research and Resource Center.

Navajo Court – 505 North Sixteenth Street

The Navajo Court was an early auto court built in cabin court style. It was in business by 1926 and grew from just a few cabins to at least fourteen. The owner offered free rent to some individuals who were willing to work on the property. By 1954 the Navajo was no longer renting cabins. The facility was demolished in the 1950s.

Today the Goodwill administration facility utilizes the real estate.

Navajo Hotel – See Sixth Avenue Hotel

Navajo Courts circa 1950 (Author's Collection)

The Navajo Motel still operates today (Photo by Author 2012)

Navajo Motel – 3232 East Van Buren Street

The Navajo Motel was open by 1946. The facility utilized single-story, strip-motel type construction. Four strip-style buildings were erected, and an additional building was used for the office and manager's quarters. The Navajo Motel has endured through time and still operates as the Navajo Motel today. The motel may have closed intermittently, but it has always remained the Navajo.

Near Town Motel – See Pasadena Motel

New Dennis Hotel – See Dennis Hotel

New Hunky Dory Court – See Hunky Dory Auto Court

New Ivanhoe Hotel – See Thibodo House

New Mills House – See Farley House

New Windsor Hotel – See Sixth Avenue Hotel

New York Hotel – 242 East Madison Street

The New York Hotel was operating by 1920 on the corner of Madison and Third Streets. The facility contained 36 rooms and a dining facility. Ground floor store fronts were also rented. The area became one of the higher crime areas in Phoenix, but the hotel endured many years. It stopped accepting guests in the mid-1970s. The hotel was eventually demolished to make room for the construction of the America West arena. Today this is the US Airways Center.

Newton's Inn – 917 East Van Buren Street

The Newton's Inn was opened in the summer of 1963. The facility was built to adjoin the existing Newton's Prime Rib restaurant. L.J. Newton, the main investor, owned six restaurants in Arizona at the time. The investment group raised capital in the amount of $850,000 and carried no mortgage. The facility was built in two-story motor hotel style utilizing block construction. Sixty-eight sleeping rooms, an 80-seat coffee shop, lobby, and banquet room were included in the complex. The facility was upscale with large rooms and even ice machines in each room.

The Newton's Inn operated until 1993 when the facility moved to an apartment business model. The facility was demolished by 1999. Today the Newton's Inn real estate is part of a modern apartment complex.

Nightingale Court – 4201 East Washington Street

The Nightingale family operated a gas station at 4201 East Washington starting about 1948. By 1952 they had added cabin rentals to the business. Only four units were built. By 1966 the court was closed. The new city mass transit facility utilizes the real estate today.

Nine-O-Nine Court – See Atherton Court

Nordrach (The) – 42 South Second Avenue

The Nordrach building began as the Pneumo-Chemic Sanitarium opened in 1898. The facility was sold in 1901, but continued accepting invalids. In 1903 the business converted to a lodging facility and took on the Nordrach name. Advertising immediately included a "no invalids" statement.

The two-story brick structure featured screened porches and regular meals. Its previous use as a sanitarium made the facility quite comfortable. It even included a basement, which is unusual in Phoenix. The Nordrach operated until 1919 when it was razed. The three-story Savoy Hotel was built in its place.

Today the area contains the Calvin C. Goode Municipal Building. Second Avenue no longer exists in that area.

Normandie Hotel – 137 North First Street

The Normandie Hotel was located on the southeast corner of Monroe and First Streets. The hotel was a substantial building taking up half the block. It was built in two-story hotel-style and featured a cooling system and shower baths. The Normandie Hotel was operating by 1923. Prior to that time the facility was known as the Rex Arms Apartments. It is not known if the building remained the same or if the Normandie was a new build.

In 1960 the Normandie was demolished and became a parking lot. The Hyatt Regency Phoenix is located on the property today.

Norms Hotel – See French Rooming House

North Central Manor – 5534 North Central Avenue

The North Central Manor was open by 1952 at the corner of Marshall and Central Avenues. The facility consisted of five buildings placed as to create a central courtyard. The courtyard included a recreational area with a pool. Operated mainly as apartments, the Manor was also advertised to short-term renters for a few years from 1953 to 1956.

It operated for many years as apartments, but was demolished in the 1990s. Today the address is a high-end residential area.

North Central Motor Lodge – See Ivory Palaces Motor Lodge

Norway Hotel – 1738 West Van Buren Street

A short-lived hotel existed at 1738 West Van Buren Street from 1949 to 1951. Little is known about the facility other than it existed. By 1951 the hotel had become the assembly hall for the Advent Christian Church.

Today a gas station resides on the property.

O&E Tourist Court – Calico Cat Court

Oak Avenue Court – 1305 Oak Avenue (North Sixteenth Drive)

The Oak Avenue Court was a small, seven-unit motel located on what is now North Sixteenth Drive. Oak Avenue was renamed in the 1950s. The facility was long-lived, being in business by 1939 and closing about 1986.

Today the area is residential.

Oakland Motel circa 1960 (Author's Collection)

Oakland Motel building in 2012 (Photo by Author)

Oakland Motel – 2448 West Van Buren Street

The Oakland Motel was open by 1948. The motel utilized two buildings placed in an L-shape. Construction was of the single-story, strip motel style. By 1973 the motel had become apartments.

Today the property is a used car business. One of the buildings has been demolished, but the other still exists.

Oasis Motel – See Counhan Court

Occidental Hotel – See Perkins Rooming House

Ohio Motel – 211 North Twenty-First Street

The Ohio Motel was in operation by 1948. The facility consisted of six duplex cottages and an owner's home. This resulted in twelve rental units. It appears the area was used for trailer sales prior to the motel's construction. By 1953 the Ohio became the El Ray Motel.

The El Ray was out of business by 1984. Today the real estate is utilized by the I-10 easement.

OK Court – 1617 West Buckeye Road

The OK Court was accepting guests by 1940. The court utilized eight cabins arranged in one row along the west property line.

In 1944 a guest at the court was beaten and relieved of his wallet while buying cigarettes near the court. Interestingly, the perpetrators were described as wearing zoot-suits and were not apprehended.

By 1957 the court was no longer in business. Today the area is an undeveloped lot.

OK Tourist Court – 201 North Twelfth Street

The OK Tourist Court was in business by 1931. The facility consisted of a grocery store and six rental cottages. By 1945 the court became the Peck Auto Court.

In the spring of 1939 James Cartier, a court guest, was killed. The five-year-old boy was crossing the alley on the sidewalk at the north edge of the court when he was struck. The driver was released as it was deemed an accident.

By 1950 the court moved to an all-apartment business model. The buildings were demolished in the early 1980s. Today the real estate is residential.

Old Faithful Inn – 1916 East Van Buren Street

The Old Faithful Inn opened in 1952 with a formal opening on the thirteenth of September. The facility consisted of twenty-six units with red brick walls. Construction was of the cottage court style with individual buildings arranged in a U-shape. A two-story apartment area existed at the bottom of the U, most likely used as the owner's or manager's quarters.

Old Faithful Inn circa 1960 (Author's Collection)

The Old Faithful closed by 1980 and was demolished by 1995. Today, nothing but the palm trees remains of the facility.

Olivet Hotel – 1012 North Central Avenue

The Olivet Hotel was open by 1929. The facility was a two-story building located at Roosevelt Street and Central Avenue.

The hotel was closed by 1971 and demolished in short order. The land functioned as a parking lot for some time. Eventually the road easement in the area changed putting the property in First Avenue, and the park between First and Central Avenues.

Orange Auto Court – 2008 East Van Buren Street

The Orange Auto Court was one of the early auto courts in Phoenix. By 1931 it was renting cabins to transient guests and also feeding them at the Orange Café. In the early 1950s the court changed its name to the Ahoy Tourist Motel, probably in an attempt to compete.

The Orange Auto Court made the news in 1943 when two young boys were bitten by a rabid dog near their cabin.

The Ahoy Tourist Motel did not last long and by 1957 the facility had closed. It became a trailer sales business immediately after its closing. Today the property is part of the I-10 easement where it meets Van Buren Street.

Oregon Hotel – See Raymond Hotel

Oriel Hotel – See Denver Hotel

Ortiz Court – See Hurds Court

Paducah Hotel – 14 North Sixth Street

By 1951 the Paducah Hotel was in operation on North Sixth Street. The facility was built on the property of a previous small rooming house. The hotel was a smaller downtown property and was two stories in construction.

The Paducah Hotel played a part in the murder of Henry Bischoff by Honor Robinson in 1958. Vera Whipple and Bischoff traveled to Phoenix from Washington and stayed with Robinson. The three conspired to create a robbery ring. At some point Robinson became attracted to Whipple, and the two shared carnal affection in the Paducah Hotel. When Bischoff discovered the affair, he and Robinson had an argument. Shortly afterward, Robinson lured Bischoff to Papago Park on the pretense there was a robbery job to do there. Instead, Robinson shot him twice in the back, killing Bischoff. Robinson was convicted of murder and placed on Arizona's death row.

By 1972 the Paducah Hotel no longer accepted guests. It was demolished in short order. Today the Arizona Science Center is located on the property.

Palace Auto Court – 1925 East Van Buren Street

The Palace Auto Camp was in business by 1926 to cater to the new traveling motorists. The facility offered services to those camping on the grounds. Like most auto camps that wanted to stay in business, the Palace started offering cabin rentals. By the mid-1930s the camp was renamed the Palace Auto Court.

The Palace Auto Court operated until 1949 when the facility became the Halls Auto Court. It was soon after converted to a strip-style motel and named the Halls Motel. The motel was demolished in 2006. The property is now a vacant lot.

Palgrave House – See Grand View Hotel

Palm Circle Court – See Menear's Court

Palm Garden Court – 1533 Grand Avenue

The Palm Garden Court was in operation by 1939. The facility was built in the cabin court style utilizing individual cabins as units. The Palm Garden Court was closed and demolished by 1955 to make room for the Bali-Hi Motor Hotel.

Palm Lane Motor Court circa 1950 (Author's Collection)

Palm Lane Motor Court – 3037 East Van Buren Street

The Palm Lane Motor Court opened in 1941. The court utilized multiple buildings with two units per building. These were aligned along the property lines to create a central courtyard in the center. The Palm Lane served transient guests until 1963. At that time the facility was demolished to make room for the new Chilton Inn.

Palmdale Court – See Washington and Hollywood Courts

Palmesa Hotel Court – See Sandman Motel

Palms Auto Court – 1214 East Van Buren Street

The Palms Auto Court was an early auto court established by 1925. The facility enlisted the usual cabin court style construction. By 1952 the Palms was no longer renting cabins. The long established service station on the location continued to operate.

The area formerly occupied by the Palms Auto Court is now a used car lot.

Palms Hotel – See Benson Lodge

Palms Rooming House – See Gordon Rooming House

Palomine Inn – 1520 West Van Buren Street

The Palomine Inn was opened in 1938. The court was built in Spanish style with stucco walls and tile roofs. It was built in cottage court style with individual buildings. The property also contained a restaurant, lounge with entertainment, and a beauty shop. The Palomine was one of the properties built by contractor Andy Womack. Womack built courts and homes to sell.

Palomine Inn circa 1960 (Author's Collection)

The Palomine was closed by 1994 and quickly demolished. Today a modern restaurant sits on the property where the Palomine once stood.

Panama (The) – 220 East Adams Street

The Panama was a large rooming house opened by 1916. It was closed by 1931, demolished, and replaced by a parking lot.

The Phoenix Convention Center utilizes the property today.

Papago Vista Motel – 5445 East Van Buren Street

The Papago Vista Motel was operating by 1948. The motel consisted of nine rental units built in single-story, strip motel style and a four-room manager's quarters. A 32-seat cafe was also located on the premises. The Papago Vista was closed as a motel by 1971. All traces of the Papago Vista were gone by 1990.

Today the real estate is part of a condominium complex.

The Paradise Inn circa 1950 (Author's Collection)

Paradise Inn – 6150 East Camelback Road

The Paradise Inn was a multi-building resort complex located at the foot of Camelback Mountain. The facility opened by early 1945. It was built in Spanish style architecture and was located just east of the Jokake Inn. The Paradise was one of the premier resorts in Phoenix and offered full-service amenities such as meeting rooms, a restaurant, lounge, and golf course. The resort was part of the Alsonette Hotel Chain beginning in 1949.

The resort was demolished to build the Phoenician Resort. However, part of the golf course was incorporated into the Phoenician's facility.

Paris Hotel – See Espanol Hotel

Park Central Motor Hotel circa 1965 (Author's Collection)

The last remaining building from the Park Central Motor Hotel complex (Photo by Author 2014)

Park Central Motor Hotel – 3033 North Seventh Avenue

In 1959 the Park Central Terrace Apartments were converted to the Park Central Motor Hotel. The original apartments were built in 1955. The facility was a mix of two-story and single-story buildings built in motor inn style with exterior entrances. One hundred rental rooms were available plus a 60-foot pool. In 1960 a restaurant was added to the complex.

The hotel also operated the Western Hotel Training School, which trained students in all aspects of hotel operations. In the early 1990s most of the facility was demolished to make room for a hospital. One of the buildings still exists today.

Park Hotel – See Grand View Hotel

Park Lane Motor Hotel circa 1940 (Author's Collection)

Park Lane Motor Court – 1601 West Van Buren Street

Spanish style cottages defined the Park Lane Motor Court when it opened in 1936. Touted as specifically for tourists, the fourteen-unit court offered single- and double-room units with kitchenettes. Within a few years the property would be accepting long-term guests as well as transients. This was the normal course for Phoenix auto courts. The rental business would give the court a consistent base income. Tourism and transient business would provide the profits.

The Park Lane was closed by 1987 and quickly demolished. Today the area is a parking facility.

Park Motel – 5344 East Van Buren Street

The Park Motel was renting rooms by 1947. The facility rented both motel units and trailers. Papago Park adjoined the motel, which gave the facility something to advertise and accounts for its name.

The Park Motel was closed by 1971 and the facility catered to trailers only afterward. All traces of the Park Motel were gone by 1989.

Parker Cabin Court – See Culver Street Court

Parker House – 333 (455) North Second Avenue

The Parker House began operation as the Eldorado Hotel by 1903, and possibly even earlier. Its original address was 455 North Second Avenue. By 1904 the facility took on the Parker House name. Addresses in the area were renumbered about this time and the Parker took on the 333 North Second Avenue address. The facility was a 70-foot by 40-foot building located on two lots. It contained twenty-eight rooms, a dining room, and kitchen. By 1908 the Parker was renamed the Woodford Hotel. The name changed again to the Lebanon Hotel by 1929.

By 1961 the facility was no longer in business. Today a parking facility is located on the property.

The Parkmore Motel buildings, now operating as apartments (Photo by Author 2014)

Parkmore Motel – 312 North Eighteenth Avenue

The Parkmore Motel consisted of seven units in two buildings of brick construction. They were operated as apartments for most of their existence. However, the facility utilized the Parkmore Motel name and operated as such for a few years in the early 1950s.

Today the Parkmore buildings still exist and are used for apartments.

Parkview Court – 3424 East Van Buren Street

The Parkview Court was in operation by 1930. The court utilized Spanish influenced architecture in a cabin court style. Joyland Park was located across the street and is the reason for the court's name. The Parkview Court outlived Joyland Park by a decade.

In 1957 the Parkview Court was demolished to build the new Desert Rose Motel. Today the real estate still holds the Desert Rose buildings, which are utilized as apartments.

Parkway Motel – See Mar-Di-Kay Motel

Pasadena Motel operating as the Classic Motel in 2012 (Photo by Author)

Pasadena Motel – 1865 East Van Buren Street

The Pasadena Motel was built in 1948 on the property of the Eastside Court and the Arizona Gem Shop. Built in the newer single-story, strip motel style, the Pasadena Motel was a very modern building at its opening. One area near the street was built in two-story fashion. In 1951 the motel became known as the Eighteen Sixty-Five Motel. The name lasted until 1954 when the owners settled on the Near Town Motel. In 1991 the facility moved to an apartment sales model. Recently, the property began renting as a motel again.

The Pasadena Motel has avoided the wrecking ball and still exists as the Classic Motel.

Patio Hotel – See Stag Hotel

Patrick Hotel – 325 West Washington Street

In September of 1923 the Patrick Hotel began accepting guests. The building began in 1911 as the Patrick Building, a two-story office and ballroom building. In 1923 the building was remodeled to include the 38-room hotel. The roof was raised to create a third floor with sleeping rooms. The second floor ballroom was converted to sleeping rooms as well. It formerly held one of the largest dance floors in the city. The lobby was also located on the second floor. A furniture company utilized the ground floor and continued to do so after the hotel opened.

By 1963 the Patrick hotel was no longer in business. The hotel, along with the entire block, was soon demolished to create downtown parking. Today a modern parking structure utilizes the property.

Patrick Hotel circa 1948 (Author's Collection)

Patton Grand Rooms – 324 West Washington Street

The Patton Grand Opera House opened in the fall of 1898. By early 1900 the facility became the Dorris Theatre. While the facility was operated under the Patton Grand name, rooms were advertised for rent in the building.

The Phoenix Municipal Court building is located on the property today.

Pauline's Court – 305-07 North Twentieth Street

Pauline's Court was a short-lived facility located just north of Van Buren Street on Twentieth Street. It was in business by 1955 and gone by 1959. By 1956 the facility became the Mareci's Court. It appears that part of the court became part of the Essex Johnny's Apartments in 1959.

The area holds a machine shop today.

Pearson Hotel (Jefferson Street) – See Elgin Hotel (Jefferson Street)

Pearson Hotel – 15 South First Avenue

The Walker building was constructed at the corner of Washington Street and First Avenue about 1911. The second floor was fitted with apartments and rented as such. By 1937 these apartments became the Pearson Hotel. By 1948 the hotel was no longer in business. The building was razed in the early 1970s to create Patriots Square Park.

Today the area is part of the CityScape development.

Peck Auto Court – See OK Tourist Court

Pecks Court – 1717 West Maricopa Street

Pecks Court was in operation by 1945, just west of Seventeenth Avenue. This was a popular location for motels as Seventeenth Avenue, and Buckeye Road was the main highway to San Diego at the time. The facility was a cabin court with about nine cabins.

Like most small courts in the area, Pecks Court accepted both short-term and long-term renters. It is very likely that the facility contained all long-term renters by the mid-1960s.

The court was demolished in the 1970s. Today the property contains industrial buildings.

Penn's Court – 745 Grand Avenue

By 1923 there were rooms for rent at 745 Grand Avenue. The facility was a mix of at least one small house and cabins for rent. These were likely rented as apartments until about 1947 when the facility took on the name Penn's Court and advertised to transients. By 1955 the court was out of business.

It is likely that the court was affiliated with the former Happy Place Cottages, which operated under the Penn's Court name as well.

Today the court no longer exists, and the area is part of a metal fabricating machine company.

The Pennsylvania Motel, now apartments (Photo by Author 2014)

Pennsylvania Motel – 3239 East Van Buren Street

The Pennsylvania Motel was opened in 1948. The facility utilized single-story, strip-motel construction laid out in a shallow U-shape. Being built on the corner, access to rooms was from Thirty-Third Street.

The Pennsylvania was closed to motel business by 1978 and became apartments. Today the original Pennsylvania building is still in use as apartments.

Perkins Rooming House – 130 North Central Avenue

The Perkins Rooming House opened for business in December 1896. The facility contained twenty rental rooms and was located across the street from the Adams Hotel. By 1899 the facility changed names to the Occidental Hotel.

By 1948 the Occidental was closed. Today a retail building called The Hub is located at the site.

Mountain View Motel, formerly Perma Rest Motel, circa 1955 (Author's Collection)

The Perma Rest Motel as it looks today (Photo by Author 2014)

Perma Rest Motel – 3344 (3360) West Buckeye Road

By 1948 the Perma Rest Motel was in business. The facility was a single-story, strip-style motel and appears to have had eight rental units. By 1955 the motel had been renamed as the Mountain View Motel, and by 1966 it became the Daytonian Motel. The Daytonian didn't last long as the facility became apartments by 1967.

The original Perma Rest Motel buildings still exists. They were utilized as apartments until 2012 and are now vacant.

Phillips House – 325 North Fourth Avenue

The Phillips House was operating by 1899 at 449 North Fourth Avenue. The house rented rooms and included a restaurant. By 1906 it appears the facility's address was changed to 325 North Fourth Avenue. North Fourth Avenue does not contain any 400 or 500 addresses to this day.

Like many lodging facilities in Phoenix, the Phillips House was a seasonal property. It opened for a fall and winter season. Summer months were used for maintenance and improvements. It appears the house became either long-term rentals or a home in the mid-1920s.

Today Fire Station Number One is at the location.

Phoenician Hotel – See Ritz Hotel

Phoenix Airport Travelodge - See Hiway House.

Phoenix East TraveLodge circa 1970 (Author's Collection)

The East TraveLodge operating as a Super 8 in 2012 (Photo by Author)

Phoenix East TraveLodge – 965 East Van Buren Street

The second TraveLodge in Phoenix opened in the summer of 1960. The facility was built in two-story motor hotel fashion with 60 rooms. The TraveLodge was built on property that formerly held the Klose Inn Auto Court.

In 1966 the husband and wife managers were robbed at gunpoint. They were tied up, and the woman was strangled until she passed out. The gunman used a hunting knife to destroy the man's left eye. Both survived the attack. The attacker was eventually caught and convicted.

The facility remained a TraveLodge until 1990 when it became the American Lodge. By 2005 the property had taken a Super 8 flag.

Today the Phoenix East TraveLodge buildings still exist as the Super 8 motel.

Phoenix Hotel – See Byers House

Phoenix Hotel – 242 East Washington Street

The Phoenix Hotel was the first lodging facility in Phoenix. It was opened in 1872 and was built by John Gardiner. Gardiner emigrated from England in 1862 and moved around quite a bit before settling in Phoenix in 1870. His primary business was overland shipping. During his stay in Phoenix, he shipped goods throughout Arizona with his five-wagon shipping business. Of course Gardiner dabbled in other businesses, one of which was the Phoenix Hotel.

The hotel was located at Washington and Third Streets and utilized single-story adobe construction. Rooms were laid out along the perimeter of the building with a central court area. The center was utilized for guests' enjoyment and included a swimming pool of sorts. Water was directed into the court area from one of the canals and filled a large swimming hole. Water ran off from the pool back into the canal system.

The exterior of the hotel was modernized in 1891. Along with the modernization, the name was changed to the Pioneer Hotel. By 1893 the Pioneer Hotel closed and was demolished in short order to make room for the new Capitol Hotel. The new hotel was also owned by the Gardiners.

Today the real estate is home to the Phoenix Symphony Hall.

Phoenix Motel – See Kirby's Motel

Phoenix Motor Lodge – 348 North Fourteenth Avenue

By 1947 kitchenette rooms were being rented under the name Phoenix Motor Lodge. The lodge utilized single-story, strip-motel construction in an L-configuration. It appears to quickly have changed names to the Kings Land Lodge. The facility became the El Rancho Annex by 1952. It was affiliated and operated through the El Rancho Motel located on Van Buren Street, about a block away.

By 1965 the facility no longer operated as a motel. It was demolished in the mid-1990s. Today the real estate is an undeveloped lot.

Phoenix Municipal Auto Camp - Christy Park

The Phoenix Municipal Auto Camp was created by the City of Phoenix with help from the Chamber of Commerce to aid in the control and accommodation of early motorists. The facility provided space for camping, gas, water, and sewers. The camp was located at Christy Park near Six Points (the intersection of Nineteenth Avenue and Grand Avenue). It operated in the early to mid-1920s before other accommodations became available.

Phoenixona Motor Lodge – See Lanny's Court

Pickwick Gables – 2142 West Van Buren Street

Pickwick Gables was open by 1931. After an addition in 1934, the facility featured nine rental cottages. Each cottage varied in size with two-, three-, and four-room buildings. A five-room owner's residence and office was located on the property as well.

Pickwick Gables began advertising as apartments in 1964, although it may have accepted transients from time to time. The building began to be removed in the 1960s, and all of the Pickwick Gables buildings were removed by the end of the 1970s.

Pickwick Gables circa 1935 (Author's Collection)

A storage-unit business is now located on the property where the Pickwick Gables once stood.

Pink Palace Motel – See Hutch Motel

Pioneer Hotel – See Phoenix Hotel

Pioneer Lodge – 5200 East Van Buren Street

The Pioneer Lodge opened with some difficulty in 1948. Its original application for construction was denied in early 1947. In any event, the motel opened and included fourteen units built in single-story, strip motel style. By 1953 the facility was renamed the DeManana Motel. The property endured until 1972 when it was closed. By 1976 the motel had become the Erotica Motel. The motel was complemented with an adult store. By 1988 the Erotica was closed. It was demolished by 1992.

Today the property is part of the Loop 202 easement where it meets Van Buren Street.

Plaza Hotel – 509 North First Street

The Plaza Hotel on First Street was opened in 1940. It took the name of a hotel on North Second Street that had recently changed its name to the White Hotel. The new hotel was a two-story brick structure. For many years the hotel also rented apartments and advertised itself as the Plaza Hotel Apartments at times.

By 1967 the Plaza no longer functioned as a hotel and likely remained as apartments. The Plaza Hotel building was demolished in 2007. Taylor Place, an Arizona State University dormitory, is now located on the property.

The Plaza House (Fry Building) operating as a sports bar in 2012 (Photo by Author)

Plaza House – 144 East Washington Street

The Plaza House utilized the second floor of the Fry building, located on the northwest corner of Washington and Second Streets. The Fry building was built in 1891, and upstairs rooms were likely rented soon after. However, the first appearance of the Plaza House name in historical records was in 1899. Around 1910 the Plaza started utilizing Eighteen North Second Street as the advertised address. Soon afterward the facility started being referred to as The Plaza or the Plaza Hotel. By 1938 the business became the White Hotel.

In 1943 a murder took place in one of the rooms at the White Hotel. Harry Bounds, an ex-convict, inflicted fatal wounds upon his wife by beating her. Bounds had spent two years in prison for the attempted murder of his former wife by cutting her throat with a knife. With the help of testimony from other hotel guests, the jury convicted Bounds of first degree murder.

In December of 1944 Elmer Hubbard, a White Hotel resident, was notified that his son was returning home from the war in the Pacific. This was good news as his son had been aboard the Aircraft Carrier Princeton during the Battle of Leyte Gulf in the Philippines. The Princeton was sunk during the battle, and H. E. Hubbard had survived the incident.

By 1995 the White Hotel stopped renting rooms. The Fry building still exists and is listed on the National Register of Historic Places. Today a pizza restaurant and sports bar is located in the building.

Polk House – 215 East Polk Street

The Polk House was a rooming house in operation by 1905. Its size and construction is unknown. By 1915 the facility became known as The Home. The name was soon changed to The Avon. The Avon functioned as both apartments and transient rentals. However, by 1921 The Avon was strictly apartments.

Today Polk Street does not exist in the East 200 block. The area where the Polk House once stood is utilized by the Phoenix Sheridan Hotel and the Arizona Republic newspaper building.

Pollard Court – See San Antonio Court

Rainbow Motel, formerly the Polly Court, circa 1960 (Author's Collection)

The Polly Court operates as the Rainbow Motel today (Photo by Author 2012)

Polly Court – 2262 (2402) Grand Avenue

The Polly Court was renting rooms by 1937. The facility consisted of a cabin court and trailer facilities. By 1949 the court had become the Arrow Motel. In the 1950s the court was updated by converting the cabins along the east property line to a single-story strip building. Stucco walls and Spanish design set the theme for the motel. By 1952 the business had become the Rainbow Motel.

Today the Rainbow Motel still exists and is still renting rooms on a weekly basis. One of the cottages was demolished in 2012, leaving the facility with seventeen rental units.

Portal Grande Motel – 212 North Twenty-First Street

The Portal Grande Motel was in operation by 1947. The facility consisted of two apartment-style buildings that held the rental units. Also on property was an owner's residence.

All of the buildings were demolished in 1966. Today the real estate is utilized by the I-10 easement.

Porter Hotel – 12 South Central Avenue

By 1909 the Porter Hotel was utilizing the upstairs rooms of the Porter Building as sleeping rooms. The facility was a two-story brick building. The Thibodo House also utilized the same building with an entrance on West Washington Street. The two facilities were advertised together for a couple of years as one hotel with two names. This gave the convenience of two entrances and the competitive advantage of two names. By 1913 the Porter Hotel name was changed to the Main Hotel.

By 1915 the rooms became part of the Thibodo.

Portland Hotel – 525 North Central Avenue

The Portland Hotel was opened in 1898 on North Central Avenue. The facility was advertised as a family hotel, meaning they accepted women and children.

The Portland seems to have been a short-lived facility. After 1901, no mention of it can be found. Today the real estate is part of the Walter Cronkite School of Journalism facility.

Portland Hotel – 11 (7) South Third Street

The Portland Hotel was in business by 1916. The facility was a two-story brick building with sleeping rooms on the second floor. The ground floor contained store fronts, like most small downtown hotels.

In 1947 a California woman who had previously suffered from amnesia disappeared from the Portland Hotel. Her husband said she left the room to get coffee and never returned. What became of her is not known.

The Portland was no longer operating by 1977. It sat vacant for a few years and was demolished in the early 1980s. The Phoenix Convention Center utilizes the real estate today.

Potter Motor Court – 323 North Twentieth Street

The Potter Motor Court began as long-term cottage rentals and was operating by 1940. The facility began utilizing the Potter Motor Court name by 1949. The court was a small array of cabins of varying sizes.

By 1962 the court was closed. It was demolished in short order. Today the property holds a warehouse that sells automotive parts.

One of Price's Cabins, now operating as apartments (Photo by Author 2014)

Price's Cabins – 1535 West Buckeye Road

John Price placed cabin rentals on his property in the 1950s. They were generally rented as apartments, but did accept short-term travelers from time to time. By 1977 the facility was renamed the Stewart's Cabins. By 1984 Stewart's Cabins dropped from listings and are shown as apartments-only.

The location is still rented as apartments today, and the buildings are original.

Produce Hotel – 141 South Third Street

The Produce Hotel was built on the property of the old Grand Canyon Hotel by 1949. It may have been known as the Chesterfield Rooms when it was first built. The facility was a two-story brick building.

The Produce operated three hotel annexes. Annex A was at 300 East Madison Street. Annex B was at 344 East Madison. Annex C was located at 704 East Madison Street. The annexes were likely older rooming houses and were all located on the second floor of their respective buildings. In 1963 a man was shot to death in the Produce Annex C. James Smith shot Foster Jacobs during a disagreement over a dice game.

By 1977 the hotel was no longer functioning. It was demolished within a few years.

Jefferson Street was rerouted when the Phoenix Convention Center was built. The Produce hotel was where the street is now located. None of the Annexes still exist today.

Pueblo Grande Court – See Kozy Kourt

Pueblo Motel – See Gardner's Motel

Pullman Auto Court – 1930 East Washington Street

The Pullman Auto Court was accepting guests by 1930. The court consisted of seventeen long and narrow cabins utilized as rental units. It also contained a four-room cottage used as the owner's quarters.

The Pullman was out of business by 1961 and demolished in short order. Today a modern industrial building is located on the property.

Pyramid Motel circa 1965 (Author's Collection)

The Pyramid Motel operating as a TraveLodge in 2012 (Photo by Author)

Pyramid Motel – 3307 East Van Buren Street

The Pyramid Motel was opened in 1960. The motel was built in two-story motor inn style. Rooms were configured in one strip along the west property line. The initial construction included twenty rooms, the lobby and manager's quarters, and a fifty-foot pool. By 1965 the Pyramid had thirty units to rent.

The facility retained the Pyramid name through 2010. It then became a Travelodge. In 2013 the Pyramid Motel building was added to the United Methodist Outreach Missions (UMOM) New Day Center facility next door. The UMOM location now consists of the former Bagdad Inn, the Caravan Inn East, and the Pyramid motels.

Rainbow Auto Court – 2022 East Van Buren Street

The Rainbow Auto Court was opened in 1929. Little is known about this court since limited historical data is available. However, it's very likely that the facility was built in the cabin court style. At the time of construction, virtually all auto courts utilized this style. The Rainbow was gone by 1939.

Today the property is part of the I-10 easement where it meets Van Buren Street.

Rainbow Motel – See Polly Court

Ramada Coronet Hotel – See Coronet Hotel

Ramada Inn - 3801 East Van Buren Street

The Ramada Inn was opened in 1959 as a resort facility by the five-year-old Ramada Inn organization. The corporate owned facility was Ramada Inn's lead property, as it was located across the street from Ramada's world headquarters and reservation center. The facility was a 250–unit, full-service hotel with all the amenities, including a convention center and miniature railroad. The banquet facilities could accommodate conventions of up to 1,000 people. The hotel was used as both a resort facility for tourists and convention goers, as well as to impress potential franchisees.

Ramada Inn circa 1960 (Author's Collection)

The Ramada Inn was closed in 1990. Demolition of the facility began in 1998, with the property now being utilized by the Gateway Community College complex.

Ranch House Motel circa 1950 (Author's Collection)

The Ranch House (rear building) operating as an adult business in 2012 (Photo by Author)

Ranch House – 2909 East Van Buren Street

By 1946 the Ranch House Motel was open for business. The motel consisted of three buildings. The office and owner's quarters building was near the road. Two guest buildings were built in single-story, strip motel style. They were arranged in an L-configuration.

The Ranch House was closed by 1971. The facility probably closed at least partly because the original owner died in September 1965.

Today the property is an adult business. At least one of the buildings still exists.

Ranchero Motor Motel – 2210 West Buckeye Road

By 1949 the Ranchero Motor Motel was operating on Buckeye Road. The facility was a sixteen-unit, single-story, strip-style motel with a four-bedroom home for the owners. By 1963 the motel became the Red Arrow Motel. The facility was renovated in 1967, and new furnishings were installed. Additional units were added as well.

In 1968 the motel was robbed at gunpoint by a "hippie" wearing a leather jacket with a white cross on the back. The perpetrator warned the manager not to tell the police. It took her seven hours to report the forty-five dollar theft.

By 1978 the Red Arrow became Orta's Apartments and stopped catering to transient guests. It was demolished in the 1990s. The address now holds a modern industrial building.

Rancho De Oro Court – 3325 East Van Buren Street

Open by 1948, the Rancho De Oro was a cabin court with a center courtyard and many trees. By 1958 the property would be demolished to build the Caravan East Motel complex.

Today the area is part of the New Day Center, a facility for the homeless.

Raymond Hotel – 535 East Jefferson Street

By 1928 the Raymond Hotel was in business. It was owned by H.H. Rice and was unusual as it catered strictly to African Americans. Rice was well-versed in the hotel business as he had previously operated a boarding house at Thirty-Five South Second Avenue. The hotel may have been known as the Oregon Hotel for a couple of years, around 1933. By 1935 it became the Rice's Hotel. The facility also operated an annex located a couple of doors down at 527 East Jefferson Street. It is rumored that famous black Americans like Jackie Robinson and Louis Armstrong stayed at the hotel. Rice also purchased the Bonner Hotel.

The Rice Hotel was long-lived, but by 1982 it was closed and soon demolished.

Today the Jefferson Street easement has moved. The real estate the Raymond Hotel stood on is where the Chase Field parking structure is located and in the new Jefferson Street easement.

Reading Hotel – See Colonial Hotel

Red Arrow Motel – See Ranchero Motor Motel

Deserama Motel, formerly the Red Barn Motel, circa 1970 (Author's Collection)

Red Barn Motel – 2853 East Van Buren Street

The Red Barn Motel opened in 1957 and included 52 rooms. Construction style was single-story, strip-motel as this style had gained popularity and appeared more modern. The Red Barn was built partially upon the former Sahuaro Court grounds. The Red Barn included a restaurant as part of the complex as well.

In 1964 the Red Barn became the Deserama Motel. The Deserama made the papers in 1971 when a guest was issued a drug charge. An employee of the motel noticed a man place a carton of milk on the window sill of room number 33. Police were called to investigate and four ounces of heroin, valued at $100,000, was found inside. The guests in the room were brought up on federal drug charges, but a court eventually dismissed them.

The Deserama was closed and demolished in 2007. It is now just another vacant lot.

Red Horse Motel – 4130 East Van Buren Street

The Red Horse Motel was in operation by 1949. The facility utilized single-story, strip-style construction. There were twelve units and a two-room manager's quarters. By

1955 the motel's name had changed to the El Don Motel. Additions were made to the motel in the 1960s by extending the building to front and rear.

The El Don was out of business by 1984 and demolished by 1986. Today the real estate holds a modern office building.

Red Mug Motel – See Hodges Court

Red Rooster Motel – See Desert Rest Motel

Red Wing Court – 1898 West Buckeye Road

By 1930 the Buckeye Road Court was in business on the northeast corner of Buckeye Road and Nineteenth Avenue. The court had changed its name to the Red Wing Court by 1934. Individual rental buildings defined the facility as a standard cabin court. It contained about eight cottages arranged in an L-shape. The small court operated until the late 1940s or early 1950s. It was demolished soon after it closed.

Today an automotive parts warehouse is located on the property.

Redman's Guest Lodge, now a residence (Photo by Author 2014)

Redman's Guest Lodge – 53 East Roanoke Avenue

Redman's Guest Lodge was a lodging house utilizing the Redman's home. The facility was a regular house in which the owners rented out rooms and provided meals. By 1968 the facility became the Chancewell Manor Lodge. The Chancewell catered to guests with health problems, specifically arthritis. At this time it was operated by a nurse.

The facility operated until the early 1980s. At that time it moved to a boarding house business model. Today the house still exists as a private residence.

Reeds Court – 2722 West Buckeye Road

By 1946 Reeds Court was in operation. The facility consisted of a cabin court, trailer facilities, and a gas station.

In 1955 a fire destroyed one of the cabins. A couple and their infant narrowly escaped the blaze by climbing through a window.

By 1960 the court became the Golden Boy Mobile Lodge. Obviously it had become more of a trailer facility than auto court. By 1961 the business became the L&E Lodge. This was short-lived and by 1964 the facility moved to an apartment business model.

Today the area is an automotive repair business.

Regency Motel – See Vivian Court

Rest Haven Auto Court – 2230 East Van Buren Street

By 1935 an auto court was in business at 2230 East Van Buren. Originally named Roosevelt Court, the facility consisted of thirteen units built in the cabin court style. The cabins were aligned along the property lines to create a center parking and courtyard area. In 1937 the court gained its long-lived Rest Haven name. By 1966 the facility was closed and quickly demolished.

Today the area is mostly vacant land.

Rex Hotel – 316 East Madison Street

The Rex Hotel was a downtown hotel in business by 1932. The configuration of the hotel is not known. However, it was likely a two-story building with sleeping rooms on the upper floor like most of the other small downtown hotels. By 1951 the Rex Hotel was no longer in business. The building still existed until about 1980 when the Jefferson Street alignment was moved. This necessitated the demolition of the entire block.

Today the area is utilized by the Phoenix Convention Center and Jefferson Street. The location is on the north side of Jefferson Street between Third and Fourth Streets. The location of Jefferson Street at that point is just a few feet north of the old Madison Street alignment.

Rice's Hotel – See Raymond Hotel

Rincon Apartment Hotel – See Moeller Hotel

Rita's Court – See Hodges Court

Rite Spot Court – 2038 East Van Buren Street

Very little is known about the Rite Spot Court. It operated between 1943 and 1950. Newspaper articles show it was open in 1943 when one of the cabins was destroyed by fire. A two-year-old boy was critically burned and his mother injured during a rescue.

The Rite Spot may have been absorbed into another motel or simply demolished. Today the land once occupied by the Rite Spot is part of the I-10 easement where it meets Van Buren Street.

The former Ritz Hotel as it looks today (Photo by Author 2014)

Ritz Hotel – 642 North Third Avenue

By 1931 the Ritz Hotel was operating. It utilized a large, two-story home that was built in 1901. Rooms were both heated and cooled. The hotel also offered a dining room. In 1940 the hotel was renamed the Phoenician. It operated as a hotel until the mid-1960s when it moved to an apartment business model.

Today the Ritz building still exists as a home.

Ritz Tourist Court – See Motel Inn

Riverside Court – 67 West Watkins Road

The Riverside Court started as a home. By 1943 five cabins existed on the property as rentals. About 1955 the area took on the name Riverside as it was close to the Salt River. The property contained many trees and was advertised as comfortable and shady. By 1960 the court operated twenty-two rental units.

The court closed by 1969 and was quickly demolished. Today the area is partly industrialized and partly vacant.

Roberts Auto Court – 2201 West Buckeye Road

By 1930 the Roberts Auto Court was in business. The facility was a small cabin court with several cabins for rent. By 1948 the court no longer rented cabins to the transient market. It was soon cleared of its cabins, and an auto auction company was started on the property.

Today the real estate holds a used truck sales business.

Robinhood Motel – See Zila Motel

Rock Center Motel – See Grand Avenue Court

Rodeway Inn on Grand Avenue circa 1970 (Author's Collection)

The former Rodeway Inn, now operating as a US Vets location (Photo by Author 2014)

Rodeway Inn – 3400 Grand Avenue

The Rodeway Inn on Grand Avenue was the second Rodeway to be opened in Phoenix. Rodeway Inns was a Phoenix-based chain, which was started in 1962. The facility was built in two-story, motor hotel style, and opened in 1968. The colonial designed facility held 84 rental units in a three-building complex.

The Rodeway became a Howard Johnsons Motel by 1997. This lasted several years until the facility became an Americas Best Value Inn by 2007. In 2012 the former Rodeway Inn was renovated and became a US Vets location. US Vets provides housing for homeless veterans.

Rodeway Inn – 424 West Van Buren Street

The nation's first Rodeway Inn was opened on West Van Buren Street in 1962. This was the start of another Phoenix-based motel chain that Mike Robinson was involved in. The facility was constructed in two-story motor inn style. The layout utilized a space-saving modified U-configuration.

The Rodeway Inn, circa 1965 (Author's Collection)

The Rodeway Inn operates as the Americas Best Inn today (Photo by Author 2012)

By 1967 the motel was renamed the Kelly Inn. Kelly Inns were another new Phoenix-based chain. By 1979 the motel changed names again, this time to the Budget Inn. Finally, by 2010 the motel had become the Americas Best Value Inn. The motel operates as such today with its original buildings intact.

Rodeway Inn Airport – 1202 South Twenty-Fourth Street

The construction of the Rodeway Inn at Sky Harbor Airport was approved in September 1968. Construction began soon afterward, and the hotel opened in late 1969. The facility contained 142 units built in two-story motor inn style. The Rodehouse Restaurant and Lounge opened in January 1970 and completed the facility. The hotel was the third Rodeway Inn to be built in Phoenix. Rodeway Inns was a Phoenix-based hotel chain.

By 1998 the hotel had been demolished and a parking lot built in its place. The parking lot remains today as the Copperhead Lot. The current location of the lot is the Southwest corner of Buckeye Road and Copperhead Drive. The Twenty-Fourth Street easement was moved in 2000 due to an airport expansion.

Rogers Guest Home – 373 North Second Avenue

The Rogers Guest Home was a house that accepted mostly convalescent guests. It was in operation by 1935. The house was used previously as a minor boarding house by the Zook family. About 1958 the facility was demolished and became a parking lot for the YMCA. It remains so today.

Romney Motor Hotel – See Chilton Inn

Romney Sun Dancer Hotel – See Sun Dancer Hotel

Romona Hotel – 319 East Washington Street

In 1920 the Romona Theatre was opened as new construction where the old Gold Hotel stood. The complex included many other businesses under the Romona name. For a couple of years, furnished rooms were rented at the rear of the building under the name Romona Hotel.

Today the area is part of the Phoenix Convention Center.

Roosevelt Court – See Rest Haven Auto Court

Roosevelt Hotel – 724 East Roosevelt Street

The Roosevelt Hotel was opened in 1947. The hotel operated nine units, but the configuration of the building is not known. It did offer a pool and laundry facilities. By 1953 the facility became the Roosevelt Apartments and no longer accepted short-term renters. The facility was demolished in the late 1950s.

A commercial building built in 1961 is currently on the real estate.

Rose Alice Motor Court – See Dew Drop Inn

Rose Bowl Motor Court circa 1940 (Author's Collection)

Rose Bowl Motor Court – 2645 East Van Buren Street

The Rose Bowl Motor Court opened in 1939 as part of Van Buren's motel row. It was built in the cabin court style utilizing individual buildings. Tile roofs and stucco gave the facility a Spanish look.

The Rose Bowl made the news in 1944 when a car was stolen from the property. The thieves had also robbed a gas station at Twenty-First Street and Van Buren.

The adjacent Lazy A Motel shared the Rose Bowl's address starting in 1967. They operated as separate motels until 1984 when the Lazy A name was dropped, and its rooms became part of the Rose Bowl.

By 1991 the Rose Bowl Motel closed, and it was demolished by 1998. Today the property is part of the Salvation Army complex.

Rose Court – See Colorado Court

The Rose Lane Village, now condominiums (Photo by Author 2014)

Rose Lane Village – 6135 North Central Avenue

The Rose Lane Village was built as apartments on the corner of Rose Lane and Central Avenue. The facility utilized separate two- and three-bedroom buildings as rental apartments. Amenities included carports, shuffleboard, and a swimming pool. It was advertised as "complete hotel service if desired" through the 1950s and 1960s. By 1972 the facility became condominiums.

Today the buildings still exist as condominiums.

Rose Marie Motel circa 1950 (Author's Collection)

Rose Marie Motel – 4127 East Van Buren Street

The Rose Marie Motel opened by 1949. The facility utilized cabin construction with individual buildings as units. Covered parking was available between the cottages. The Rose Marie also rented trailer pads in the rear.

By 1986 the Rose Marie was closed and demolished. Today the property is a parking area.

Rose Tourist Court – 1549-55 West Van Buren Street

By 1929 the Rose Tourist Court was in business. The facility was a cabin-style court with ten cabins and a home. The cabins were placed all around the perimeter of the property. Mary Schabel was the longtime owner and operator of the facility until her death in 1966.

In 1939 thieves knocked out a window screen, blinded the guest in the cabin with a flashlight, and stole his pants. The teenage culprits had committed crimes all over the area and were eventually caught. They apparently stole pants due to the fact that pants usually contain cash.

The Rose Court was closed and demolished shortly after Mary's death in 1966. A funeral home chapel now sits on the property where the Rose Tourist Court once stood.

Rosewood Village Motel – See Dew Drop Inn

Rosser Tourist Court – See Weber Court

Rosswell Hotel – 1949 East Van Buren Street

Very little is known about the Rosswell Hotel. It was located on the corner of East Van Buren and Twentieth Street. The facility was a large home that was utilized as a hotel starting about 1920. It became a residence again by 1925.

Today a gas station resides on the property.

Round Up Ranch – See Hialeah Court

The Rounds Rest operating as apartments in 2012 (Photo by Richard Christensen)

Rounds Rest Motel – 3318 (3336) West Buckeye Road

The Rounds Rest Motel was in business by 1948. The facility included ten one- and two-bedroom units. Each unit was fitted with a kitchenette.

By 1972 the Rounds Rest was no longer in the motel business. Today the buildings still exist and are used as apartments.

Route 80 Motel – See Alanoma Lodge

Royal Crest Lodge – 1015 South Seventeenth Avenue

The Royal Crest Lodge was opened in 1938 as the Apartment Hotel. The facility utilized cabin court construction with cottages of up to five rooms. By 1941 the court was renamed the Kitchenette Court. The facility became the Royal Crest Lodge by 1948. The court became the J&E Motel by 1976. By 1983 the court was renamed as the Las Casitas Motel. This was short lived as the facility went to an apartment business concept by 1984.

The Royal Crest was demolished by 2009. Today the real estate where the Royal Crest Lodge once stood is a modern apartment complex.

The Royal Palms Bungalows operating as apartments in 2012 (Photo by Author)

Royal Palms Bungalows – 108 North Twenty-First Avenue (2105 West Monroe Street)

The Royal Palms Bungalows were in operation by 1930. The facility contained eight large cottages with multiple rooms. They were rented as apartments through the years. However, they were advertised to tourists from 1945 to 1947. The attempt to utilize the facility as a motel may have worked, but it certainly was short-lived.

The construction of the court was of high-quality brick. This is evident in the court's longevity. The facility still operates as apartments with the original buildings.

Royal Palms Inn circa 1950 (Author's Collection)

Royal Palms Inn – 5200 East Camelback Road

The Royal Palms began as a winter home for Delos Cooke, a New York financier and his family. Cooke built a fifteen-room mansion on the property and imported 900 palm trees from the Middle East. The mansion was completed in 1929 and utilized Spanish Colonial design. Cooke did not enjoy the property for long as he passed away in 1931. Ownership varied until the mid-1940s when the property was purchased with the intent to develop it as a resort. In 1948 the facility was opened and quickly became one of the premier resorts in the Phoenix area. Many celebrities such as Groucho Marx stayed at the 100-room resort. In 1959 the resort became part of the Alsonette hotel chain joining the Jokake Inn and Paradise Inn, which were already Alsonette Hotels. In 1995 the property was purchased by Fred Unger who renovated the facility.

Today the Royal Palms still operates as an upscale resort.

Royal View Motel – 4107 (4065) East Van Buren Street

The Royal View Motel began with rental units in three buildings that were close to the road. It was in operation by 1949, and soon large cabins in the rear were added along with trailer pads. The motel changed names in 1964 to the Green Glen Motel. The property then went through an array of name changes, including Esler's Motel, Nod-Away Motel, J&J Motel, and the Van Buren Inn. The facility even closed for a while in the early1970s. The motel was closed for good by 1984 and then demolished.

Today the area is an undeveloped lot.

Rung Motel – 1120 Olmstead Lane (Vogul Avenue)

The Rung Motel was originally known as the LaGonda Apartments. About 1955 the apartments took on the motel name and were marketed as such. By 1960 the motel name was dropped, and the facility was once again apartments. The motel was located just off Cave Creek Road on what is now Vogul Avenue.

Today the area is industrial. The original building was demolished about 1990.

Ruth Street Court – 17 East Ruth Avenue

The Ruth Street Court was in operation by 1951. The facility was a cottage court located on the Arizona Canal. The court operated as apartments for the most part, but did accept short-term renters. This lasted into the mid-1960s when it returned to an apartment business model.

The court was demolished in the 1980s. Today the property is a modern apartment complex.

RV Motel – 2133 East Van Buren Street

By 1947 the RV Motel was in operation. The facility was a small, single-story, strip-style motel. A two-story owner's quarters and office was built into the center off the strip. In 1951 the motel changed its name to the Irish Motel. The Irish Motel was closed by 1986 and demolished by 1990. The property is part of the El Capri night club complex today, which immediately replaced the motel.

S&H Court – See Gingham Dog Court

Sagebrush Inn – See Benson Lodge

Sahara Hotel circa 1960 (Author's Collection)

Sahara Hotel – 401 North First Street

The Sahara Hotel was opened in early 1956 as part of the Flamingo Hotels chain. The facility was a large complex with buildings up to four stories. The hotel included convention facilities and resort amenities along with two penthouse suites. One such penthouse suite was used by Marylyn Monroe in 1956 while filming in Phoenix.

The Sahara became part of the Ramada Inn chain even though it retained its name as the owners of the Flamingo chain were also involved in the creation of the Ramada Inn chain. The hotel soon became the Ramada Sahara Hotel and in 1977 became known as the Ramada Inn - Downtown. The Ramada Inn became a dormitory for the downtown campus of Arizona State University in 2006. The facility closed in 2008 and was purchased by the City of Phoenix and Arizona State University in 2010.

The Sahara was demolished in 2010 to create a downtown parking lot. The university plans to use the property in the future for expanding the downtown campus.

Sahuaro Court – See Aut-O-Tel Camp

St. Elmo Lodging House – See Glenwood Lodging House

St. Francis – See Steinegger Lodging House

The St. James building in 2012 (Photo by Author)

St. James Hotel – 21 East Madison Street

The St. James Hotel was built in 1929. It utilized two-story brick construction with a distinctive neon hotel sign located in the front center. Of course the neon portion may have been added at a later date. The hotel was a popular, moderately priced property when first built. Through the years it serviced lower and lower quality clientele. By 2005 the hotel was closed.

The City of Phoenix instituted a morality ordinance that was enforced throughout the city in its early years. This was instituted to help stop prostitution in the city. Looking through arrest records of the area, it appears that most lodging facilities experienced vice arrests at some time or another. The St. James was no exception. In 1944 records show that a fourteen-year-old girl who was married for four months was arrested along with a Corporal from Luke Field. They were charged with a violation of the city's morals ordinance. Many times the arrests were made at the request of the hotel management or other guests.

The hotel was purchased by the owners of the Phoenix Suns in 2005. In 2012 the St. James Hotel was slated for demolition to produce a parking lot for the nearby US Airways Center. After demolishing the Madison Hotel next door, and some activism by preservationists, the owners decided not to demolish the St. James. The agreement is to save a small portion of the hotel for posterity. The hotel is listed on the National Register of Historic Places.

St. Louis Hotel – 607 East Jefferson Street

The St. Louis Hotel started in business in 1923. The facility included a café and offices, and was built in the familiar downtown hotel style with interior room entrances. The St. Louis catered to the African American business market.

By 1977 the hotel was closed and demolished. Chase Field utilizes the real estate today.

Salt River Hotel – see Alturas Hotel

Samoan Village Motor Hotel circa 1965 (Author's Collection)

Samoan Village – 3901 East Van Buren Street

The Samoan Village Motor Hotel was built in 1963 on part of the former Autopia Motor Park grounds. The facility utilized motor inn style, two-story construction in a U-shape. A central recreational area was decorated in a Polynesian theme. The complex utilized grass buildings, natural wood beams, lava rock wall covering, and simulated grass wallpaper. A restaurant, lounge, and banquet facilities were included at a total construction cost of $750,000.

A name change took place in 1973 with the Samoan Village becoming the Aloha Resort. The Aloha Resort remained until 1982 when the facility was closed. By 1996 the buildings were demolished.

Today the property once used by the Samoan Village is part of the Gateway College campus.

The San Antonio Court, vacant, in 2012 (Photo by Author)

San Antonio Court - 2134 West Washington Street

The San Antonio Court was open by 1929. The facility consisted of six brick cottages and an owner's quarters in the rear. It appears the San Antonio was built as part of a three-court complex, including the Washington and Hollywood courts. It's likely the same developer built them to sell separately. By 1931 the facility became the Dobson Court.

By 1955 the court was split into two facilities. The west three cottages remained the Dobson Court, and the east three became the Pollard Court. The Pollard Court was assigned the address 2124 West Washington. It appears both courts were still under the same ownership. The Dobson units were quickly marketed as apartments under the name Erb Apartments.

By 1964 the Pollard Court became apartments along with the Erb Apartments. Today the San Antonio buildings still exist but are vacant.

San Carlos Hotel still operates today. (Photo by Author, 2012)

San Carlos Hotel – 202 North Central Avenue

The San Carlos was one of the large downtown hotels built prior to the Great Depression. Up until that time most construction was concentrated in the downtown area. Phoenix experienced a building boom in the 1920s. The hotel was opened in March 1928 and consisted of seven stories with an owner's penthouse on top. It was built in the Italian Renaissance style with 128 rental rooms. The hotel was built on the property previously utilized for the first Phoenix school.

When the San Carlos opened, it was the most modern and upscale lodging facility in the city. It featured elevators and air conditioning, both firsts for a high rise hotel in Phoenix. Rooms were fitted with water taps that delivered ice-chilled water. Many celebrities stayed at the San Carlos, including Mae West, Marylyn Monroe, Clark Gable, Humphrey Bogart, and Cary Grant.

The ground floor featured the lobby, a restaurant, and lounge. An outdoor pool was located on the third floor for privacy. Space was also rented to various businesses through the years, including a shoe store, a barber shop, and a ladies apparel store.

Today the San Carlos Hotel still operates as a boutique hotel property. It was fully renovated in 2003. The facility competes for the downtown convention-goer and corporate business, but is also popular with history and ghost buffs. Supposed paranormal activity is said to take place due to a woman jumping to her death from the roof in 1929. The San Carlos is a rare example of Phoenix lodging history that is still functioning in its original capacity and still well kept.

Sandman Motel circa 1970 (Author's Collection)

Sandman Motel – 2120 West Van Buren Street

In 1947 the Palmesa Hotel Court was in operation. By 1955 the facility had expanded and became the Sandman Motel. Thirty units were built in two-story motor hotel style. The rooms were studio-style with a combination living room and bedroom. Twenty-five of the units were equipped as kitchenettes.

The Sandman Motel still operates today (Photo by Author 2012)

The Sandman still functions as a motel under its original name and utilizes the original buildings.

Sands Hotel circa 1960 (Author's Collection)

Sands Hotel - 3400 East Van Buren Street

The Sands Hotel complex was opened in early 1955 as a large resort with two-story motor inn style buildings. The resort was modeled after a Hilton located in Havana Cuba, a popular vacation destination at the time. All rooms faced a large central recreational area and had either a patio or balcony. This configuration was new at the time, and many resort hotels would incorporate the design in future years. The complex also incorporated convention facilities, office space, and stores.

In 1992 the Sands Hotel became the New Day Center operated by the United Methodist Outreach Missions (UMOM) under a lease agreement. In 1994 UMOM purchased the complex. The original Sands Hotel buildings were demolished in 2009 to make room for a new UMOM housing project, Legacy Crossing.

Santa Fe Motel circa 1960 (Author's Collection)

Santa Fe Motel – 3048 (3820) Grand Avenue

The Santa Fe Motel was in business by 1949. The facility utilized a combination of cottage and single-story, strip motel construction. The motel was under the same ownership as the adjacent Circle L Motel.

In June of 1961 a terrible storm struck the valley. During the storm four of the motel's fourteen units were destroyed by fire.

The Santa Fe Motel was closed by 1976 and demolished by 1981. Today the real estate the Santa Fe once sat on is an auto auction facility.

Santa Fe Rooms – 302 South Seventh Avenue

The Santa Fe Rooms was accepting guests by 1914. It was a two-story building located just north of the Santa Fe railroad tracks. Like most of the early downtown hotels, the Santa Fe operated for many years as a standard hotel. The older hotels that survived usually became run-down and catered to the lowest-price clientele. This was the case with the Santa Fe.

In 1956 the hotel operator, C.W. Wallace, addressed a meeting on proposed new housing codes. The new regulations would require a bathroom for every eight rooms and an electrical outlet in each hotel room. Wallace told the attendees that his hotel only had one bathroom and 75 rooms. He also stated that the hotel was admittedly a flophouse but the new law would put his guests on the street and shut down the hotel. A month later the hotel was in receivership.

By 1961 the Santa Fe was no longer in business. It was demolished within the decade. Today a machine shop is located at the address.

Sargent's Court – 1014 South Seventeenth Avenue

Sargent's Court was opened in 1938. The facility utilized cabin court construction with brick cottages. In the early years the facility included a fish pond. A grocery store was also located on the property.

By 1962 the court was no longer in business. The grocery store continued to serve the area for some time. It appears that the cabins were rented as apartments for many years after.

The facility was razed in the early 1980s. Today the real estate is undeveloped.

Savoy Hotel circa 1925 (Courtesy McClintock Collection, Arizona Room, Phoenix Public Library)

Savoy Hotel – 38 South Second Avenue

By 1920 the Savoy Hotel was in operation. The facility was a three-story structure that held 54 sleeping rooms. It was built on the site of the former Nordrach Rooming House.

In 1935, a 74-year-old man was injured by his own gun shots at the Savoy. He entered his wife's room and began firing his pistol at her. The 29-year-old woman was uninjured.

The Savoy underwent a $30,000 remodel in 1936. The hotel was refurnished, air conditioning was added, and a twenty-six-foot neon sign was added to the roof. The renovations modernized the facility and left it one of the better mid-priced hotels in the city.

In August of 1939 the hotel entered into a lease agreement with Milner Hotels, Inc. Milner operated 137 hotels at the time and would soon become the largest hotel chain in the world. The hotel was renamed the Milner Hotel. By 1950 the hotel was renamed as the Earle Hotel. It was still under a lease with Milner Hotels, but the company utilized the names Earle, Reed, and Milner in its chain. It was determined the Earle Hotel name was a better fit for the property.

In 1956, two years before the Milner Hotels lease was up, the owner offered the hotel to the City of Phoenix for $180,000. Upon completion of the lease in 1958 the city approved the purchase and began utilizing the property for office space. The final sale price was $178,900. The hotel was demolished in the 1960s.

Today the area contains the Calvin C. Goode Municipal Building. Second Avenue no longer exists in that area.

Schell & Gish Rooming House – 714 East Polk Street

The rooming house at 714 East Polk was operating by 1916. The facility was a collection of small homes and apartments. Thirteen rooms were available for rent. The house quickly went to an apartment business plan. The buildings were demolished in the 1960s.

Today the Arizona State University Preparatory Academy utilizes the property.

Sea Breeze Tourist Village circa 1940 (Author's Collection)

Sea Breeze Motor Inn - 2701 East Van Buren Street

The Sea Breeze opened in 1938 with an early use of two-story motor inn style construction. The facility also had a cabin area near the pool and recreation area. Old photos show that the facility was expanded at some point with the addition of new guest room buildings. The facility was also part of the Best Western referral chain.

The Sea Breeze had an unusual name for a desert motel until you realize it was owned by the SeBree family. The Sea Breeze was purchased by an adjacent lodging property, the Desert Hills Motor Inn. The new owners demolished the Sea Breeze buildings in 1965 to make way for a major expansion which included a convention center. The property, which was once the Sea Breeze Motor Inn, is now owned by the Salvation Army.

Seaside Court – See Kozy Kourt

Seattle Hotel – See Thibodo House

The Sefton Hotel, now operates as offices (Photo by Author 2014)

Sefton Hotel – 1308 East Van Buren Street

The Sefton Hotel was built in 1949. The property was different from most Van Buren properties as it was built in true hotel-style with interior entrances.

The original owners of the property, Robert and Ina Sefton, were reported missing in March of 1961. The couple had not returned from a fishing trip to Tiburon Island, Mexico. An air-sea search was conducted by the United States Coast Guard. Mexican officials located the Sefton's car at a marina in Puerto Penasco where they kept their sixteen-foot boat. On March 26th, the Sefton's bodies were found on the shore near Puerto Penasco.

The Sefton Hotel continued to operate through 1969. The building has had several uses through the years. It received an exterior renovation in 2014, and functions as offices today.

Seidler Court – See Copemoar Court

Seventeenth Avenue Court – 1408 North Seventeenth Avenue

Cabins were being rented at 1408 North Seventeenth Avenue by 1938. The court may have been rented as apartments for the first few years. Eventually it took on the Seventeenth Avenue Court name and started catering to transient guests. The facility was a cabin court with nine rental units.

By 1970 the court was no longer in business. It was demolished before 1976. Today the address is a parking lot.

Seventh Avenue Hotel – See West End House

Seventh Street Hotel – 313 South Seventh Street

The Seventh Street Hotel was a short-lived lodging facility. It was open by 1917 and became a grocery store and restaurant by 1923. The size and configuration of the hotel are not known.

Today a wholesale food service business is located on the property.

Shady Haven Court – 501 North Seventeenth Street

By 1948 the Shady Haven Court was operating. The facility included a few cabins and trailer spaces. The Shady Haven concentrated on trailers and by 1957 the cabins became long-term rentals.

Today the area is not developed.

Shady Lane Court – 3250 (4240) Grand Avenue

The Shady Lane Court was accepting guests by 1936. The facility consisted of a cabin-type court, a trailer park, and a grocery store.

In 1946 a kerosene stove started a fire in one of the cabins. Two children were inside at the time while their mother was at a nearby cabin rented by her mother-in-law. The mother entered the blazing cabin and rescued her two-month-old baby girl. She re-entered the cabin twice more, but was not able to save her seventeen-month-old daughter. She could hear the child's cries, but was unable to find her. The child was later found under her bed where she hid from the flames.

The Shady Lane Court was no longer providing lodging by 1951. The area was cleared of buildings in the 1950s. The property is part of the Costco complex on Grand Avenue today.

Shady Park Auto Camp circa 1927 (Author's Collection)

Shady Park Motel – 1937 East Van Buren Street

By 1926 the Shady Park Auto Camp had been established. This was another early camp that catered to the new motoring tourists. The camp soon added rental cabins and around 1939 changed their name to Shady Park Auto Court. This was a necessary move to stay competitive in the area.

Although the Shady Park retained its cabin court layout, the facility was renamed the

Shady Park Motel in the late 1950s. There is no doubt this was a change to remain competitive, at least in advertising and reservations.

The Shady Park closed by 1989, and all remnants of the facility were demolished by 2007. Today the area is an undeveloped lot.

Shafer Hotel – See Williams Hotel

Shannon Court – 2160 East Van Buren Street

Shannon Court was an early and long-standing auto court that appeared by 1927. The facility initially started as an auto camp and grocery store. Auto camps were the usual alternative to hotels at the time. They provided basic amenities to traveling campers.

By 1932, Shannon Auto Camp had added cabin court facilities and changed their name to Shannon Auto Court. The court was laid out in a large U-shape following the lot lines of the property. The Shannon Court operated for many years, finally being closed and demolished by 1977.

Today the area is a used car lot facility.

Sharon Court – See Wingfoot Court

Shaughnessy Auto Court – 1508 Grand Avenue (1106 North Fifteenth Avenue)

By 1928 the Shaughnessy Auto Court was operating on Grand Avenue. The facility was built in the usual cabin court style of the time. About a dozen cabins were placed along Fifteenth Avenue and another dozen placed in a parallel line to the west. An area in between comprised an oval drive for cabin access. The Shaughnessys quickly eliminated the row of cabins along Fifteenth Avenue to introduce new businesses on their property. By 1961 the remaining court converted to an apartment-style business plan.

Today the area is multiple-use and at least one cabin still exists.

Shelton Court – 1429 South Seventh Street

The Shelton Court was in business by 1949. The small facility was built in cabin court style with seven cabins. All cabins were lined up along the property line with ample space between them.

By 1953 the court moved to an apartment business plan and stopped advertising to short-term renters. The cabins were demolished in the 1960s.

Today an industrial pipe company is located at the address.

Shir-Mar Court – See Johnsons Court

Silver Arrow Court circa 1935 (Author's Collection)

Silver Arrow Court – 2017 (2013) West Van Buren Street

By 1930 the Las Casitas Auto Court was in business on West Van Buren Street. The facility was built in cabin court style. A mixture of Spanish styling and heavy art deco architecture defined the property. By 1935 the facility was renamed the Silver Arrow Court.

The Silver Arrow was closed by 1987 and demolished by 1990.

Silver Bell Court – 1735 Grand Avenue

The Silver Bell Court was in operation by 1937. The facility had been rented as apartments for some time prior to 1937. It appears that the court was a mix of different size cabins and cottages with up to five rooms. Trailer and pad rentals were also added to the court in later years. By 1952 the court changed its name to the Standard Motel.

The Standard Motel was closed and demolished in 1958 to make room for the construction of the Hiway Inn. Today the property still holds the Hiway Inn buildings which are utilized as homeless housing.

Silver Crest Court – 2025 East Monroe Street

By 1952 there were apartments being rented at 2025 East Monroe. These would be the start of the Silver Crest Court. The court consisted of ten brick apartments in one- and two-bedroom configurations.

In 1965 a long-term guest at the Silver Crest was killed in his room. He accused his girlfriend of looking at other men and attacked her. She retaliated by fatally stabbing him twice with a pocket knife.

The Silver Crest catered more and more to apartment dwellers and by 1967 it was strictly apartments. Today the real estate is part of the I-10 easement.

Silver Dollar Court - 2529 East Van Buren Street

The Silver Dollar Court was opened in 1941 as an auto court style facility. The individual cabins were created in a Spanish style. At some point in time, the space between the cabins was utilized to create more rental rooms. This method was popular as it made the facility look more modern, like a strip-style motel. The facility still retained its Spanish-style facade.

Sun Villa Court, formerly the Silver Dollar Court, circa 1955 (Author's Collection)

The only part left of the Silver Dollar Court is the office building (Photo by Author 2012)

The Silver Dollar changed its name to the Silver Moon Court in 1948. This was to last only a short time since the name changed again in 1950 to the Sun Villa Court.

The Sun Villa made headlines in late 1964 when the husband and wife owners were discovered murdered at the motel. Their sixteen-year-old son was later convicted of tying them up and murdering them by stabbing and shooting the couple.

The Sun Villa closed in 1997 and was later used as apartments. Most of the facility was demolished in 2005. Only the office remains in an otherwise vacant lot.

Silver Moon Court - See Silver Dollar Court

Silver Spur Motel – See Flint Motel

Six Points Auto Camp – 1810 Grand Avenue

The Six Points Auto Camp was renting cabins by 1928. The facility was a cabin court with about a dozen buildings. The court gained its name due to its proximity to the intersection of Grand Avenue and Nineteenth Avenue known as the Six Points area.

In 1939 a man was shot in the head at the court. He survived his injury. The perpetrator told police the man had attempted to strike him. The shooter was arrested and charged with intent to commit murder. The charges were dropped when the shooter was found to be insane and committed to the state hospital.

The Six Points was closed by 1950, and the buildings were demolished. The address now holds a spa supply business.

Sixth Avenue Hotel – 546 West Adams Street

The Sixth Avenue Hotel opened in 1893 at the northeast corner of Adams Street and Sixth Avenue. The dining room opened on April first that year and featured an Easter dinner. The dining room was run by the former operator of the Can Can Restaurant in Tombstone. The original build included 40 rooms in a brick, two-story structure. By 1915 the hotel was renamed the Bassler Hotel. In 1920 it became the Navajo Hotel under a lease agreement. The lease holder gave up the lease in June of 1923, and the hotel's contents were auctioned off. After a renovation, the facility became the Windsor

Hotel that same year. In 1935 the hotel received a major upgrade and exterior modernization. The third floor was completed, and a deco façade was created on the building. Around 1950 the hotel was remodeled again and was given the name the New Windsor Hotel.

Windsor Hotel, formerly the Sixth Avenue Hotel, circa 1940 (Author's Collection)

The Sixth Avenue, still operating as the New Windsor in 2012 (Photo by Author)

The New Windsor is listed on the National Register of Historic Places. It still operates as a hotel, and caters to low income and elderly patrons. Some of its residents have lived there for many years.

Sky Harbor Court – See Gingham Dog Court

The Sky Harbor View Court operating as apartments in 2012 (Photo by Author)

Sky Harbor View Court – 2532 East Washington Street

By 1940 cabins were being built at 2532 East Washington. The Sky Harbor View Court held ten cabins and twenty-two trailer spaces by 1945. An additional small, strip-style motel building was added by 1949.

By 1985 the facility became the Sky Harbor Apartments. The Sky Harbor View buildings still exist today and are still rented as apartments. The facility is one of only a few examples left of early mixed-use lodging facilities that are still in good condition. Phoenix literally had hundreds of these types of businesses at one time.

Sky Riders Hotel circa 1965 (Author's Collection)

Sky Riders Hotel – 2901 Sky Harbor Boulevard

The Sky Riders Hotel was opened in 1954 with 44 rental units built in two-story motor inn style. The facility was located on leased airport property and was advertised as the first airport hotel in the world. It was literally the first building next to the terminal. In 1954 the hotel expanded by adding another 35 rooms. Hotel owners in Phoenix protested the expansion explaining they felt the hotel was unfair competition due to its location on public property. Nevertheless, the addition was approved. The hotel expanded again in 1962 to a total of 180 rooms. The hotel played upon its airport location by decorating in an aviation theme. A pool, lounge, restaurant, and meeting facilities were all located at the hotel.

In 1955 the Sky Riders Hotel was robbed by a pair of thieves, one known to the police as the "pig-eyed robber" due to his distinctive eyes. The night desk workers were tied up and robbed. No one was harmed, but almost one thousand dollars was stolen.

In 1973 the aging Sky Riders Hotel was sold and renovated. Gone was the aviation theme in favor of a southwestern look. Tennis courts were added, the lobby was tripled in size, and the hotel was dubbed the Sheridan Airport Inn.

In 1991 the hotel was demolished as part of the airport improvement plan. This included new terminals and the demolition of the old terminal (terminal number 1). The West Economy outdoor airport parking lot is located on the property which formerly held the Sky Riders Hotel.

Sleepy Hollow Motel – 3035 East Washington Street

The Sleepy Hollow Motel was a small facility built around an existing home. The cottages were placed alongside the home and at the rear of the property. There were about six rental units.

By 1963 the Sleepy Hollow was closed and was demolished in short order. The land has been vacant ever since.

Small Hotel (Second Street) – See Headley Hotel

Small Hotel – 414 West Jefferson Street

The building that became the Small Hotel was the Phelps Apartments for many years. By 1947 it became the hotel. The hotel was a two-story structure with porches. The facility was no longer utilized as a hotel or apartments after the mid-1950s. However, aerial photos show the building still stood for many years. Another hotel became the Small Hotel shortly after the Jefferson Street hotel closed. It is not known if the two hotels had the same ownership.

Today the area is part of the United States District Court complex.

Smith's Hotel – See French Rooming House

Snow White Court – 1320 South Twenty-Fourth Street

The Snow White Court was a small court consisting of just a few cabins. It was in business by 1947 but was short-lived. By 1951 it was no longer advertised.

Due to an airport expansion project, the Twenty-Fourth Street easement was moved in 2000. The area where the Snow White Court once existed is now on Copperhead Drive, south of Buckeye Road. It is part of the airport facilities located south of where the road is closed today.

Sombrero Motel – See Del Ano Motel

Sorrell Court – 2319 West Tonto Street

The Sorrell Court was accepting patrons by 1949. The facility was a cottage court with eleven cottages and a main owner's residence. By the mid-1950s the court started operating on an apartment-only basis. The buildings remained for many years, but were demolished in the 1990s.

Today the area is residential with several homes on the property.

Sourant Lodge – 3279 East Camelback Road

In the early 1950s the large home that existed among the orange groves began to be utilized as a guest lodge. The facility was rural at the time with lush green space and a resort atmosphere. Accommodations included one- and two-room units. A swimming pool was added at some point as well. The Sourant was always marketed as apartments, but did accept shorter term guests through the 1950s. The facility appears to have become apartments-only in the 1960s.

The Sourant Lodge was demolished in the 1970s. New apartments were built and still exist on the property.

Southwest Court – 2137 East Van Buren Street

The Southwest Court was opened in 1938. The facility consisted of twelve individual cottages and ten trailer pads. By 1960 the court was no longer in business, being replaced by Harrys Capri.

Today the property is part of the El Capri dance club complex.

Spiral Motel – See Greenway Manor Court

Spur Motel – See Drake Motel

Stables Motel – 4729 North Seventh Street

By 1953 the Stables Motel was accepting guests. Rooms had already been rented at the existing stables on the property for a few years prior. The Sombrero Playhouse, a theatrical venue, was located next door to the Stables Motel. Because of the Stables proximity to the Sombrero Playhouse, many semi-famous actors stayed at the facility. The motel took full advantage by advertising, "Where the Stars Spend the Winter".

The motel closed by 1965 but was not demolished until the early 1980s. Today the Valley Commerce Center is located on the property.

Stacy Hotel – 203 West Jefferson Street

The Stacy Hotel was operating by 1914. The facility was a two-story brick building. By 1949 the hotel became the Astor Hotel. It lasted until 1962 when it was demolished to make room for a new county government complex.

Today the building on the real estate is the Central Court Building.

Stag Hotel – 27 West Madison Street

The Stag Hotel was built in 1931 on the site of an established rooming house. The facility was a two-story brick building that utilized the art deco styling popular at the time. A restaurant was also located in the building. The hotel was renamed the Patio Hotel by 1935.

The Stag Hotel operating as a restaurant in 2012 (Photo by Author)

In 1942 a hotel night clerk, Frank Mathein, died after a confrontation at the hotel. Mathein attempted to eject two men sleeping in the lobby. An argument ensued and one of the men punched Mathein in the head. The police were summoned and the men were ejected. Mathein claimed he was fine and refused to press charges. A short while later Mathein suffered a fatal stroke.

The Patio Hotel was long-lived, closing by 1982. Today the 1931 building still exists as the Sing High restaurant.

Stag Hotel – 203½ North Central Avenue

In the spring of 1910, the Craig Building was opened on the northeast corner of Central Avenue and Monroe Street. The building was a two-story structure with retail space on the ground floor. The first resident of the ground floor was the Adams Pharmacy. The second floor opened in the early summer of 1910 and became the Stag Hotel. The Stag was considered upscale and catered to "gentlemen only".

A month before the Stag opened, the Adams Hotel nearby was destroyed by fire. The Craig Building was utilized as temporary quarters for the Adams Hotel.

By 1912 the hotel had become the Del Ray Hotel. This name endured for many years, but by 1936 the facility was renamed the Marx Palace Hotel. At some point the facility started accepting female guests.

In 1939, Louise Frederikson, a hotel guest, fell from the hotel balcony. She collided with a parked car and then the concrete. The woman survived and immediately told authorities that she was pushed. Other hotel guests were questioned and some detained. The following day she was in much better health and explained that she had fainted at the railing. She could not remember telling the police she was pushed the previous day. The detained guests were still charged with drunkenness.

By 1969 the hotel was closed. Demolition took place in the 1970s. Today the area where the Stag Hotel stood is a parking area.

Stagecoach Inn Motel – See Aricopa Motel

Stallings Auto Camp – 1710 East Van Buren Street

In 1929 the Stallings Auto Camp opened on East Van Buren Street. It was late for a new facility to call itself an auto camp in 1929 as auto courts were becoming popular. By 1933 the facility was renamed the Home Court. The court was built in the usual cabin style with a central court area. Home Court was not long-lived and by 1939 it was no longer in business. The cabins survived into the early 1980s when they were finally demolished.

The area once occupied by the Stallings Auto Camp is now a used car lot.

Stan's Court – See Tamarack Inn

Standard Motel – See Silver Bell Court

Star Auto Court – 2830 (2908) West Van Buren Street

The Star Auto Court was open by 1931. The facility started out as a six-unit court of unknown construction style. By 1951 the court had become the Bell Motel.

In 1966 a man driving along Van Buren Street had a cardiac arrest. As he passed away the car crashed into the motel and destroyed one of the rooms.

Floyd Smith, the owner of the Bell Motel, was killed in 1973 when he was hit by a car in front of the motel.

The Bell Motel became more and more dependent on long-term rentals. By 1983 the facility was renamed the Bell Apartments. Demolition took place by 1992.

Today there is an auto shop at the location.

Star Lodging House – 47 East Jackson Street

The Star Lodging House was in business by 1893. The facility was of unknown size but did serve food as well as rent sleeping rooms.

In 1899 a man from Michigan arrived at the Star Lodging House. He came to look for his son who had been sending him letters. The son's correspondence espoused his prosperity in Arizona. He explained how he owned a 600-acre ranch near a silver mine, about 20 miles from Phoenix. The man could not locate his son to surprise him. It became apparent that the stories were fantasy as there is no silver mine that close to Phoenix.

In 1906 there was a gun battle at the Star Lodging House. During an argument between two men sharing a room, a pistol was pulled and shots fired. The shooter left the building, shooting at people as he left. He took refuge in an outhouse on the property when police arrived. The man continued to shoot at the police and guests until he was finally apprehended. During the shootout, the man fired approximately 37 shots riddling the hotel with bullets and nearly hitting many people. Miraculously, no one was hurt.

The Hotel also operated an annex located nearby at 11 East Jackson Street. It was known simply as the Star Lodging House Annex. The annex appears to have been utilized from about 1931 through the demise of the facility.

By 1921 the Star Lodging House was no longer renting rooms. Today the area has a warehouse on it.

Star Lodging House Annex – See Star Lodging House

Starlite Motel – See Desert Rest Motel

State Hotel – See Colonial Hotel

State Motor Lodge – See Greenway Manor Court

Steering Wheel Motel – See Lorena Auto Court

Stefford's Cottages - 19 East Alice Street

By 1949 the Stefford's Cottages were in business. The facility consisted of five cottages. By 1955 the court became the Fuller Cottages. Soon three of the cottages were demolished and replaced with a new single-story strip building. The new structure utilized block construction and held six rental units. The name was changed to the Cactus Court when the new building was opened.

By 1965 the court was rented only as apartments. The buildings were demolished in the early 1980s. Today the real estate is undeveloped.

Steinegger Lodging House – 27 East Monroe Street

The Steinegger Lodging House was opened in 1889. It was a two-story brick structure and contained twenty sleeping rooms. Two bathrooms served the hotel guests.

The Steinegger family was one of the original settlers in the Phoenix area. Alexander Steinegger was settled in the area even before Phoenix was created. He participated in the vote for the original town site. He also purchased one of the original lots sold at auction. By trading some his out-of-town property, he was able to procure some downtown real estate.

Steinegger Lodging House circa 1915 (Author's Collection)

By 1897 the facility became the Alamo House. Many times the Alamo House would rent its rooms unfurnished. In 1909 the name changed again to The Francis. A major renovation occurred in 1911 with sixteen additional rooms built. Many of the new rooms included their own bathrooms. The façade of the building was rebuilt in concrete. The facility took on the name St. Francis after the remodel. By 1930 the hotel took on its final name, the Golden West Hotel.

The Steinegger Lodging House in 2012 (Photo by Author)

The Golden West operated until about 2008 when it was closed. The facility had remained in the possession of Alexander Steinegger's heirs for its entire and considerable lifespan. Today the building still exists, but is closed. It is the oldest existing lodging facility building in Phoenix. Attempts are being made by preservationists to save the building.

Stenlake Rooming House – 356 North Fourth Avenue

The Stenlakes likely started renting rooms in late 1904. A dining room was added in 1905. The facility grew to include fifteen sleeping rooms, a dining room, kitchen, a public room, and two bath rooms. By 1948 the property was sold to the Mark family and became the Marks Hotel. By 1959 the facility became the Fourth Avenue Hotel.

The hotel began operating exclusively on an apartment basis by 1980. Demolition occurred in the early 1980s. Today the area is undeveloped.

Steyaert Tourist Home – See Swindall Tourist Home

Stone Motel circa 1950 (Author's Collection)

Stone Motel – 2114 (2044) East Van Buren Street

The Stone Motel was built in 1946. The construction consisted of short, strip motel style buildings with a total of 35 rental units. Each building was covered in stone facing, and the property was fenced with a short stone wall. The facility functioned as a motel and also as a showplace for Barkers Artcraft Stone Company, which was located at the same address.

The address on this property can be confusing. The facility was originally assigned 2044 East Van Buren. However, the motel was located on the northwest corner of Twenty-First Place and Van Buren. This is east of the Twenty-First Street intersection, so it was reassigned to 2114 East Van Buren. After I-10 was built, the 2114 East Van Buren address moved across Twenty-First Place to the east. This is where the address now remains, but it is not the location of the Stone Motel. This location was a Valley National Bank branch at the time the Stone Motel existed.

The Stone Motel operated until the mid-1970s when it was converted to an alcohol and drug recovery center. It was demolished by 1984. The area is now part of the freeway ramp system exiting I-10 and joining Highway 51 and Loop 202.

Stop Motel – 3662 Grand Avenue

The Stop and Park Trailer Park was operating before 1950. However, the trailer park did offer cabin rentals. By 1955 the park became the Stop Motel, a cabin court and trailer park.

In 1956 a family living in the motel met with tragedy. Late one night a family member fell and was hurt. Eight members of the family and three friends loaded themselves in a car and headed for the hospital. Just up the road, the car had a terrible collision with a train at the Thirty-Fifth Avenue crossing. All eleven people lost their lives, five of which were staying at the Stop Motel long-term.

By 1966 the Stop Motel was closed and quickly demolished. A dance club was built on the location and opened in 1967. The club still stands on the property today.

Strand Hotel – See Grand View Hotel

Stroud Rooms – See Hoffman House

Sun Court – 2006 East Van Buren Street

By 1931 the Sun Court was in full operation. The facility was laid out in cabin court style with individual cabins. By 1955 the property had become known as Mary's Motel and by 1958 as the Eldorado Motel. The Eldorado was closed and demolished by 1983.

Today the area is part of the I-10 easement where it meets Van Buren Street.

The Romney Sun Dancer Hotel circa 1970 (Author's Collection)

Sun Dancer Hotel – 803 East Van Buren Street

The Sun Dancer Hotel opened in early 1966. The facility consisted of two buildings. The rear building was three stories and held 41 sleeping rooms. A single-story building in front held the lobby, restaurant, and coffee shop. A lounge was located in a basement, below the lobby.

The Sun Dancer was a partnership agreement between Wayne Romney and another individual. Soon the hotel's name changed to the Romney Sun Dancer Hotel. It's likely the partnership had been dissolved leaving Romney as the owner.

In 1973 the night clerk at the Sun Dancer was robbed at gun point. The robber made off with some money but no one was hurt.

The Sun Dancer kept its name until 1993 when the facility became used as apartments. By 1999 the buildings had been demolished. Today the area is a modern apartment complex.

Sun Down Court – 2330 West Buckeye Road

By 1948 the Sun Down Court was in operation. It was a small, single-story, strip-style building with a two-story section in the center. The two-story portion was likely an owner's quarters.

By 1964 the Court moved to an apartment business model. It was demolished in 2000 and is a parking lot today.

Sun Terrace Court – 3239 West Van Buren Street

The Sun Terrace Court was open by 1948. The facility included ten rental units built for apartment-style buildings. By 1972 the court became an apartment building rather than catering to travelers.

The Sun Terrace was closed by 1984 and demolished by 1996. Today the property is a used car lot.

Sun Valley Court – 2006 East Buckeye Road

By 1953 the Sun Valley Court was advertising to the traveling public. The facility was previously utilized as apartments and was still more of an apartment business than motel. It consisted of thirteen one-bedroom rental units and three store fronts along Henshaw (Buckeye) Road. By 1964 the court took on an apartment business model and became the Sun Valley Court Apartments. The facility's name changed to the Cha Kel Court by 1965. It still functioned mainly as apartments.

The Cha Kel lasted into the 1980s and was demolished by 1986. A parking lot is located on the real estate today.

Sun Valley Court – 2309 West Buckeye Road

By 1947 the Sun Valley Court was operating. It was a small court which included five cabins and a three-bedroom home. The Sun Valley name was dropped about 1952, around the time another facility on Buckeye Road took on the name. After that time the cabins were rented as apartments only.

The Sun Valley Court's office and owners quarters as they look today (Photo by Author 2014)

Today the area is a used car business. The offices are in the original home, but the cabins are long gone.

Sun Valley Motel – See Beach Court

Sun Valley Motel Apartments – 1016 North Third Street

The Sun Valley Motel Apartments was opened as the Beebe Apartments by 1941. The name and business model changed by 1948 when the apartments began operating partially as a motel. The facility consisted of two strip-style apartment buildings that were likely two-story structures.

By 1973 the Sun Valley no longer accepted short-term business. It operated as apartments for some time, but was demolished in the early 1980s. The new Scientology building is located on the property today.

Sun Villa Motel - See Silver Dollar Court

Sunny Lane Motel – 3224 West Monroe Street

The Sunny Lane Motel was a small facility with two duplex buildings. The buildings were originally marketed as apartments. By 1957 the apartments took on the motel name and were being marketed as such. By 1966 the motel stopped operating.

The buildings were razed in the 1980s. Today the area is industrialized.

Sunset Auto Court – 2305 West Van Buren Street

The Sunset Auto Court was a cabin court of which little is known. The court was in operation by 1929 and gone by 1935.

An upholstery shop is located at the address now.

Sunset Motel – 3818 East Van Buren Street

The Sunset Motel opened in 1946. The facility utilized multiple duplex buildings in its construction. Buildings were of Spanish design with walls of stucco. The office and manager's quarters were located in the center of the complex.

The Sunset Motel closed by 1990, and it was demolished by 1992. Today the land is a parking lot.

Sutton Court – 1126 South Nineteenth Avenue

By 1932 the short-lived Sutton Court was in business. The facility was a cabin court with about a dozen units. It became the Harris Court by 1935. By 1938 the court was gone.

Today a fast-food restaurant is on the real estate.

The Swindall Tourist Home built in 1913 still exists (Photo by Author 2012)

Swindall Tourist Home – 1021 East Washington Street

The home located at 1021 East Washington was built in 1913 and utilized intermittently as a tourist home. Rooms for rent at the home were first advertised in 1920 under the Steyaert family ownership. Later, the home was marketed as the Swindall Tourist Home under the Swindall family ownership. This started in 1940 and lasted into the 1980s. Both the Steyaerts and Swindalls catered to African American clientele.

The home still exists today.

Tahiti Inn – 2900 East Van Buren Street

The Tahiti Inn facility consisted of two styles of motels. In 1959 the Franciscan Lodge became the Tahiti Inn Huts. The huts consisted of a cabin court arranged in a U-configuration. The second motel style was located next door and simply called the Tahiti Inn. This facility was a modern, two-story motel built in the motor hotel style. It contained 73 units and was built in 1959.

The Tahiti Inn operating as a TraveLodge in the 1980s (Author's Collection)

The Tahiti Inn operating as a Days Inn in 2012 (Photo by Author)

At some point the huts area was split away from the more modern Tahiti Inn. Today the huts area is a steel company. It's possible to still see the drive that ends at the property line where it led to the huts. One or two huts appear to still exist as offices.

The Tahiti Inn went on to become the Phoenix Airport TraveLodge in 1977. By 2000 the motel was known as the Park Place Motel. By 2004 it was once again a TraveLodge, and finally a Days Inn in 2010. Today the facility still operates as a Days Inn.

Tally-Ho Lodge – See Ford's Motel

Tamarack Court – 4080 (6500) Grand Avenue

The Tamarack Court was in business by 1939. The facility was a cabin court and trailer park.

By 1961 the Tamarack Court was no longer in business. Today the address is a trailer sales facility.

Tamarack Inn – 3006 (3030) West Buckeye Road

By 1941 the Tamarack Inn was operating. The facility was a cabin court with one- and two-room cottages. A grocery store was located on the property, and gas was sold at the facility as well. By 1944 the facility became Fain's Court and then the Evergreen Court by 1950. The name was changed again by 1952 to Stan's Court. Stan's lasted many years, but by 1983 it was out of business. Demolition occurred shortly after it closed.

Today the real estate is vacant.

Tamarisk Court – 1816 (1890) West Buckeye Road

Originally called Millers Court, the Tamarisk Court was in operation by 1930. The facility became Morris Court by 1932 and Tamarisk by 1938. The court consisted of a cabin court utilizing multiple room cottages and a restaurant. It held about a dozen cabins arranged in a U-pattern. By 1960 the Tamarisk was out of business and was soon demolished.

A modern automotive body parts warehouse is located on the property now.

The former Tangier Apartment Motel, now operating as apartments (Photo by Author 2014)

Tangier Apartment Motel – 1402 East Jefferson Street

The Tangier Apartment Motel was opened by 1958. The facility was built in single-story, strip-style construction. It included two buildings aligned parallel to each other. A public area was located between the buildings. By 1965 the facility became the J and R Motel.

The J and R moved to an apartment-only business model by 1983. Today the Tangier buildings still exist and are rented as apartments.

Tent City Auto Camp – 602 North Eighteenth Street (1760 Villa Avenue)

The Tent City Auto Camp was an early auto camp operating by 1923 under the ownership of the Gallsworthy family. It started strictly as a camping facility for motorists and is the first such camp built for the purpose in Phoenix. The facility provided basic amenities such as a space, water, and restroom facilities. The term "tent city" at the time did not have the negative associations it has today. As a matter of fact, a very popular beach resort in San Diego was named Coronado Tent City at the time. As the market changed, motorists demanded more amenities, including housing. Tent City soon added cabins to the complex. At least one building on the grounds was built using hundreds of discarded oil cans from local service stations. A large house and travel trailer area was eventually added to the complex.

By 1948 the facility turned into a trailer-court-only property, and the name was changed to Tent City Trailer Court. The trailer court operated for a few years. It was replaced in the 1950s with apartment housing which still exists today.

Terry Ann Motel – See Eli Motel

The Terry's Court buildings as they look today (Photo by Author 2014)

Terry's Court – 311-15 West Jones Avenue

Terry's Court was constructed in 1949. The facility consisted of fourteen cottages of varying sizes. These were arranged around the property lines with a center parking area. The court began as an auto court but became Terry's Apartments in about 1954.

Today all but one of the original buildings still exists.

Texan Motel – See Zila Motel

Theatre Motel circa 1950 (Author's Collection)

Theatre Motel – 3602 East Van Buren Street

The Theatre Motel was selling rooms by 1948. The motel was built in single-story, strip motel style, which was becoming popular at the time. Thirty-one units were built in two rows. All of the Theatre Motels units were kitchenettes and included both a living room and bedroom. The motel was built to complement the existing drive-in theatre on the property.

The Theatre Motel was closed by 1988 and demolished by 1989. Today the property holds a modern apartment complex.

Thibodo House – 11½ West Washington Street

The Thibodo House was renting rooms by 1909. The facility was located in the Thibodo Block named after the first physician in Phoenix. He and a partner doctor arrived in Phoenix in 1872. Eventually Dr. Thibodo built the Thibodo Building on Washington Street, between Central and First Avenues. He operated his drug store and office from the location.

The Thibodo was located in a two-story brick building and utilized the second story. A restaurant was located on the first floor. The facility went through a number of name changes. By 1917 it was named the Denver Hotel Annex, obviously a part of the Denver Hotel. It quickly became the Tourist House by 1919. About 1927 it became the Chicago Rooms, and then the New Ivanhoe Hotel by 1929. By 1930 the facility was named the Seattle Hotel, and finally the Day Hotel a few years later. By 1942 the facility was no longer renting rooms.

The Porter Hotel was located adjacent to the Thibodo. Interestingly, for a couple of years around 1910, the two facilities were advertised together as one facility with two names and entrances. The Porter Hotel only survived a few more years and may have been absorbed into the Thibodo.

Today the real estate is utilized by the CityScape complex.

Thompson Court – See Wildwood Lodge

Thompson Motel – See Travelers Motel

The Three Palms Motel, operating as apartments (Photo by Author 2014)

Three Palms Motel – 3902 West Buckeye Road

By 1948 the Three Palms Motel was in business. The facility was a single-story, strip-style motel with six units. By 1973 the Three Palms switched to a long-term rental business model. The facility still exists today and is rented as apartments.

Three Wells Motel – 3151 West Buckeye Road

The Three Wells Motel was in operation by 1955. The complex eventually included eight motel units, a café, and two houses.

The Three Wells experienced some excitement in October of 1966. Three people were arrested at the motel for theft of firearms. The three were moving the stolen guns from one vehicle to another when the arrest occurred. They had stolen around 275 guns from a warehouse in Phoenix.

By 1976 the Three Wells was closed and most of the property was cleared. All the remaining buildings were demolished in the early 1980s. Today the real estate holds a modern metal building and building supply business.

The Thunderbird Lodge now operates as apartments (Photo by Author 2014)

Thunderbird Lodge – 834 North Second Avenue

The Thunderbird Lodge was opened in 1941 as the McRae Apartments. The building was a two-story structure with twelve apartments. Construction consisted of a concrete ground floor and wood for the second floor. It was built on the property of a previous apartment building. In 1953 the apartment building moved to the lodge business plan and was renamed the Thunderbird Lodge. The facility provided both room and board. This was an obvious attempt to gain the business of higher-rate winter visitors.

By 1971 the lodge switched to an apartment business plan. Today the Thunderbird Lodge building still exists and continues to operate as apartments.

Thunderbird Motel circa 1950 (Author's Collection)

Thunderbird Motel – 2601 East Van Buren Street

The Thunderbird Motel opened in 1948 in the middle of Van Buren's motel row. The facility utilized separate buildings with covered garages between them. This was a popular building style for motels as the trend changed from cabin courts to strip motels. By 1992 the motel stopped serving transient guests, and by 2002 the Thunderbird had been demolished.

Today the property is used for an automotive business. The skeleton of the last Thunderbird Motel sign still exists on the property.

Tierra Verde Motel – 3424 West Buckeye Road

By 1948 the Tierra Verde Motel was accepting guests. The facility contained five kitchenette units available for rent. They were separate buildings placed in a row along the west property line.

By 1971 the Tierra Verde was no longer a motel and was demolished in short order. Today the real estate holds a used car lot.

Tilger Brothers Tourist Camp – 1023 South Seventh Avenue

The Tilger brothers opened a tourist camp on the property of their existing gas station around 1926. The facility was a true tourist camp with no cabins or units. By 1931 the camp portion of the business was shut down. It's likely the brothers decided not to invest in cabins. This would have been needed to compete in the lodging market as camps were declining.

Today the Matthew Henson Apartments utilize the property.

Tip Top Court – 3109 East Van Buren Street

The Tip Top Court was in business by 1947. The facility was a small court located at the rear of the property. It included four buildings used for rental units. The building in the front of the lot was affiliated and was used as a buffet restaurant in the early years, and a tavern later. The court lasted until 1964 when it was closed as a motel. The tavern remained for some time as did the buildings. They were finally razed in 2008.

Today the area is a vacant lot.

Toney Belle Guest Ranch – 4840 North Central Avenue

The Toney Belle Guest Ranch was opened in late 1938. The facility offered climate controlled cottages and accepted up to twenty guests at a time. Guest ranches were a popular type of tourist facility in the western states. They provided comfort and amenities sold around ranch type activities, most predominately horseback riding. Toney Belle offered a pool, croquet, and horseback riding.

When the facility was built it was on the outskirts of town. However, as the years progressed the area became built-up. By 1961 the ranch was sold, and a new 18-story apartment building was constructed on the property. Today that building still exists on the property.

Tourist Hotel – See Vermont Hotel

Tourist House – See Thibodo House

Tovrea Castle in 2012 (Photo by Author)

Tovrea Castle – 5025 East Van Buren Street

Tovrea Castle has an interesting history related to lodging in Phoenix. The castle was originally owned and built by Alessio Carraro, who started construction in 1928. The facility was intended to be a resort hotel with a cactus garden and a surrounding high-end residential development. The hotel portion, the castle, was completed in 1930 and work was to continue on the rest of the property.

Tovrea Castle main floor in 2012 (Photo by Author)

The hotel was a wooden structure consisting of three stories, a cupola, and basement. A grand staircase was built to welcome guests into the lobby area. Twelve sleeping rooms were built on the second and third levels to accommodate the guests. However, the hotel was never to accept any guests.

A large, pre-existing stockyard was located close to the castle property, which was owned by E.A. Tovrea. Both Carraro and Tovrea attempted to buy a large piece of property located between them. Tovrea wanted the property for expansion and Carraro was trying to keep a buffer between the hotel and the stockyards. Both men made the same monetary offer, but the property went to Tovrea, who quickly utilized it for sheep pens.

At this point Carraro's dream was likely not possible. The stockyard smell was unpleasant and now even closer. Carraro's wife had refused to live in Arizona and returned to San Francisco on her own. To top it off, the Great Depression was under way. When Carraro received a sealed purchase bid for his hotel, he accepted. The buyer was E. A. Tovrea, the stockyard owner.

The Tovreas turned the property into a private residence. Less than a year after the purchase E.A. Tovrea passed away leaving his wife Della to inhabit the castle. The castle remained Della's winter home until her death in 1969. She passed away due to complications of pneumonia.

A couple of months before Della's death, she was robbed at the castle. Two men entered the property and used a garden hose as a rope to scale the castle wall. A conveniently placed ladder on the second floor allowed access to the third. They finally climbed to the cupola and entered the residence. They descended through the structure to the first floor where Della confronted them. One of the men covered her mouth with his hand, and she was forced into a chair and bound. While tying Della up, one of the men accidently discharged his gun into the ceiling. The men robbed Della of approximately $50,000 worth of belongings. One man was eventually caught in California, and some items were returned. The bullet hole still remains in the ceiling at the castle.

The castle remained in the family until the City of Phoenix purchased it in the early 1990s. Today the facility still exists as a museum. As of 2012 the city is providing tours of the complex.

The former Town and Country Lodge as it looks today (Photo by Author 2014)

Town and Country Lodge – 1425 East Ocotillo Road

The Town and Country Lodge was built in 1949 as a rural guest lodge. The facility consisted of twelve rental units, two swimming pools, a restaurant, and lounge. The facility became the Desert Shadows in the 1960s. At that time it appears to have become an apartment complex.

Today most of the original Town and Country Lodge still exists as apartments.

Town House Motel circa 1970 (Author's Collection)

Town House Motel – 716 South Seventeenth Avenue

By 1948 a large cottage court was in operation at 716 South Seventeenth Avenue under the name Morreale Hotel. The name was very short-lived and was replaced by the Town House Motel by 1949. The facility was laid out in a U-configuration and included 48 units which consisted of one- or two-room cottages. A single gable roof covered all the cottages creating carports between the cottages. Over the years some of the carports were converted to rental space.

The Town House buildings in 2012 (Photo by Author)

Two major incidents happened at the Town House, both in 1965. First, a five-year-old boy was found dead in the motel pool. The boy was sleeping in one of the cabins when his mother decided to take a shower. By the time she finished showering the boy had entered the pool and drowned. Another incident involved the destruction of one of the cottages by fire. Just prior to the fire a man was seen running from the cottage. A search of the grounds revealed a bomb placed in the cellar of a second cottage. The bomb was taken to Luke Air Force Base for destruction.

By 1984 the facility had moved to an apartment business model. Today the Town House still exists and is utilized as apartments.

Townehouse Hotel – 100 West Clarendon Avenue

The Townhouse Hotel opened in March of 1963. It was the first high-rise hotel built in Phoenix in 35 years, with 25 stories. The convention center, hotel, offices, and amenities cost an estimated twenty million dollars. Built on 18 acres by Del Webb, twelve floors were dedicated to office space. Two hundred seventy-five rooms were built along with convention center seating of 3,000. A 1,200 car parking garage was erected to service the facility. Del Webb also owned the facility and had already placed its headquarters on the property.

The Hilton Garden Inn, formerly the Townhouse Hotel, today (Photo by Author 2014)

The facility was known as The Townhouse Hotel, or Del Webb's Townhouse, early on. The hotel became a Ramada Inn for a time likely due to Del Webb's ownership in the franchise. By 2001 it became known as the Lexington Hotel. About 2004 the property became the Hilton Garden Inn and still operates as such.

Townsend Motel – See Eli Motel

The Trailin Court in 2012 (Photo by Author)

Trailin Court – 3010 West Van Buren Street

By 1948 the Trailin Court was in operation. The facility was built for both trailers and motel overnights. The motel portion consisted of two cottage-style buildings and a six-unit, strip-style motel building.

The Trailin still exists as a trailer court and apartment rentals. The original buildings still exist under the name Trailin Lodge.

Trails End Court – See Graham Place

Travelers Auto Court – 1715 West Buckeye Road

Travelers Auto Court was in business by 1938. The facility consisted of a cabin court and trailer court. It appears the court stopped accepting transient guests by 1952. The cabins were still rented as apartments for many years after.

Eventually the buildings were destroyed. Today the area is vacant.

Travelers Auto Court - 1739 East Van Buren Street

In about 1930 Morris Suserud built some cabins near his grocery store on Van Buren Street. The cabins were mostly used as apartments over the next couple of years. However, they were also sporadically rented to short-term visitors. Very little information exists about the property.

The real estate now holds an abandoned building that was built after the Travelers Auto Court closed.

Travelers Lodge – See Meeks Court

Travelers Motel – 2228 East Van Buren Street

In the mid-1940s the Sun Fan Apartments became the Thompson Motel. By 1946 the facility became known as the Travelers Motel. It was somewhat abnormal to see an apartment complex turned into a motel. The usual progression is from motel to apartments as the property ages. In the Travelers case the eight-unit Sun Fan Apartments was marketed to the transient market. The motel certainly had the right location to obtain the tourist dollars coming into Phoenix.

The Travelers Motel was closed by 1984. Today the property is a vacant lot.

Phoenix TraveLodge circa 1965 (Author's Collection)

Phoenix TraveLodge operating as the Budget Lodge in 2012 (Photo by Author)

TraveLodge – Phoenix – 402 West Van Buren Street

The Phoenix TraveLodge was opened in late 1956. The facility was an L-shaped masonry structure built at a cost of $300,000. It included 40 units built in two-story motor inn style. At the time, TraveLodge utilized a managing co-owner model for its expansion phase. Each co-owner would hold fifty percent ownership and manage the facility.

By 1983 the TraveLodge had become the Budget Lodge. Today the facility still operates as the Budget Lodge.

Triangle Motor Court circa 1960 (Author's Collection)

Triangle Motor Court – 1121 South Seventeenth Avenue

By 1938 the Triangle Motor Court was in operation. The facility was built in cabin court style utilizing six cottages resulting in thirteen units. An office and manager's quarters was also built and placed at the center rear of the property. Ten of the units were kitchenettes. A single roof joined the cabins and created covered parking between them. At some point the area between the cabins was enclosed to create additional units and rental space. This was a common upgrade to modernize cabin courts to look more like strip-style motels.

Triangle Motor Court in 2012 (Photo by Author)

In 1970 two truck drivers were robbed in their shared room. Two women came to the door looking for "John". One of the men was named John, and the women were given access. Shortly thereafter two men arrived also looking for "John". They too were given access. One of the men brandished a gun and robbed the men of several hundred dollars. They were apprehended in short order.

Strangely, the Triangle took on the name Casa Del Sol Motel by 1983. This was the name of a previous motel just a couple of blocks from the Triangle. The Casa Del Sol moved to an apartment concept by 1984. Today, the Triangle Motor Court is closed and fenced off. It operated as the Casa Del Sol apartments until 2012.

The Tripp Motel Lodge now operates as apartments (Photo by Author 2014)

Tripp Motel Lodge – 417 North Twenty-Seventh Avenue

The Tripp Motel was a smattering of eight cabins located haphazardly on the property. The facility was in use by 1948 and was likely operated as apartments. The Tripp Motel name first appears in advertisements in 1951.

By 1984 the facility became apartments-only again. Today the original Tripp Motel buildings still exist and still operate as apartments.

Tropicana Motel – See Autopia

Tropics Motor Hotel circa 1970 (Author's Collection)

Tropics Motor Hotel – 1902 East Van Buren Street

The Tropics Motor Hotel opened in early 1958 with a grand opening on the first of March. The facility was very modern and built in two-story motor hotel style. The complex included a coffee shop, restaurant, and cocktail lounge. Fifty rooms were built and most were fitted with twenty-one-inch console televisions. The Tropics was one of the early "themed" motels. Obviously the theme was the tropics.

By 1978 the Tropics Motor Hotel was closed, but the lounge remained open for some time. The facility was demolished by 1995. Today the property is vacant other than the palm trees which were once part of the facility's landscape.

Turista Motel circa 1960 (Author's Collection)

Turista Motel – 4180 Grand Avenue

By 1954 the Turista Motel was accepting guests. The facility was a cottage-type court with some kitchenettes. The complex included a gas station and trailer court as well.

The Turista became the Grand Valley Motel by 1969. The facility lasted many years but was finally closed by 1990.

Today the address is a vacant lot.

Turley Auto Court – See Bridges Auto Court

Twilight Lodge – See Wildwood Lodge

Twin Palms Court – See Antry's Auto Court

Twin Palms Lodge – 504 North Sixth Street

The Twin Palms Lodge began as O'Reillys Boarding House around 1932. The home existed prior to that date under other ownership and could have been a boarding house. By 1945 the large home took on the Twin Palms Lodge name. The lodge catered mostly to long-term renters, but did accept short-term visitors at times. By 1955 the Lodge was no longer accepting guests. It was demolished in the 1960s.

Today the University of Arizona College of Medicine uses the real estate.

Twin Wheels Motel – See Maricopa Motel

U-Wanna Motel – 5249 South Central Avenue

The U-Wanna Motel was in operation by 1949. The facility was a mix of small cottages and trailer spaces.

The motel was closed in the mid-1980s and demolished. Modern buildings are located on the property today.

Ulloa Rooms – 800 East Washington Street

The Ulloa Rooms was a small cabin court open by 1951. The facility utilized an unknown number of twelve-foot by twelve-foot cabins. By 1961 the facility became known as Johns Court.

In 1965 a long-term resident died in a cabin explosion. He had turned off a space heater and later attempted to heat water for tea using an open flame. The cabin exploded due to a poor gas connection utilizing a rubber hose. The incident provoked discussion in the city and helped enact housing regulations in Phoenix.

By 1965 the facility moved to an all-apartment business model. Today a modern apartment complex exists on the property.

Ultra Motel – 5333 East Van Buren Street

The Ultra Motel was operating by 1948. The facility was a cabin court utilizing individual buildings as units. The Ultra was out of business and demolished by 1969.

Today the real estate is part of the Riverwalk residential development.

Union Hotel – See Farley House

US Auto Court – 1629 East Van Buren Street

The US Auto Court started as an early auto camp in 1925. The facility was one of the original auto camps that popped up in Phoenix in the 1920s. The name of the camp when it was opened is unknown. By 1930 the facility had followed the competition and added cabins. At this time the court operated under the name Cottage Auto Camp. The name was soon changed to the US Auto Court and operated as such for many years, but by 1982 the court was closed. It was razed in short order.

In 1963 the facility made local news as the owner, an 81-year-old grandmother, was arrested, handcuffed, and jailed briefly. Her crime was refusing to upgrade her cabin heaters with vents to comply with city regulations. The court appeared again in the news in 1966 when a woman committed a Christmas Day suicide in one of the cabins.

Today the land on which the US Auto Court stood is being utilized by a used car lot.

Utah Hotel – See Elmo Rooming House

Utica Motel – 5317 East Van Buren Street

By 1947 the Utica Motel was in operation. The construction of the facility is unknown. The facility lasted until 1964 when the motel was razed. Modern apartments are on the property today.

Vagabond Motor Hotel circa 1970 (Author's Collection)

The Vagabond operating as the Phoenix Sunrise in 2012 (Photo by Author)

Vagabond Motor Hotel – 3644 East Van Buren Street

The Vagabond Motor Hotel was opened in 1962 by the owner of the Arizona Palms Motel across the street. The facility utilized two-story motor inn style construction. A former lodging facility, the Yaqui Motor Lodge, was demolished to make room for the new 42-unit motel.

The Vagabond's name changed around 1975 to the Western Six Motel. By 1980 the motel became known as the Phoenix Six Motel and by 1999 as the Phoenix Sunrise Motel.

Today the original Vagabond Motor Hotel buildings are still in use as the Phoenix Sunrise Motel.

Val Villa Lodge – See M & P Motel

Valley Court – 3842 East Van Buren Street

The Valley Court was accepting guests by 1947. It was a small court with four buildings utilized for rental units.

By 1964 the court was closed, and the property soon became part of the Ramada World Headquarters complex. Today the area is a parking lot.

Valley Inn – See Vinton Manor Apartment Hotel

Valley Lodging House – 123 West Jefferson Street

The Valley Lodging House was one of the most popular rooming houses in Phoenix. It was located close to the city courthouse and opened in 1902. The facility also housed a dining room. The house operated for many years but became less viable after 1930. The only mention in the historical record after that date is in 1938 when a fire destroyed one of the rear screen porches.

Today the East Court Building stands on the property.

Valley Motel – See Del Coosha Court

Van Buren Motel – See Lorena Auto Court

Vee Gee Auto Court – (6300) Grand Avenue

The Vee Gee Auto Court was in operation by 1937. The facility consisted of eleven cement block cottages and the Jayhawk Trailer Camp.

The fate of the Vee Gee is not known. It may have closed after 1947 or it may have been renamed. Grand Avenue addresses changed about the same time, and the new address is not known.

The Vendome Hotel (with porches) circa 1908 (Courtesy Library of Congress)

Vendome Hotel – 319 West Washington Street

The Vendome Hotel was opened in October 1889. Construction was of two-story wood frame and brick, creating 20 guest rooms. The facility was built and operated by G. Herrett, an immigrant from New Brunswick, Canada.

In 1893 a mysterious theft occurred at the Vendome. A guest retired for the evening after locking both his windows and doors. He left the skeleton key in the keyhole on the inside of the door. He placed his purse containing $6,000 in checks and cash under his pillow. In the morning the purse was gone, but the door and windows remained locked, and the key was still in the door.

By 1924 the facility no longer functioned as a hotel. Today the property is utilized as a downtown parking garage.

Verde Motel – 2133 West Van Buren Street

By 1930 the new cabin court, Fosters Court Verde, was open for business. The facility included two- and three-room cottages fitted with kitchenettes. Carports and laundry facilities were also located on the property. By 1959 the court was renamed simply the Verde Motel.

The Verde was closed by 1984. The buildings were demolished in the late 1990s. Today a used car facility is located where the Verde Motel once stood.

Vermont Hotel – 22 East Madison Street

The Vermont Hotel was opened by 1899. The facility utilized a single-story front area which held the lobby and restaurant. An attached two-story brick building in the rear held the sleeping rooms. By 1931 the business became the Tourist Hotel.

The Vermont was demolished by 1956 and became the parking lot for the St. James Hotel across the street. Today the area remains a parking lot.

Villa Motor Hotel - 2970 East Van Buren Street

The Villa Motor Hotel was opened in 1948 as a cottage court style facility. Individual cabins were built in a Mediterranean style with stucco walls and tile roofs. Access was gained through an arched driveway into the court area. The facility was built at the same time as the adjacent Airways Motor Hotel, which was built in similar style. It's likely the two motels had the same original ownership.

Villa Motor Hotel circa 1955 (Author's Collection)

The Villa operates as apartments today (Photo by Author 2012)

The Villa operated under the original name until 1975 when it was renamed the Seven Motor Inn. The facility used the new name until 1995 when the motel was closed. The property was quickly reopened as apartments.

The original Villa Motor Hotel buildings still exist and operate as temporary apartment housing under the name JG Temporal Housing.

The Villa Vista Motel operating as apartments in 2012 (Photo by Richard Christensen)

Villa Vista Motel – 3330 West Buckeye Road

By 1948 the Del Reo Lodge was in business. It soon took on its long-lived name, the Villa Vista Motel. The facility started with a six-unit, single-story, strip-style building. Eventually two strip-style buildings were located on the property.

In 1965 some excitement took place at the Villa Vista. Alfred Moore, a liquor control agent, attempted to intervene when he spotted Fernando Dominquez accosting a woman at Sixteenth Place and Buckeye Road. Dominquez shot at the agent four times with two bullets entering Moore's back. Those shots proved fatal. The woman was Dominquez's ex-wife, and he had forced her to accompany him to the Villa Vista Motel. Over the next nineteen hours he threatened her life and took liberties with her. Police were made aware of Dominquez's location and kicked down the door to the room. Gun shots were heard, and Dominquez was found dead of self-inflicted wounds in the motel bathroom. The woman survived the ordeal.

By 1984 the business switched to an apartment business model. Today the original buildings still exist and are rented as apartments.

Vinton Manor Hotel circa 1955 (Author's Collection)

Vinton Manor Apartment Hotel – 3312 North Central Avenue

By 1950 the Vinton Manor Apartment Hotel was operating. The facility utilized two-story buildings constructed in hotel style. The complex did include a third-story penthouse on a portion of the building. It contained approximately fifty rental units and four penthouse suites. By 1963 the Vinton became the Valley Inn.

The Valley Inn became apartments-only by 1966 and was demolished quickly. Today the entire block the Vinton Manor was on is part of a high-rise office building complex.

Virginia Court – 705 South Nineteenth Avenue

The Virginia Court was a small three-building court in business by 1928. The property also held a grocery store and restaurant. The facility operated mostly as apartments but did advertise to the transient market from 1931 to 1956. By 1959 the facility was no longer in operation.

A scrap metal company is on the property today. The original buildings were removed in the 1960s.

Virginia Hotel – 60 South Third Street

The Virginia Hotel was a small downtown hotel of which little is known. It was in business by 1928. The facility changed names to the Hollywood Hotel by 1931.

By 1981 the Hollywood ceased to function as a hotel. It was quickly demolished and the property used as a parking lot. Today the Collier Center utilizes the real estate.

Virginia Rooming House – 44 South Central Avenue

By January 1905 the Virginia Rooming House was accepting guests. The facility was a two-story brick building located on the northwest corner of Central Avenue and Washington Street. The rooming house utilized the second floor, and various tenants utilized the ground floor. A restaurant was on the ground floor for many years. By 1916 the Virginia became the Angeles Hotel.

Angeles Hotel, formerly the Virginia Rooming House circa 1930 (Courtesy Arizona State Library, Archives and Public Records, History and Archives Division, Phoenix, #97-0853)

By 1948 the hotel was no longer functioning and the second floor was rented to several businesses. The building was demolished in the early 1970s along with the entire block to build Patriots Square Park. Today the real estate is part of the CityScape complex.

Vista Linda Court – 2926 (2930) West Buckeye Road

By 1947 the Vista Linda Court was in business. The facility was a cottage court utilizing duplex buildings as rentals. The property also included an office building with an owner's apartment. The original build included thirteen units. By 1950 the court took on the name of Comfort Motel. Expansions resulted in seventeen units by 1966.

The Vista Linda operating as the Lexxus Motel in 2012 (Photo by Author)

In 1961 a renter's 13-year-old boy was rescued from South Mountain Park. The boy went exploring on the mountain with a group of other children. During his climb, his support gave way and he fell twenty feet to a ledge. He was stranded on the ledge for two hours before a helicopter from Luke Air Force Base rescued him. He ended up with a head injury and broken legs.

The Comfort became apartments by 1984. However, it recently has taken on the name Lexxus Motel and is renting to the transient market today.

Vivian Court – 308-10 North Fourteenth Avenue

By 1930 the Vivian Court was accepting guests. The court was a very early example of single-story, strip motel style construction. It was built using two strip buildings facing each other like many later motels. The court area between was very narrow and parking was not available in that area. The facility was an all-brick construction consisting of twelve units. Each unit consisted of three rooms. By 1949 the court was renamed the Regency Motel.

The former Vivian Court, now operating as apartments (Photo by Author 2014)

The building at 314 North Fourteenth Avenue was under the same ownership and was part of the complex. It was rented for a time as apartments and then became part of the Regency Motel. That building was demolished.

The Regency operated as a motel and apartment for many years. By 1984 the motel was out of business. Today the Vivian Court buildings still exist and are rented as apartments.

Waggoner Eastside Court – 2018 East Van Buren Street

In 1936 AC Waggoner added a cabin court facility to his existing grocery business. The court operated successfully for some time, but by 1953 the facility was closed.

The Waggoner Eastside Court had its share of troubles. In 1939 a five-year-old girl staying in one of the cabins was struck by a vehicle in the road. She passed away about a week afterwards. In 1943 a four-month-old boy was smothered to death in one of the cabins. Several other small children apparently piled on top of him. Additionally, two of the cabins were destroyed in fires in 1940 and 1945.

The property is now part of the I-10 easement where Van Buren Street intersects.

Wanada Lodge – 1227 East Maryland Avenue

The Wanada Lodge was accepting guests by 1940. The facility was a rural guest lodge with multiple buildings and shady areas. The amenities at the Wanada Lodge are not known. By 1960 the facility was being operated as apartments. This did not last long as the lodge was demolished in 1962 to make way for a new condominium complex. This construction still exists today.

The Wanda Auto Court as it looks today (Photo by Author 2014)

Wanda Auto Court – 350 North Fifty-Third Street

By 1950 the Wanda Auto Court was accepting guests. The facility was a small cabin court consisting of six units. Each cabin was placed in a row along the rear property line. Cabins consisted of single-room units and two-room units.

The property operated as a motel until 1969 when it switched to an apartment business model. The original Wanda Auto Court buildings still exist but are not in use.

Warren Motel – See Best-Yet Motel

Washington Circle Auto Court – 1718 East Washington Street

The Washington Circle Auto Court was in business by 1946. The facility was a cabin court consisting of nineteen units and a two-bedroom brick duplex. At some point the name was shortened to Washington Court.

By 1957 the court was no longer in business. It was razed in the 1960s. Today the area is a parking lot.

Washington Court – See Washington Circle Court

The Washington Court buildings as they look today (Photo by Author 2014)

Washington Court – 2136 West Washington Street

The Washington Court was open by 1929. The facility consisted of six brick cottages and an owner's quarters in the rear. It appears the Washington was built as part of a three-court complex including the San Antonio and Hollywood courts. It's likely the same developer built them to sell separately. By 1932 the Washington and Hollywood Courts were combined to create the Palmdale Court.

The Washington Court became apartments by 1968. Today the original Washington Court buildings still stand but are vacant.

Washington Hotel – 228 North First Street

The Washington Hotel was in business by 1913. While the property was a long-lived one, little information is available about it. It was a two-story brick structure located at Van Buren and First Streets. It's likely the sleeping rooms were located upstairs and other businesses utilized the ground floor. One such business was the Washington Hotel Barber Shop.

By 1970 the Washington Hotel was no longer operating. The building was demolished to build the Valley Center, which opened in 1972.

Today the Chase Tower (formerly the Valley Center) resides on the entire block. It is the tallest building in the state of Arizona.

Waverly House – Third Avenue and Adams Street

The Waverly House was a lodging facility that provided both room and board. Little is known of the facility. It operated from 1906 to 1908, but likely longer. Which corner it was on is not known.

Way West Motel circa 1957 (Author's Collection)

Way West Motel - 5313 North Seventh Street

The Way West Motel was accepting guests by 1951. The facility started with cottage-style buildings that were likely duplex configuration. This original build held sixteen rental units and were placed along the northern property line. By 1952 the name was changed to the Jo Lyn Motel. In the late 1950s a single-story, strip motel building was built along the southern property line. This raised the total rental units to 38. About the same time, certainly by 1957, the name changed again, this time to the Westernaire Motel.

The facility was closed by 1986 and quickly demolished. Today the Paragon Plaza is located on the real estate.

Weber Court – 3939 East Van Buren Street

The Weber Court was in business by 1937. The facility consisted of at least four single-story strip buildings with rental units. In the early 1940s the name of the court changed to the Rosser Tourist Court.

In the fall of 1944 the owner, Ida Rosser, was notified that one of her sons was killed in action in France. Another son was reported as missing in action, and two other sons were still in service.

In 1951 the court was renamed the Les De Lane Court. This lasted until 1954 when the court took its final name, the Modern Court. By 1960 the facility was closed and became a trailer sales business.

Today the real estate is part of the Gateway Community College campus.

Wells Cottages – See Copemoar Court

West Buckeye Court – 2140 West Buckeye Road

By 1948 the West Buckeye Court was in business. The facility included cabins for rent and trailer spaces. Some of the cabins were kitchenettes. A restaurant was also located on the property. By 1958 both the court and the café took on the name Lena's. By 1961 the motel became the Phoenix Court Apartments and moved to a long-term renter business model.

In 1958 a fist fight ensued just outside the café. A third man left the café with a pistol to stop the argument. A fourth man, Walter DeWitt, told him to put the gun down and was shot. The shooter, Bobby Brooks, was charged with first degree murder and convicted of manslaughter.

Today the area is mostly vacant. However, the café continues to operate as the El Horseshoe Restaurant.

West End Cottages – 918 North Fifteenth Avenue

By 1930 the West End Cottages was in operation. The facility was built in cabin court style utilizing twelve cabins arranged in a U-shape. Furnishings from the cabins were sold off in late 1965. By 1969 all the cabins were razed, and a vacant lot appeared.

Today the property is still a vacant lot.

West End House – 701 West Washington Street

The West End House was open by 1889, and possibly earlier. The facility was one of Phoenix's many smaller hotels.

In 1889 William Doheney shot and killed his father in the West End House. A family squabble had ensued for some time, and it climaxed at the hotel where they lived. After four years of trials and legal wrestling, Doheney was found not guilty of his murder charge. The jury found he was justified by reason of self-defense.

The West End House was the temporary location for Native American education prior to the opening of the Phoenix Indian Industrial School. The 1891 class had 42 students enrolled. Work started on the permanent school in December 1891.

By 1920 the hotel started utilizing the address Sixth South Seventh Avenue. It quickly took on the name Seventh Avenue Hotel.

In 1948 the hotel was sold and became part of the Arizona Military District Headquarters building. The hotel, along with an adjacent building, was renovated for the headquarters. Today the real estate is undeveloped.

The last building left from the West Side Motel (Photo by Author 2014)

West Side Motel – 3012 West Van Buren Street

By 1939 at least one cabin was available for rent behind the service station at 3012 West Van Buren Street. Soon the cottages had grown to six, and a grocery store was added. It's likely the cabins were rented as apartments until 1948 when the facility began being advertised as the West Side Court. By 1953 twelve units were available on the property.

By 1969 the West Side Court had become apartment rentals and trailers. Today a restaurant is located on the former real estate of the West Side Motel. It uses one of the original buildings.

West Siesta Motel – See Motel Inn

West Winds Lodge - 2216 North Sixteenth Street

The West Winds Lodge was in business by 1947. The facility utilized single-story, strip motel construction. It included ten rental units. Around 1961 the lodge became the Westwinds Motel.

The West Winds Lodge, now operating as the Westwinds Apartments (Photo by Author 2014)

The Westwinds operated under the motel name for many years. By 1982 it dropped the motel name and stuck with apartments. Today the facility still exists and is operated as the Westwinds Apartments.

Western Acres Motel – 2135 West Buckeye Road

By 1948 the Western Acres Motel was in business. The facility included eleven rental units. The units were built in four buildings.

The Western Acres was closed by 1981 and demolished by 1986. The area is a pallet sales business today.

Western Air Court – 2916 West Buckeye Road

By 1949 the Western Air Court was in business. The facility was a mixture of cottages and trailer spaces. By 1961 the Western Air became apartments.

Today the property contains a pallet sales business.

Western Motel – See Eli Motel

Western Motel Apartments – See Anglin Motel

Western Village circa 1955 (Author's Collection)

Western Village Motor Hotel – 1601 Grand Avenue

The Western Village Motor Hotel was one of the first resort-style facilities built in Phoenix. The facility opened in 1949 with 39 rental units. Two-story motor inn style buildings were used in the construction. In 1951 a fifteen-unit addition was built along with a restaurant. The original builder saw the need for a resort-type facility on the west side and built it.

The Western Village eventually became part of the Master Host Inns chain, a referral chain based in Texas.

The Western Village was closed, burned, and demolished by 1991. Today the real estate holds the Phoenix World Outreach building.

Westernaire Motel – See Way West Motel

Westminster Lodging House – 19 West Van Buren Street

The Westminster was a lodging house that began operations by 1897. It featured screen porches for the sleeping comfort of guests. By 1918 the facility was no longer in operation.

Today the Civic Space Park utilizes the real estate.

Westward Court – 1850 West Grant Street

The Westward Court was a small auto court consisting of three buildings and a home at the rear. The total number of rental units was six, and it was operating by 1939. In the early 1950s the court started renting exclusively as apartments and took on the name Davidson Apartments.

The Westward Court buildings were demolished in the early 1980s. Today a gas station is located on the property.

The Westward Ho Court operates as apartments today (Photo by Author 2012)

Westward Ho Court – 802 South Seventeenth Avenue

The Gavin Court was opened in 1939. The facility was a small cabin court consisting of five brick buildings, including the office and manager's quarters. By 1942 the facility became the Westward Ho Court. Surprisingly, the motel was able to retain its name even though the largest hotel in town had the same name.

By 1980 the facility had become an apartment building. Today the Westward Ho Court buildings still exist as apartments.

Westward Ho Hotel now operates as assisted living (Photo by Author 2014)

Westward Ho Hotel circa 1940 (Author's Collection)

Westward Ho Hotel – 610 North Central Avenue

The sixteen-story Westward Ho opened in 1928 and immediately became the tallest building in Arizona. When the project was announced in late 1926, the facility was slated to be called the Roosevelt Hotel. Ownership of the hotel changed during construction, and the Roosevelt name was dropped.

The hotel was an upscale property with 350 rooms. Of course the facility included full banquet and meeting facilities and multiple restaurants. The Thunderbird Room was a large, twelve-hundred-person convention room in which many large functions occurred.

In the 1940s the Hotel added a four-story structure to the west side of the property. The new building was called the Patio Suites and brought the Westward Ho's total room count to five hundred. Another three-hundred-room, eighteen-story expansion was announced in the 1960s, but was never built.

By 1980 the Westward Ho became federally assisted housing. It remains so today. In 1982 the building was added to the National Register of Historic Places.

Westward Lodge – 848 North First Avenue

The Westward Lodge started as a home prior to 1930. It was a large home with many rooms, including seven lavatories. It became apartments under the name Kenneth-Anne by the early 1930s. About 1938 it became the Town House but was still operating as apartments.

In 1939 the owner was put on trial for working a woman more than 48 hours in a week. The owner plead guilty. By 1940 the facility had changed hands and became the Westward Lodge. It started accepting transient guests. In 1963 the longtime owner passed away. Two years later the contents of the lodge were auctioned off. The building was demolished.

Today the address remains unimproved.

Westwinds Motel – See West Winds Lodge

Westwood Court – See Loma Alta Court

Wharton Hotel – 38 North Central Avenue

By 1897 the Wharton Rooming House was renting rooms. The facility was a two-story structure and included eighteen rental rooms. The hotel apparently went by the name Avalon Rooms for a short time around 1926. By 1928 the facility became known as the Como Hotel. The name changed again by 1934 to the American Hotel. The facility was no longer a hotel by 1935. It became the home of the Benevolent and Fraternal Order of Antelopes.

The Ernst and Young building is on the Wharton Hotels property now.

White Hotel – See Plaza House

White Oak Lodge circa 1955 (Author's Collection)

White Oak Lodge – 5310 North Central Avenue

The White Oak Lodge was in business by 1950. The facility consisted of a single-story, strip-style motel building used for rental units. A second building located forward of the rentals was utilized for a lobby and owner's quarters. A large pool located between the buildings was the centerpiece of the property. Relaxation was the theme of the White Oak as it was located in a rural area.

The White Oak was closed by 1970 and demolished in the 1970s. A modern apartment complex is on the real estate today.

White Rose Court – 1738 East Washington Street

The White Rose Auto Court was operating by 1938. It was built in cabin court style and included approximately twenty cabins.

By 1961 the court was no longer in business. Today the real estate is not developed.

White Way Court – 1661 Grand Avenue

The White Way Court was in operation by 1938. The facility utilized cabin court style construction. By 1948 the court was no longer in business.

The real estate utilized by the White Way Court is now part of the I-10 Easement.

Whitehouse Lodge – See The Ivon

Whites Auto Camp – 1840 East Van Buren Street

Whites Auto Camp was in business by 1926. The facility was an early auto camp that catered to camping guests who traveled by car. Whites offered the basic needs of the traveler such as water and sewer. It appears that the facility decided not to upgrade to a cabin court like most auto camps did. By 1934 the camp no longer greeted guests. However, Thomas White continued to live on the property for many years afterward.

Today the St. Luke's Medical Center owns the property.

Whites Motel – See Eli Motel

Whittles Motor Court – See Motor Inn Auto Court

Wideman's Cottages – 10042 North Seventh Place

Cottages began appearing at the location in the 1940s. Eventually there were about eight cottages and a home on the property. In the 1950s they were marketed to both short-term and long-term renters. The site was demolished in the 1990s.

Today residential homes are on the property.

Wilberta Court – 1118 East Monroe Street

By 1931 the Wilberta Court was in business. The facility was a seventeen-unit cabin court using individual buildings as units. The court was renamed as the Lewis Court by 1936. This lasted a couple of years, but by 1938 the name changed again to the Morgan Court. By 1952 the court moved to an apartment business structure.

The buildings were demolished in the 1970s. Today the area is residential.

Wildwood Lodge – 4200 (4100) East Van Buren Street

By 1934 the Wildwood Lodge was in business. The facility consisted of fourteen cabins and a home on five acres. By 1944 the court had become the Thompson Court and then the Twilight Lodge shortly afterward. By 1957 the facility was closed and became a trailer sales business and trailer court.

Today the property is a parking lot.

Wilkins Court – See Camelback View Auto Court

Williams Court – See Elvas Motel

Williams Hotel – 602 West Van Buren Street

It appears the Raymond Hotel was open by 1908. The hotel does not appear in records until 1916, but a 1937 newspaper advertisement mentions that the owner has been at the property for twenty-nine years. The facility was likely a small, hotel-style building with interior corridors, although little information about the property exists. By 1920 it became the Williams Hotel. The hotel held this name until 1953 when it was renamed the Shafer Hotel. The facility was closed and demolished by 1958 when the City Center Motel was built on the real estate.

Today the property holds the replacement for the Shafer Hotel, the City Center Motel.

Williams House – Washington Street between First and Second Avenues

The opening date of the Williams House is not known. It certainly was open by 1891 and was located on the north side of Washington Street between what are now First and Second Avenues. This was directly across the street from the courthouse at the time. The facility was a two-story wooden structure. It contained the hotel, a restaurant, and a shoe store.

In July of 1893 a midnight fire destroyed the Williams House. The fire was likely caused by an overturned lamp. All guests escaped the fire with only a couple of minor injuries. The hotel was insured for $2,500.

Today the Wells Fargo Building and the Maricopa County Sheriff's Office are located in the area of the Williams House.

Willmoth Court – See Lincoln Auto Court

Willow Avenue Court – 1520 North Willow Avenue (North Seventeenth Drive)

The Willow Avenue Court was in operation by 1939. It was built in a mixed style with fifteen units consisting of rental cabins and a single-story strip building. The court was named the Willow Avenue Court because North Seventeenth Drive was formerly Willow Avenue. When the street name changed in the 1950s, the court changed its name to simply Willow Court.

The court began operating as apartments-only in the mid-1970s. The buildings began to be demolished at that time with the final buildings razed in the 1990s. Today the real estate is utilized as a parking lot.

Wilson Court – 2521 East Adams Street

The Wilson Court was a six-cabin court with eight units. It was built in the 1940s and operated as apartments for the most part. For a few years in the early 1950s it was marketed to tourists. It then returned to an apartment business plan.

Today the area is a parking lot. The buildings were demolished in the 1980s.

Wilsons Court – 2925 West Buckeye Road

By 1952 the Wilsons Court was accepting guests. The facility was a twelve-unit court with small cabins and at least one larger cottage apartment.

In 1960 an elderly man living at the court was killed in a fire. Neighbors spotted the fire, broke down the door, and retrieved the man from the kitchen floor. By then, however, it was too late.

In 1969 the court was sold to settle the estate of the owner. It did not reopen and was demolished in the 1970s. Today a trucking company uses the real estate.

Wilsons Court – 3401 West Van Buren Street

Wilsons Court was a small cabin court open by 1944. By 1952 the property had become a hardware store, and the cabins were demolished.

Today the real estate contains a modern building with several businesses in it.

Windmill Hotel Motor Inn – See Crescent Court

Windsor Court – 1222 North Third Street

The Windsor Court was in business by 1929. The construction style of the facility is not known. From aerial photos it appears the court consisted of four single-story strip motel buildings. However, this style would have been very rare at the time of construction. It's more likely the court was a series of cottages with a single gable roof over more than one cottage. This was a popular construction style at the time because it created a covered parking area between the cottages.

By 1973 the court ceased to function and was razed soon after closing. Today the Deck Park Tunnel is directly below the property. A parking lot is located there now.

Windsor Hotel – See Sixth Avenue Hotel

Windsor House – Central between Monroe and Adams

The Windsor House was an early hotel located in the center of the block on Centre (Central) Street between Monroe Street and Adams Street. The facility offered both single rooms and suites, and also offered a dining room. Records show it existed from 1890 to 1893, but was likely open longer.

In January of 1891 Eda Rexilius and William Tedford were married in the Windsor House. The marriage took place after one of Eda's friends offered her one hundred dollars to get married within 24 hours. She won the money.

It is unknown which side of Central the Windsor House resided on. The facility certainly does not exist today.

Wing Auto Camp – 1643 East Van Buren Street

Ong Wing, owner of the Wing grocery store, briefly opened an auto camp next to his store. It appears to be a very brief endeavor existing in 1928.

It was very common for business owners to try and maximize the uses of their properties. Auto camps were easy add-on businesses since the initial investment, beyond the property, was negligible. However, many owners didn't take into account the difficulty or lifestyle change adding a twenty-four-hour business can inflict.

The property is still utilized as a grocery store. The buildings from the Wing Auto Camp are long gone.

Wingfoot Court – 3335 (3405) East Van Buren Street

In 1947 the Wingfoot Court was opened. The facility was a ten-cottage motel. Buildings were aligned from the front to the rear of a narrow lot. By 1952 the court became the Sharon Court. The court endured until 1958 when it was closed and demolished to make room for the Bagdad Motel.

The land where the Wingfoot Court once stood now holds the New Day Center.

Wings Motor Court – 1732 West Grant Street

By 1951 rooms were being rented on an apartment basis at 1732 West Grant. Soon the facility would be marketed to tourists and named the Wings Motor Court. The facility consisted of duplex bungalows. By 1963 the Wings became the Hotel Court Motel.

The Hotel Court was out of business by 1973 and quickly demolished. Today the real estate is used by a general contracting company for outside storage.

Wings Motor Court – 522 South Seventeenth Avenue (1706 West Lincoln Street)

By 1947 the Wings Motor Court was operating with five units along with the Lincoln Arizona Oil Company. The facility utilized small, cottage-style buildings located at the northwest corner of Lincoln Street and Nineteenth Avenue. By 1956 the facility had changed its name to the Cloverleaf Apartments and moved to a long-term rental business plan.

Eventually the buildings were demolished and industrial buildings were placed on the site. Today the Interwest Safety Supply Building is located on the property.

Winston Inn and Court – 1342 East Jefferson Street

The buildings at 1342 East Jefferson Street were originally the Booker T. Washington Hospital. The facility had room for thirty patients as well as cabins for tuberculosis patients. It included an emergency room and was operated for the benefit of the African-American population in the city of Phoenix. By 1942 the hospital was no longer in operation, and the facility became the Winston Inn. The Winston operated as a meeting and conference center with a restaurant. The cabins were converted to a tourist court. The facility was closed by the mid-1950s. It was demolished shortly after it closed.

The real estate has remained vacant since the 1950s. Today it is utilized for parking. A few of the original hospital palm trees still remain.

Winter Garden – See Montezuma Place

Winterhaven Court – 1714 East Van Buren Street

Winterhaven Court was a short-lived auto court which opened in 1935. By 1941 it had become a sheet metal company and was a grocery store in the 1950s.

The area now holds an auto glass company.

Wollpert Hotel – 215 South Second Street

The Wollpert opened as a rooming house by 1916. The size and configuration of the hotel is not known. By 1929 the facility became known as the Eddie Hotel. It took on the name Commercial Hotel by 1935.

The Wollpert was purchased by the City of Phoenix by 1943. It was utilized as a detention clinic for the police department. Today the area is within the US Airways Center complex.

Wonderland Court – 2535 East Van Buren Street

The Wonderland Court was a cabin-style court that opened in 1941. The facility sat in the middle of a row of many motels on the south side of Van Buren Street. The Wonderland was closed by 1983, and the buildings were demolished by 1991.

The property is now a vacant lot.

Woodford Hotel – See Parker House

Wrangler Motel – See Green Parrot Auto Court

Wright's Lodge – see Monte Vista Lodge

Yaqui Motor Lodge circa 1940 (Author's Collection)

Yaqui Motor Lodge – 3650 East Van Buren Street

The Yaqui Motor Lodge opened in 1938. It consisted of two strip-style buildings with a courtyard between them. The court utilized Spanish architecture.

The Yaqui was demolished in 1962, and the property became part of the Vagabond Motel complex built that year. The Vagabond still exists as the Phoenix Sunrise Motel.

Yavapai (The) – 376 North Third Avenue

The Yavapai was a nine-room home of brick construction. Rooms were rented through the years, and it became known as the Yavapai in the 1910s. It continued to be utilized as a guest home until it was converted to a funeral home in about 1930.

Today the property holds equipment used by the APS power company.

Yavapai Cottage Court – See Craus Bungalows

Yellow Rose of Texas Court – See Lincoln Auto Court

Zeller Bachelors Court – 930 South Seventh Street

Zeller Bachelor Court began about 1930 under the name New Batching Apartments. The facility consisted of a mix of multiple room cottages and cabins. In 1941 two of the buildings were destroyed by fire, and one of the renters was killed. By 1950 the facility changed its name to Zeller Bachelor Court. This was likely changed to attract more short-term renters. Ownership did not change.

The court was out of business by 1977 and quickly demolished. Today a parking lot and industrial storage are located on the property.

Zila Motel – 3221 East Van Buren Street

The Zila Motel was operating by 1947. The motel utilized a single-story strip building along the western property line with ten rental units. An office and owner's quarters was located forward and center on the lot. Eight of the ten units were kitchenettes.

The property went through many name changes. By 1948 the facility was named the Casa Rosita Motel. In 1950 the name changed again to the Texan Motel. By 1952 the name became the Circle Motel. Finally, the facility became the Robinhood Motel.

In 1966 the Robinhood Motel was demolished. Today the area is a vacant lot.

Zira Court – 2836 East Van Buren Street

The Zira Court was open by 1944. The facility utilized individual buildings with a mix of gable and flat roofs with covered parking between the buildings. A two-story office and manager's quarters building was also a feature of the property.

Zira Court circa 1945 (Author's Collection)

The Zira Court operating as the Budget Motel in 2012 (Photo by Author)

The Zira Court operated until 1972 when it was no longer utilized as a motel. In 1983 the buildings again became a motel under the name Pueblo Inn Motel. In 2010 the facility became the Budget Motel.

The original Zira Court buildings still operate today as the Budget Motel.

Section Three

Listing by Address

Adams Street - East

29   Leland House

220   Panama House

510   Downtown Motel

1310   Dixie Court

1609   Adams Court

2105   Elva's Motel, Williams Court

2146   Dusty Trail Motel, East Adams Motel

2521   Wilson Court

Adams Street - West

221   Gilbert House

246   Alhambra Rooming House, Kelso House

546   Sixth Avenue Hotel, Bassler Hotel, Navajo Hotel, Windsor Hotel, New Windsor Hotel

Alice Street - East

19   Stefford's Cottages, Fuller Cottages, Cactus Court

Apache Street - East

1113   Garland Smith Court

Buckeye Road - East

1102   Lantana Auto Court

2006   Sun Valley Court, Cha Kel Court

2010   Millers Auto Court

2198   Airport Haven Court

2220   Air Line Modern Cottage Court,   59 Trees Court

Buckeye Road - West

709   Golden Rule Court

801   Greenhaw Auto Court

1507   Horse Shoe Auto Court

1535   Prices Cabins, Stewart's Cabins

1617   OK Court

1715   Travelers Auto Court

1724   Circle Inn Court, Buckeye Motel

1816   Tamarisk Court, Millers Court, Morris Court

1898   Red Wing Court, Buckeye Road Court

2114   Best-Yet Motel, Warren Motel, Angela Hotel

2135   Western Acres Motel

2140   West Buckeye Court, Lena's Court

2148   Barbara Court

2201   Roberts Auto Court

2210   Ranchero Motor Motel, Red Arrow Motel

2212   Lanny's Court, Phoenixona Motor Lodge

2309   Sun Valley Court

2330   Sun Down Court

2400   Mar-Di-Kay Motel, Parkway Motel

2412   Maria Motel

2425   El Lynn Motel, Motto Guest Lodge, Freeway Motel

2722   Reeds Court, Golden Boy Mobile Lodge, L&E Lodge

2723   Hughes Rooms

2828   C and M Motel

2916   Western Air Court

2925   Wilsons Court

2926   Vista Linda Court, Comfort Motel, Lexxus Motel

2933   Ford's Motel, Fillion Motel, Box A Motel, Campbell Motel, Talley-Ho Lodge

3006   Tamarack Inn, Fain's Court, Evergreen Court, Stan's Court

3125   Jacksons Court

3151   Three Wells Motel

3158   Colony Motel, Cloud Motel

3159   Cottonwood Court, J&O Court

3308   Alanoma Lodge, Route 80 Motel

3318   Rounds Rest Motel

3330   Villa Vista Motel, Del Reo Lodge

3344   Perma Rest Motel, Mountain View Motel, Daytonian Motel

3424   Tierra Verde Motel

3430   Hi Chi Motel

3902   Three Palms Motel

3926   Homedale Court

Broadway Road - East

214   Monte Vista Court

2921   Gardner's Motel, Pueblo Motel

Camelback Road - East

2390   Arizona Manor Hotel

3279   Sourant Lodge

4222   Camelback Lodge

5200   Royal Palms Inn

6000   Jokake Inn

6150   Paradise Inn

Cave Creek Road

9315   Anglin Motel, Motel Apartments

Central Avenue - North

27   Hoffman House, Stroud Rooms

38   Wharton Hotel, Avalon Rooms, Como Hotel, American Hotel

109   Adams Hotel, Phoenix Hilton Hotel, Wyndham Phoenix Hotel, Renaissance Phoenix Hotel

130   Perkins Rooming House, Occidental Hotel

202   San Carlos Hotel

203   Stag Hotel, Del Ray Hotel, Marx Palace Hotel

515   Apache Hotel

515   Central Avenue Hotel, Annex Hotel

525   Portland Hotel

610   Westward Ho Hotel

713   El Cerrito Hotel

1001   Coronet Hotel, Ramada Coronet Hotel

1012   Olivet Hotel

3312   Vinton Manor Apartment Hotel, Valley Inn

3601 Ivory Palace Motor Lodge, North Central Motor Lodge

4027 Hide Away Court

4321 Central Plaza Inn, St. Francis Hotel, Holiday Inn

4710 Hollywood Guest Manor

4840 Toney Belle Guest Ranch

5310 White Oak Lodge

5534 North Central Manor

5614 Arizona Ranch House

6135 Rose Lane Village

6630 Fresno Guest Ranch

8502 Butler's Guest Ranch

8511 Arbor Court

Central Avenue - South

12 Porter Hotel, Main Hotel

14 Denver Hotel, Oriel Hotel

32 Central Hotel

44 Virginia Rooming House, Angeles Hotel

49 Commercial Hotel, Luhrs Hotel

109 Jefferson Hotel

135 Kersting Hotel, Compton Hotel, Morrison Hotel

4220 Central Motel

5225 El Comanche Motel

5249 U-Wanna Motel

5403 Admiral Motel

Clarendon Avenue - West

100   Townehouse Hotel, Ramada Inn, Lexington Hotel, Hilton Garden Inn

Culver Street - West

1830   Culver Street Court , Parker Cabin Court

Earll Drive - East

1740   Earll Court

Fairmount Avenue - East

1114   Copemoar Court, Seidler Court, Wells Cottages

Fillmore Street - East

1459   Delmar Court

Garfield Street - West

1501   Dicks Court

Grand Avenue

745   Penn's Court

765   Egyptian Motor Hotel, Oklahoma Hotel, Las Palmas Motel

1223   Dew Drop Inn, Rosewood Village Motel, Rose Alice Motel

1325   Desert Sun Hotel, Porter House Hotel

1331   Didit's Court

1501   Caravan Inn – West, Oasis Motor Hotel

1508   Shaughnessy Court

1509	Evergreen Court
1515	Bali-Hi Motor Hotel
1533	Palm Garden Court
1560	Coliseum Inn
1601	Western Village Motor Hotel
1625	Grand Avenue Cottage Court
1628	Blue Point Court, Court Carol, Grand Avenue Court
1635	Black Diamond Auto Cabins, Fern Glen Court
1661	White Way Court
1701	Happy Place Cottages, Penn Court
1735	Hiway Inn, Hiway Inn Coliseum
1735	Silver Bell Court, Standard Motel
1801	Ideal Auto Court
1810	Six Points Auto Camp
1950	Far West Auto Court
2250	La Fiesta Bungalow Court
2262	Polly Court, Arrow Motel, Rainbow Motel
2308	Arizona Auto Court
2450	EZ In Motel
2812	Best Rest Court
2830	Grand Avenue Court, Alhambra Court, Rock Center Motel
3040	Circle L Motel
3048	Santa Fe Motel
3060	El Ranchito Motel, Godsoe Motel, Delmar Motel
3138	Cottonwood Court, A Motel
3250	Shady Lane Court

3308 Detroiter Tourist Court, Illini Motor Court

3400 Rodeway Inn, Howard Johnson, America's Best Value, US Vets

3514 Elena Court

3604 Midway Court

3648 Court Motel

3662 Stop Motel

3710 Crooks Court

3744 Mokan Motel

3776 Hodges Court, Rita's Court, Red Mug Court

4080 Tamarack Court

4180 Turista Lodge, Grand Valley Motel

4250 Horseshoe Motel

1826 Minnie's Court

Grant Street - West

1732 Wings Motor Court Hotel, Court Motel

1850 Westward Court

2217 Lorena's Motel

Harrison Street - West

420 Arizona Lodging House

Hatcher Road - East

1212 Ewing's Tourist Court

Indian School Road - East

6121 Ingleside Inn

Jackson Street - East

47 Star Lodging House

Jackson Street - West

24 Hardwick Hotel

1822 Jackson Motor Court

Jefferson Street - East

219 Jefferson Rooms, Espana Hotel, Annex Hotel

222 Espanol Hotel, Paris Hotel

319 Jefferson Rooming House, Alexander Hotel, Imperial Rooms, Mission House Hotel, Imperial Hotel

335 Hayes Rooms

535 Raymond Hotel, Oregon Hotel, Rice's Hotel

607 St. Louis Hotel

702 Kemp Hotel

707 Duran Hotel

717 Little Harlem Hotel

1342 Winston Inn and Court

1402 Tangier Apartment Motel, J&R Motel

1601 Leap Sampson Auto Camp

Jefferson Street - West

32   Elgin Hotel, Pearson Hotel, Miller Hotel

123 Valley Lodging House

203 Stacy Hotel, Astor Hotel

401 Barstow Rooms

414 Small Hotel

427 Gordon Rooming House, Palms Rooming House, Attaway House

Jones Avenue - West

311 Terry's Court

Latham Avenue - West

1605 Kirby's Motel, Phoenix Motel

Laurel Avenue - North

1214 Corral Motel, Kitchenette Motel

Lincoln Street - East

2216 Hurds Court, Ortiz Court

Lincoln Street - West

2107 Lincoln Auto Court, Yellow Rose of Texas Court, Willmoth Court, Conway Court

Linden Street - West

1618 Corral Court, Linden Court

Madison Street - East

21   St. James Hotel

22   Vermont Hotel, Tourist Hotel

35   Madison Hotel

205   Commercial Hotel, Headley Hotel

242   New York Hotel

316   Rex Hotel

1747   Mesquite Court

Madison Street - West

27   Stag Hotel, Patio Hotel

909   Hutch Motel, Pink Palace Motel, Alamo Motel

Maricopa Street - West

1717   Pecks Court

Maryland Avenue - East

1227   Wanada Lodge

Maryland Avenue - West

335   Arizona Ambassador Hotel

McDowell Road - East

202   Los Olivos Lodge, EconoLodge, Quality Inn

Missouri Avenue - East

2400   Arizona Biltmore Hotel

Mohave Street - East

231   Mohave Court, Holland Court

Monroe Street - East

27   Steinegger Lodging House , Alamo House, The Francis, St. Francis Hotel, Golden West Hotel

148   Monroe Rooming House

230   Kennedy House

245   Glenwood Lodging House, St. Elmo Lodging House

521   Bower House

948   Monroe Court

1117   Conan Auto Court

1118   Wilberta Court, Lewis Court, Morgan Court

1738   Cabrera Court

2009   Cottonwood Lodge

2021   Meremac Hotel Court

2025   Silver Crest Court

2033   Menears Court, Palm Circle Court

2117   Michiana Motel

2125   Hide Away Motel

2133   Harmony House Motel, Sunrise Motel

2146   Gel Mar Court

2203   Johnsons Court, Shir-Mar Court

2401   Lane Court

Monroe Street - West

227   Mona Lisa Rooms

3224 Sunny Lane Motel

Moreland Street - West

84   Melville Guest Lodge

Ocotillo Road - East

1425 Town and Country Lodge

Olmstead Lane

1120 Rung Motel

Polk Street - East

215   Polk House, The Home, The Avon

415   Millers Motel

714   Schell & Gish Rooming House

Roanoke Avenue - East

53   Redman's Guest Lodge, Chancewell Manor Lodge

Roosevelt Street - East

724   Roosevelt Hotel

4801 Desert Grove Auto Court

Roosevelt Street - West

1545   Glow Court

Ruth Avenue - East

17   Ruth Street Court

Sky Harbor Boulevard

2901   Sky Riders Hotel, Sheridan Airport Inn

Thomas Road - East

2512   Biltmore Motel

4935   Lo Lo Mai Lodge

Tonto Street - East

113   Central Park Court

Tonto Street - West

2319   Sorrell Court, Desert Shadows Lodge

Van Buren Street - East

716   Gillis Tourist Home

803   Sun Dancer Lodge, Romney Sun Dancer Hotel

804   AutoLodge Motel, Economy Inn

917   Newton's Inn

938   Hyatt Chalet , Chalet Lodge, Super 6 Hotel, Super 7 Hotel

965   Klose Inn Auto Court

965	Phoenix East Travelodge, American Lodge, Super 8
1214	Palms Auto Court
1308	Sefton Hotel
1601	American Camp
1617	Colorado Court, Rose Court
1629	US Auto Court, Cottage Auto Camp
1643	Wing Auto Camp
1709	Floods Court, Constantini Court
1710	Stallings Auto Camp, Home Court
1714	Winterhaven Court
1723	Fenix Auto Camp
1727	Delozier Auto Court
1729	Craft Court, Clemens Court
1735	Mexico Cafe Auto Court
1736	Mutt and Jeff Camp
1739	Travelers Auto Court
1803	Coronado Court
1840	Whites Auto Camp
1850	Montezuma Place, Montezuma Motel
1863	Eastside Court
1865	Pasadena Motel, Eighteen Sixty-Five Motel, Near Town Motel, Classic Motel
1867	Forney's Court, Midway Auto Camp, Dewitt's Tourist Court
1902	Tropics Motor Lodge
1903	Liberty Motel
1916	Old Faithful Inn
1924	Hitching Post Court

1925 Halls Motel, Palace Auto Court

1925 Palace Auto Court, Halls Auto Court

1937 Shady Park Motel

1940 Korner Court

1949 Rosswell Hotel

2004 Antry's Auto Court, Twin Palms Motel, L-Bar-K Motel

2006 Sun Court, Mary's Motel, Eldorado Motel

2008 Orange Auto Court, Ahoy Tourist Motel

2018 Waggoner Eastside Court

2020 Bridges Auto Court, Turley Auto Court

2021 Lucille's Motel, Helen's Cottages

2022 Rainbow Auto Court

2038 Rite Spot Court

2045 Lorena Auto Court, Van Buren Motel, Steering Wheel Motel

2104 Cross R Motel, C&E, Bob's Motel

2114 Stone Motel

2125 Del Coosha Court, Valley Motel

2133 RV Motel, Irish Motel

2137 Southwest Court

2139 Drive In court

2160 Shannon Court

2220 Camp Phoenix Court

2228 Travelers Motel, Thompson Motel

2229 Camp Joy

2230 Rest Haven Auto Court, Roosevelt Court

2247 Holiday Inn, Airport Central Hotel

2360 Green Parrot Auto Court, Jay Hawk Motel, Wrangler Motel

2364 H and R Auto Court

2364 Kon Tiki Hotel

2433 Mission Motel, Paradise Motel

2501 Columbia Court

2501 Flamingo Hotel, Flamingo Economy Motel, Flamingo Airporter Motel, Skyline Motel, Rodeway Inn

2515 Log Cabin Auto Court

2529 Silver Dollar Court, Silver Moon Court, Sun Villa Motel

2535 Wonderland Court

2601 Thunderbird Motel

2625 Arizona Motel

2635 Lazy A Court

2645 Rose Bowl Motor Court

2701 Sea Breeze Motor Inn

2745 Desert Hills Hotel

2823 Frontier Lodge

2834 Desert King Court, Keystone Lodge, Copa Inn

2835 Alamo Plaza Motor Court

2836 Zira Court, Pueblo Inn, Budget Motel

2841 Aut-O-Tel Camp, Suhuaro Court, Saguaro Court, Red Barn Motel

2853 Red Barn Motel, Deserama Motel

2900 Franciscan Lodge, Tahiti Inn Huts

2900 Tahiti Inn, Franciscan Lodge, TraveLodge, Park Place Hotel, Days Inn

2909 Ranch House

2913 El Molino Court, Dunes Motel

2915 Hudson Lodge, Dunes Motel

2922 Airways Motor Hotel, Desert Pool Motel, Fantasyland Motel, Relax Inn

2949 Del Camino Lodge, Kinds Court, Dunes Motel

2970 Villa Motor Hotel, Seven Motor Inn

3001 Calico Cat Court, O&E Motel, Bellevue Motel, Hawthorne Motel

3037 Chilton Inn, Romney Chilton Inn, Romney Hotel, Wards Hotel, Best Inn, EconoLodge

3037 Palm Lane Motor Court

3109 Tip Top Court

3148 Hiway House, TraveLodge

3221 Zila Motel, Casa Rosita Motel, Texan Motel, Circle Motel, Robinhood Motel

3232 Navajo Motel

3239 Pennsylvania Motel

3301 Motor Inn Auto Court, Whittle's Motel, Jaime's Motel

3307 Pyramid Motel, TraveLodge

3323 Caravan Inn – East, Days Inn

3325 Rancho De Oro Court

3335 Bagdad Inn, Caravan Inn, Super 8

3335 Wingfoot Court, Sharon Court

3400 Sands Hotel

3401 Blue Crown Auto Court

3411 Crest Lodge

3424 Desert Rose Motel

3424 Parkview Court

3513 El Rita Motel

3515 Joyland

3541 ABC Court

3541 Desert Sky Hotel, Quality Inn, EconoLodge, Economy Inn, Rodeway Inn, Travel Inn

3543 Camelback View Auto Court, Joe's Court, Wilkins Court

3547 Gaylord Motel, Parkview Inn, Best Inn

3547 Graham Place, Trails End Motel

3553 Kidd's Auto Court, Kings Motel

3602 Theatre Motel

3613 Aztec Motor Court

3641 Beach Court, Sun Valley Motel

3644 Vagabond Motel, Western 6 Motel, Phoenix 6 Motel, Phoenix Sunrise Motel

3650 Yaqui Motor Lodge

3706 Gateway Court

3707 Lone Star Lodge

3710 Mayflower Motel

3725 Arizona Palms, Thrifty Inn, Western Lodge

3751 Alamo Auto Court

3801 Ramada Inn

3810 Greenway Manor Court, Spiral Motel, State Motor Lodge

3818 Sunset Motel

3830 Imperial 400 East, La Casa Real

3842 Valley Court

3901 Autopia Motor Park, Continental Guest Lodge, Tropicana Motel

3901 Samoan Village, Aloha Resort

3939 Weber Auto Court, Rosser Tourist Court, Les De Lane Court, Modern Court

4107 Royal View Motel, Green Glen Motel, Esler's Motel, Nod-Away Motel, J&J Motel, Van Buren Inn

4120 Desert Star Motor Hotel, Comfort Inn, Ramada Limited, Howard Johnson

4127	Rose Marie Motel
4130	Red Horse Motel, El Don Motel
4131	Desert Rest Motel, Red Rooster Motel, Starlite Motel
4140	Flint Motel, Silver Spur Motel
4150	Golden West Lodge
4200	Wildwood Lodge, Thompson Court, Twilight Lodge
4311	Aricopa Motel, Stagecoach Inn
4433	Meeks Court, Travelers Lodge
4630	Edgerton's Motel, Bronco Motel
4638	Moon Kist Court
5021	Fortune Cottages
5025	Tovrea Castle
5130	Desert View Motel
5139	McLean Auto Court, Eastside Tourist Court
5147	Hilltop Court
5200	Pioneer Lodge, DeManana Motel, Erotica Motel
5218	Cottage Court, Minnesota Cottage Court
5315	Motel 6
5317	Utica Motel
5333	Ultra Motel
5339	Lariat Lodge
5344	Park Motel
5445	Papago Vista Motel
6600	Dixie Camp

Van Buren Street - West

19	Westminster Lodging House
424	Rodeway Inn , Kelly Inn, Budget Inn, America's Best Value
600	City Center Motel, Best West Inn
602	Williams Hotel, Raymond Hotel, Shafer Hotel
950	Desert Inn
1208	Greenway Motor Hotel
1300	El Rancho Motor Hotel
1520	Palomine Inn
1537	Mayfair Motor Hotel
1549	Rose Tourist Court
1552	Harvard Motor Court
1601	Park Lane Motor Court
1617	Motel Inn, Ritz Tourist Court, Auto Rest Motel, Los Flores Motel, West Siesta Motel
1738	Norway Hotel
1741	Greens Motel
1809	Henderson Court
1814	Bel Aire Motel
1825	Capitol Auto Court
1837	HoMotel Court
1930	McCoy's Motor Court, Casa Royale Guest Home, Royal Rest Motel
1939	Circle K Motor Hotel
1945	Lampliter Motel
2012	Cocanut Grove Motel, Coconut Grove Motel
2017	Silver Arrow Court, Las Casitas Motel
2041	Canary Court, Gunnel Tourist Camp

2120 Sandman Motel, Palmesa Motel

2125 Del Ano Motel, Sombrero Motel

2133 Verde Motel, Fosters Court Verde

2142 Pickwick Gables

2222 Gold Spot Inn, Tourist Court

2305 Sunset Auto Court

2448 Oakland Motel

2511 Lazy S Lodge , Plaza Motel Apartments

2519 Eli Motel, Chippewa Motel, Cy-Erna Motel, White's Motel, Townsend Motel, Terry Ann Motel, Western Motel, Lo-Ra Motel, Cactus Motel

2608 BB Motel, Avalon Motel, Englund Motel

2830 Star Auto Court, Bell Motel

3000 MaryBill Auto Court, Angelo's Court

3010 Trailin Court

3012 West Side Motel

3020 Long Rest Motel

3024 Gary Auto Court

3030 Loma Alta Court, Westwood Motel, Circle Inn

3100 Howard's Court, Halls Court

3239 Sun Terrace Court

3501 Wilsons Court

3602 Bobs Van Buren Motel

402 TraveLodge Phoenix, Budget Lodge

Villa Avenue

1755 Miller Auto Camp

Washington Street - East

22	Anheuser Hotel, Majestic Hotel
23	Downtown Hotel
122	Central Hotel
136	Bank Exchange Hotel
144	Plaza House, White Hotel
210	Amuzu Hotel
225	Gregory House
233	Alturas Hotel, Salt River Hotel
242	Capitol Hotel
242	Phoenix Hotel, Pioneer Hotel
309	Lemon Hotel, Mills House, Arcade Hotel
309	Gold Hotel
319	Romona Hotel
446	Maxwell House
502	Grand Hotel
720	Mascot Hotel
800	Ulloa Rooms, John's Court
1021	Swindall Tourist Home, Stayaert House
1022	Hammons Rooms
1229	Gardner's Hotel
1604	Corona Cottage Court
1608	Good Luck Auto Court
1612	Mary's Cottage Court
1718	Washington Circle Court, Washington Court
1726	Davis Court, Jack's Tourist Court

1738 White Rose Court

1811 Bills Cottage Court, Bucks Court

1818 Cottage Grove Court

1819 Last Chance Auto Court, Drive Inn Auto Court

1930 Pullman Auto Court

2209 Illinois Court

2224 Mountain View Auto Court

2333 Lewis Court, Ka Dee Modern Court

2502 Hialeah Court, Round Up Ranch

2532 Sky Harbor View Motel

3000 Gingham Dog Court, Sky Harbor Court, S&H Court

3025 Market Motel, Al's Apartment Motel

3035 Sleepy Hollow Motel

3150 Carlock Auto Court

4201 Nightingale Court

4216 Midway Court

4401 Kozy Kourt, Seaside Court, Pueblo Grande Court

4417 M and P Motel, Val Villa Lodge

4418 Counhan Court, Oasis Motel

Washington Street - West

11 Thibodo Rooming House, Denver Hotel Annex, Tourist House, Chicago Rooms, New Ivanhoe Hotel, Seattle Hotel, Day Hotel

122 Grand View Hotel, Fairmont Hotel, Dobbs House, Palgrave House, Park Hotel, Dallas Hotel, Clinton House, Strand Hotel

216 Fulton Hotel

219 Vendome Hotel

242	Mayes Hotel
311	Annex Hotel
324	Patton Grand Rooms
325	Patrick Hotel
401	Dixie Hotel, Moss Rooming House, Fourth Avenue House
431	French Rooming House, Norm's Hotel, Smith's Hotel, Bell Hotel
438	Elmo Rooming House, Globe Hotel, Cecil Hotel, Utah Hotel
530	Irving House
534	Ambassador Hotel
618	Farley House, New Mills House, Union Hotel
701	West End House, Seventh Avenue Hotel
1656	Kimball Hotel
2025	Castella Court, Jayne's Court
2118	Craus Bungalows, Yavapai Cottage Court, Guess Court
2134	San Antonio Court, Dobson Court, Pollard Court
2136	Washington Court, Palmdale Court
2138	Hollywood Court, Palmdale Court

Watkins Road - West

67	Riverside Court
71	Maybern Court

Yuma Street - West

1708	Cummins Auto Court, Hurley's Court, Borgouist Cabins

First Avenue - South

15   Pearson Hotel

31   Happy Home Hotel

330 Kimber House

First Avenue - North

40   Holmes Rooming House, Elite Hotel

135 Colonial Hotel, Reading Hotel, State Hotel

301 Holland House

848 Westward Lodge

First Street - South

109 Byers House, Phoenix Hotel

First Street - North

16   The Den

137 Normandie Hotel

228 Washington Hotel

401 Sahara Hotel, Ramada Sahara Hotel, Ramada Inn Downtown

509 Plaza Hotel

807 Lamb Hotel, Coronado Hotel

Second Avenue - South

28   Burbank Rooms, Dorris Hotel

32   Dorris Hotel, Beasley Hotel, Elgin Hotel

38	Savoy Hotel, Milner Hotel, Earle Hotel
42	Nordrach House

Second Avenue - North

11	Ford Hotel
333	Parker House, Eldorado Hotel, Woodford Hotel, Lebanon Hotel
362	Lewis Hotel
368	Copeland House
373	Rogers Guest Home
381	Bayliss Hotel, Downtowner Hotel
387	Moeller Hotel, Moeller Apartment Hotel
834	Thunderbird Lodge

Second Street - South

215	Wollpert Hotel, Eddie Hotel, Commercial Hotel
221	Headley Hotel, Headley Annex, Small Hotel

Second Street - North

15	Dennis Hotel, New Dennis Hotel, Franklin Hotel
620	Benson Lodge, Palms Hotel, Sagebrush Inn, Sullivan Hotel

Third Avenue - South

10	Arizona Hotel

Third Avenue - North

362	Emerick Hotel, Long's Guest Lodge

376 Yavapai House

642 Ritz Hotel, Phoenician Hotel

Third Street - South

11   Portland Hotel

60   Virginia Hotel, Hollywood Hotel

141 Produce Hotel, Chesterfield Rooms

143 Grand Canyon Hotel

Third Street - North

1001 Alice Guest Lodge

1016 Sun Valley Motel Apartments

1222 Windsor Court

Fourth Avenue - North

325 Phillips House

356 Stenlake Rooming House, Mark's Hotel, Fourth Avenue Hotel

645 Graystone Court

805 Embassy Square Hotel

Fifth Avenue - North

618 Fifth Avenue Court

4310 Arizona Twilighter Motel

Fifth Avenue - South

27   Bonner Hotel, Adalade Hotel

Sixth Avenue - North

385   Alwilda Lodge

650   Ivon (The), California Inn, Whitehouse Lodge

Sixth Street - North

14   Paducah Hotel

504   Twin Palms Lodge, O'Reilly's Boarding House

Seventh Place - North

10042   Wideman's Cottages

Seventh Avenue - South

302   Santa Fe Rooms

417   Lewis Courts Hotel

1020   Dabney Auto Court

1023   Tilger Brothers Tourist Camp

1110   Golden Rule Tourist Camp

Seventh Avenue - North

201   Imperial 400 Downtown, Friendship Inn, Travel Inn

3033   Park Central Motor Hotel

3130   El Cortez Apartment Hotel

Seventh Street - South

201   Colombo Lodging House

313   Seventh Street Hotel

930   Zeller Bachelors Court

1429   Shelton Court

1439   Allen's Court

Seventh Street - North

325   Monte Vista Lodge, Byron's Lodge, Wright's Lodge

4229   Franiva Motor Lodge, Corbitt's Motel

4729   Stables Motel

5049   El Rokay Lodge

5313   Way West Motel, Jo Lyn Motel, Westernaire Motel

5602   Charlesann Court

7150   Branding Iron Lodge

Eighth Street - North

210   Katherine Court

Ninth Street - North

221   Gilberts Motel

Twelfth Street - North

11   Home Court

201   OK Tourist Court, Peck Auto Court

10023 Aldridge Court, Fredley's Motel

Fourteenth Avenue - North

308   Vivian Court, Regency Motel

348   Phoenix Motor Lodge, Kings Land Lodge, El Rancho Motel Annex

Fifteenth Avenue - North

906   All States Auto Court

918   West End Cottages

4330 Kilp's Kourt

Sixteenth Drive - North

1305 Oak Avenue Court

Sixteenth Street - North

505   Navajo Court

1100 Bide-A-Wee Place

1213 Desert Breeze Motel

2216 West Winds Lodge, Westwinds Motel

7645 Cactus Rock Lodge

Seventeenth Drive - North

1517 JB Court

1520 Willow Avenue Court, Willow Court

Seventeenth Avenue - South

522   Wings Motor Court

602   Casa Del Sol Court

702   Holiday Inn

716   Town House Hotel, Morreale Hotel

801	Kings Rest Motor Court
802	Westward Ho Court, Gavin Court
810	Drake Motel, Spur Motel
901	Monterey Court
908	Arizona Motor Inn
911	Clover Court, Fountain Court
1001	Crescent Court, Windmill Hotel Motor Inn, D-Bar-G Motel
1014	Sargent's Court
1015	Royal Crest Lodge, Apartment Hotel, Kitchenette Court, J&E Motel, Las Casitas Motel
1121	Triangle Motor Court, Casa Del Sol Motel

Seventeenth Avenue - North

106	El Royale Motor Court
120	Cabana Lodge
206	La Fonda Court
1408	Seventeenth Avenue Court
1416	Franklin Court
1550	Lola's Court

Seventeenth Street - North

501	Shady Haven Court

Eighteenth Avenue - South

4	Belmont Court

Eighteenth Avenue - North

116   Martin's Tourists

312   Parkmore Motel

Eighteenth Street - North

530   Bide-A-Wee Court, Wilson's Court

602   Tent City Auto Camp

Nineteenth Avenue - South

513   Jody's Court, Bachelor Court

705   Virginia Court

811   Blue Bonnet Auto Court

903   Maricopa Auto Court

923   Hunky Dory Auto Court, New Hunky Dory Court

1126   Sutton Court, Harris Court

Twentieth Place - North

712   Lone Tree Motel

Twentieth Street - North

305   Pauline's Court, Mareci's Court

323   Potter Motor Court

Twenty-First Avenue - North

108   Royal Palm Bungalows

Twenty-First Street - North

211   Ohio Motel, El Ray Motel

212   Portal Grande Motel

Twenty-Third Street - North

330   Alameda Court, Miller Auto Court

Twenty-Fourth Street - South

1202   Rodeway Inn - Airport

1320   Snow White Court

2201   Holiday Inn, Knights Inn

Twenty-Fourth Street - North

518   Maricopa Motel, Twin Wheels Motel

Twenty-Seventh Avenue - North

401   Bungalow Court

417   Tripp Motel Lodge

Twenty-Ninth Avenue - South

1002   Bolin Court

Thirtieth Street - South

3825   Gardner's Motel Annex

Thirtieth Street - North

123 Lindsay Auto Court

Thirty-Second Place - North

109 Ernie's Cabins

Thirty-Second Street - North

1046 Bona Vista Court

Thirty-Fifth Avenue - South

909 Atherton Court, Nine-O-Nine Court

Thirty-Sixth Street - North

5100 Casa Siesta Lodge

Forty-Sixth Street - North

1502 Emerald Pool Lodge

Fifty-Third Street - North

350 Wanda Auto Court

Fifty-Sixth Street - North

4649 El Oeste Lodge

Bibliography and Resources

Anderson, J., Mahmuljin, S., & McPherson, J. (2011) Downtown Phoenix. Charleston, Arcadia Publishing.

Arizona Directory Company's Phoenix City Directory. (1895 -1943).

Arizona Independent Republic Archives. (1911 – 1947).

Arizona Republic Newspaper Archives. (1930 – 2014).

Arizona Republican Newspaper Archives. (1890 – 1930).

Arizona Room, Burton Barr Library, 1221 North Central Avenue, Phoenix, AZ.

Arizona State Library, 1700 West Washington Street, Phoenix, AZ.

Bensel Directory Company's Phoenix Directory. (1892).

Casa Grande Ruins National Monument, 1100 Ruins Drive, Coolidge, AZ.

Towne, D. (2011). Phoenix's Street of Dreams: The Visual Extravaganza that was Van Buren. www.modernphoenix.net/vanburen/vanburensigns.htm

Farish, T. (1918). History of Arizona. San Francisco. Filmer Brothers.

Garcia, K. (2008). Early Phoenix. Charleston, Arcadia Publishing.

Maricopa County Flood Control District, 2801 West Durango Street, Phoenix, AZ.

Melikian, R. (2009). Hotel San Carlos. Charleston, Arcadia Publishing.

Melikian, R. (2010). Vanishing Phoenix. Charleston, Arcadia Publishing.

Mullin-Kille Company's Phoenix City Directory. (1951 – 1960).

Phoenix Directory Company's Phoenix City Directory. (1943 – 1948).

Reiner, D. & Jacquemart, J. (2010). Tovrea Castle. Charleston, Arcadia Publishing.

Pagan, E. (2007). Historic Photos of Phoenix. Nashville, Turner Publishing.

Pueblo Grande Museum, 4619 East Washington Street, Phoenix, AZ.

Skinner Phoenix City Directory. (1903).

Tovrea Castle at Carraro Heights, 5025 East Van Buren Street, Phoenix, AZ.

Van Buren, as it used to be. (2008). www.brazilbrazil.com/vanburen.html

www.ingramcontent.com/pod-product-compliance
Lightning Source LLC
Chambersburg PA
CBHW081352290426
44110CB00018B/2352